The BUMPER BOOK of Fads and Crazes

The BUMPER BOOK of Fads and Crazes

Richard Lewis

Atlantic Books
London

Published in Great Britain in 2005 by Atlantic Books, an imprint of Grove Atlantic Ltd.

Copyright © Richard Lewis, 2005

The moral right of Richard Lewis to be identified as the author of this work has been asserted in accordance with the Copyright, Designs and Patents Act of 1988.

ISBN 1 84354 419 9

A CIP record for this book is available from the British Library,

10 9 8 7 6 5 4 3 2 1

Design by Richard Carr www.carrstudio.co.uk
Illustrations by Andrew Rae www.andrewrae.org.uk
Printed in Germany by Bercker

Atlantic Books
An imprint of Grove Atlantic Ltd
Ormond House
26–27 Boswell Street
London WC1N 3JZ

For Camille, who thinks I write books
about the sea and broken hearts.
I will try to oblige with the next one.

PRESENTS

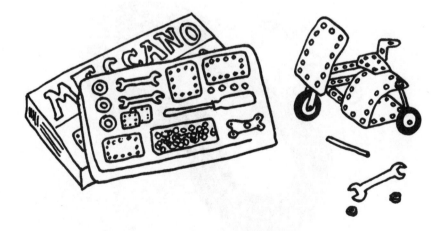

Introduction

Flavour of the month

What is a fad? Etymology tells us the word comes to us, via 'fidfad', from 'fiddlefaddle', whereupon etymology promptly says goodbye and leaves us to paddle our own canoe. In truth, a fad is a craze for a peculiar thing. But what is a craze? Well, a craze is that temporary, fleeting but widespread mania for faddish things. An enthusiasm, with the added suggestion of lunacy, gone no sooner than it arrived; when something is all the 'rage'. **Snoods, Trolls**, the Fromage Frais. Suddenly everyone is eating rocket in salads. Almost as suddenly we are agreed it tastes like ground moths and is clearly the work of the devil. The latter of course is true, which only begs the question of why we ever put the acrid vegetation into our mouths at all. This is the type of question this book proposes to address. Why? Because some questions in life are more important than others and we can't all be presenting *Newsnight*.

Why did the **Frisbee**® take off, when the **Space Hopper** seemed so well placed? Whatever happened to the **Pet Rock**? Why do **My Little Pony** figurines sell for such fortunes to collectors while **Top Trumps** are ten a penny? Who was Rubik, and what was he up to all those dark nights in his bedroom? (We now know, of course.) Why did **SodaStream** – a way to make inferior unbranded fizzy drinks at home instead of buying the celebrated Coke and 7Up – wane in popularity? (There may be a clue in the question.)

A fad can be anything from the playground craze for **Pokémon** to certain media types insisting on saying 'bobbins' every two minutes. It could be a vogue for the permanent wave or the proliferation of the

Stylophone™. Wherever the masses agree as one on a point of fathomless trivia, for the blinking of an eye, you will find the fidfad. Or fiddlefaddle.

So that's what a fad *is*. Here's what it isn't: something that once appeared innovative but which nonetheless worked itself into the general scheme of things, such as lager and nylon. A fad is also not some bygone *objet* that simply became redundant, like the shellac disc or the British woollen trade. This is not an excuse to peer, through sepia-tinted spectacles, at our grandfathers' flannel trousers. On the other hand, modern innovations that show no signs of craze-like activity will not be covered either. Television is another area that we shall leave aside. This is partly because the subject could fill an entire book. And partly because the author has already written that book (*The Encyclopaedia of Cult Children's TV*, 2001). He might be a fool but he is not a martyr. Pop-music crazes, again, could fill and have indeed filled books of their own.

We will ask why people all want the same things at the same time, we will look at the mechanics of crazes, the underbelly of marketing, at advertising and the manipulation of our emotional responses by men in suits. We will hear from harried parents, from ex-fadees, from enthusiasts and devotees. We will hear from marketing experts and fad creators. We will also listen to the fears of parenting organizations who object to the endless deluge of tie-in products and the bombardment of commercial messages directed at their offspring from the television, billboards, the internet and mobile phones.

Lastly we will ask: what was it about a certain toy, gadget, word or fashion that so captured our hearts for that fifteen minutes, and what does it tell us about ourselves? Why do we miss these ephemeral gewgaws, these singular snapshots in the zeitgeist? Perhaps, like the Sinclair Spectrum, they encapsulated our delight in a new discovery we now take for granted (the computer). Perhaps they invited us to envisage a future where fossil fuels were not ritually burnt for travel (**The Pogo Stick**).

Perhaps they showed superior ingenuity (**The Magic Eye**™) but were trampled by the lowest common denominator (**Buzz Lightyear**). Whatever its qualification for entry, each craze has been lightly seared in alphabetical order, on a bed of crisp cross-references for your reading convenience, liberally drizzled with Fad Facts and served with a side order of lists, articles and illustrations. Enjoy your fad meal. Its chef has been at pains to include the widest possible selection of crazes, although some readers may brilliantly discover omissions. Some readers may also disagree quite cleverly with the author's opinion or appraisal. If you fall into either of these categories, the author would like you to know that your feedback is not strictly required, although do feel free to post your objection to a random address on the Isle of Lewis, where mail is always appreciated. With that thought in mind, do please regress through this motley collection of fancies, whims and vogues. Jump in your memory-canoes, ladies and gentlemen, and paddle through the fiddlefaddle.

Richard Lewis, Paris, 2005

The Action Man

It's the growing-up killing machine you never grew out of. Whether yours had gripping hands, eagle eyes, blue boxers or undefined naked man-flesh down under, he was unmistakably Action Man – the only doll with boy-appeal.

The nation's favourite 'moveable fighting man' was first given orders to advance, from Leicester, in 1966. British toy manufacturers had been looking for a way to cash in on the success of America's GI Joe, by Hasbro, who had already been on the rampage stateside for two years. Two British companies produced an articulated soldier doll in response to this challenge. One was Pedigree. Aptly named, this outfit already had a successful portfolio that included the **Sindy** doll: a British rival to America's **Barbie**®. Pedigree's figure was called Tommy Gunn. The other company was Palitoy, whose twelve-inch Action Man secured the licensing deal with Hasbro – a special relationship with the United States that allowed the foot-high squaddy to bomb, bludgeon, invade and finally occupy our hearts and minds.

Introducing dolls for boys in sixties Britain was a risky strategy and one that would require immediate regime change. Dolls were for girls, that much we knew. But in a decade that spawned Women's Lib, surely a doll for boys was not out of the question? The key was to make sure the doll eschewed girly notions of babies, cooking or glamour and focused on the acceptable masculine pursuits of war, killing and the subjugation of the weak. But would Tommy Gunn be the first to stick the British flag in doll soil, or would Action Man cluster-bomb his way to dominion? Here's where the American alliance came in handy. Palitoy was able to import new GI Joe outfits and accessories quickly from Hasbro, outstripping the competition. Pedigree soon dropped Tommy Gunn, leaving the allies a clear battlefield.

The author's first Action Man came with a blond buzz cut and a scar. He acquired various changes in costume and destroyed not a few **Lego** fortresses before he was joined by a bearded naval man, with dark hair, but the same scar. Together they waged a merciless and bloody campaign of peace-keeping and western democracy, with the help of a neighbour's pontoon bridge. One kid had a Canadian Mountie. He didn't last. Action Man's head was softer than his body and could be removed. Thus the author's mother was upset one Christmas to find the fighting man's skull had toppled the fairy on top of the seasonal fir tree.

Boys with sisters, such as the author, soon discovered that Action Man could machinegun an entire **Sindy** tea party without too much effort. Though civilian casualties were frowned upon, it was only natural to sustain some collateral damage when blocking crucial supply routes (**Sindy** had the Viscount biscuits). Action Man could also be parachuted into such territory, sometimes causing regrettable but unavoidable damage to carefully placed doll furniture. It was a shame that Action Man was too big to fit inside an **Airfix** plane, but he could be made to straddle a **Hornby** train set, or his head attached to a **slot car**.

But war takes its toll on the human frame. It's not all scars and rough and tumble. Eagle Eyes Action Man, far from being a superior model, was a bizarre, mutated casualty of chemical warfare. His larger head and wide staring eyes spoke of shellshock mustard

FAD Fact Children in the United Kingdom watch 2.5 hours of television a day, more than children in any other European country and second only to the United States. (Pine & Nash)

gas. 'Volunteer needed for a special mission,' barked the Action Man Talking Commander, from holes in his torso. But who would rise to the challenge? Would it be the Argyll and Sutherland Highlanders, complete with kilts? How about the Grenadier Guards or the Household Cavalry? All were represented in Action Man clothing. Or would the plucky volunteer be an RAF man, a sailor or an astronaut?

There was plenty there to appeal to the aspirations of most boys. But how have we measured up to our youthful ambitions? Sadly, there was no Action Writer, with corduroys and thick-rimmed spectacles. Where was the Action Merchant Banker, with champagne and gym equipment, the Action Actor, complete with P45, or the Action Paparazzo, with collectible telephoto range? In the eighties, the decade that brought a new form of aspiration, Action Man lost his hold on the Toyland frontline and beat a hasty retreat.

Why? Could it have been the fact that in 1982 Britain actually went to war for real? With the conflict in the Falklands beamed to our televisions daily, our neighbours actually fighting with real guns, it's possible that it was all just a little too close to home and that playing at war lost its appeal.

It would be nice to think that, but the author suspects it was nothing of the sort. In 1977 **Star Wars** hit the screens, causing the immediate onset of space mania. Terrestrial warfare seemed limp by comparison. The following year, in response to such intergalactic enthusiasm, **Space Invaders** landed, swiftly followed by an explosion of arcade, home TV and computer games. Who wanted a bruiser in a kilt when there was the Imperial storm trooper? Who wanted to put a model gun in Action Man's hand and say 'brrrrt, brrrrt' when you could pick up your light gun and shoot at the telly (*see* **TV Games**)? In the first years of the eighties, toys changed for ever. In 1982 Clive **Sinclair** launched his breakthrough ZX Spectrum. In 1983 the third in the *Star Wars* trilogy, *Return Of The Jedi*, was released. The following year Action Man bit the **space dust**.

But, following a prolonged absence, our moveable fighting man is back. The all-new millennial tough guy has been reincarnated in a series of ultraurban and 'street' guises. Action Pimp, Action CrackDealer and Action Tramp are sadly not part of the range, though we can always hope.

FAD **RATING** ✪✪✪✪ *'Now with gripping hands.'*

The Airfix Kit

A birthday simply wasn't a birthday without the introduction of an Airfix kit to the household. Lightweight and inexpensive, the toys provided grandmothers and aunts with the perfect gift solution for boys of all ages. They could be sent through the post without fear of damage and gave the average senior citizen enough change from her pension for the usual weekly requisites: ten boxes of tissues, a leg of lamb and twenty packets of Fox's Glacier Mints. She could pick up a kit at Woolies, post it with a card and be home in time for *The Sullivans*.

When it arrived at its destination, however, the Airfix kit took on a whole new dimension. Or not, depending on your ability. Assuming Granny had got the right child and had not sent a Hawker Harrier to the granddaughter who was hoping for a horse, reactions fell into two categories.

Scenario one. You whoop with delight. With trembling fingers and a mounting sense of giddiness, you open your new kit, carefully preserving the packaging for your wall-mounted collection, and bound up the steps to the attic where your scale-model airfield diorama is nearing completion. In fact, you need only two more pieces to complete the war-time scene, and this long-awaited Spitfire is one step closer to that modellers' Nirvana. For hours, perhaps days, you are happily silent, separating tiny plastic parts from the oblong frame and, while your classmates run about like hogs in the woods, you are meticulously applying historically accurate decals with a fine brush (*see* **Dungeons and Dragons**). The noble craft of modelling fills you with a sense of peace and satisfaction, beaten only by the pride of suspending your newest achievement from a rafter with cat-gut and showing it off to your best friend, whom you later beat at chess.

Scenario two. You whoop with delight. You then break open the packaging impatiently and snap off the first part of the kit in the wrong place, thus rendering the model broken, useless, horrible and not fair. Then you carefully glue your fingers to the kitchen table with modelling 'cement', spill Humbrol enamel paint on your school trousers, throw the kit across the room, shout at your mother and go out to the woods to join your classmates, forfeiting your pudding.

These are the only two options. The author fell into the latter, but not for want of trying. For those who could make models without wanting to kill and maim the nearest sibling, the Airfix kit was a joy, a whole toy you got to make yourself, proving yourself not only capable, practical and patient, but also artistic. For those of us who found the experience akin to voluntary flagellation, the Airfix kit was the enemy. Boys who could make Airfix kits could often do sums too – and play Battleships – and are now all financially solvent local councillors and business executives (*see* **The Executive Toy**). Those who couldn't found other uses for leftover solvents. This is scientific fact.

But, oddly enough, it was lack of funds that brought the first Airfix kit into being. In 1939, the Hungarian-born entrepreneur Nicholas Kove launched a company to make cheap rubber toys filled with air. He did this under the brand name Airfix throughout the Second World War until, in 1947, he switched to making plastic combs. There Airfix might have stayed, in happy symbiosis with Brylcreem, had the company not accepted a commission to make a promotional toy tractor. Sadly Airfix could not complete the manufacture within the budget allowed, so it supplied the tractors as a kit, cannily making a virtue of the shortcoming.

This ploy seemed to work and in 1952 the company produced its first dedicated construction kit, a model of Francis Drake's sixteenth-century sailing ship the *Golden Hind*. The packaging showed the vessel in choppy waters flying a patriotic St George cross, and the kit was sold through Woolworth's for two shillings a go. Airfix followed this success the next year with a model of the Spitfire fighter plane. The good people of Britain responded with their wallets. After all, the proposition was perfect. Not just a toy but an activity, Airfix got the thumbs-up from parents. They often found they enjoyed building the kits themselves – after their offspring had flounced off. Appealing to adults meant the potential market doubled in size, and a kit meant the modeller was limited only by his ability and imagination in the full realization of the toy. An Airfix kit executed well was a thing of beauty. An Airfix kit executed by the author was a quivering travesty held together with string which would later be shot at with an air pistol or doused in paraffin, torched and set afloat down the river Frome.

THAT WAS THE YEAR...
Prehistoric Toy Crazes

4000 BCE Draughts delight Babylon. Hanging baskets also a hit (probably).

3000 BCE Backgammon. Spiky draughts from Sumeria.

2000 BCE Marbles. Egypt discovers the joy of stompsies and swapsies.

1000 BCE China goes kite crazy. Yo-yos spring up in Greece.

600 BCE India develops chess game.

In 1962 Airfix bought its rival Kitmaster and reissued that company's range of locomotive models. In the same year it expanded its remit by acquiring the rubber-doll maker Semco and slot-car company MRRC. In 1971 Airfix bought **Meccano** and **Dinky** to become the UK's largest toy-manufacturer. These last two were in deep water financially and the success of the kits was not enough to subsidize their losses.

By 1981 the toy- and game-scene had moved into the digital age and the glory years were over. Airfix went into receivership that year and was rescued by Palitoy (*see* **Action Man**). But the coupling was not successful and just six years later Airfix was sold to the paint manufacturer Humbrol, itself owned by a company that wanted to get rid of it. In 1994 the parent company flogged Humbrol to an Irish holding group; by 2003 Humbrol had been put into administration and the youth of today were busy killing their **Tamagotchi**.

At the height of its popularity during the seventies, the Airfix kit was a household name and the figurehead for a craft and modelling craze that spawned not a few dedicated retail chains. Though it is far from dead, the Airfix kit has certainly taken its rightful place in the fad hall of fame: it has moved into the domain of the serious adult collector (*see* **My Little Pony**).

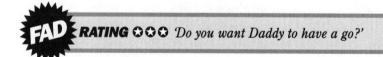

FAD *RATING* ✪✪✪ *'Do you want Daddy to have a go?'*

The Alcopop

Allegations that these sugary, fruit-flavoured alcoholic drinks were a way of peddling booze to children have always been hotly denied by their manufacturers. None the less, the tabloid newspapers waged war. In a country laid waste by 'binge drinking', they cried, surely this was the last straw. In fact, the alcopop – distinguished from normal alcohol by its lurid colouring and silly name, such as Two Dogs – is rather more a way of peddling booze to grown-ups who don't like booze. We should not be too surprised at this, for we have already witnessed the popularity of coffee for people who don't like coffee (*see* **Instant Coffee** *and* **Silly Coffee**), mashed potato for people who don't like potatoes ('For mash get Smash'), soup for people who don't like soup (*see* **Cup-a-Soup**®) and books for people who don't like books (*see* **Harry Potter**). It is to this group of products that the alcopop belongs. That it also appeals to children might be classed as a side-effect. It's like saying that cocaine is aimed at children because it looks like sherbet.

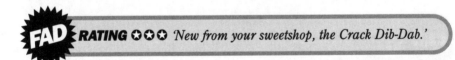

FAD **RATING ✪✪✪** *'New from your sweetshop, the Crack Dib-Dab.'*

The Atari VCS

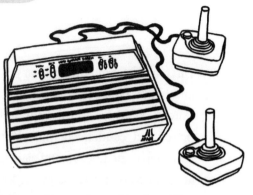

Atari's fledgling home console plugged directly into the television and made your world go chunky. This woodgrain baby (*see* **The Stylophone**™), packing a whole 4k of ROM into a box only slightly larger than a breadbin, boasted such games as *Tennis*, *Breakout*, *Outlaw* and *Chess*. First released in the UK in 1977, this loveable sideboard-sized electronic friend bipped and bopped its way into the hearts of, well, no one much until Taito licensed **Space Invaders** to Atari in 1980. This single act, which followed the sale of Atari to Warner for a modest $28 million and the subsequent firing of Atari founder Nolan Bushnell, practically made Atari's name as a home-console force to be reckoned with. But by then, others were making similar devices. While the Atari Video Computer System, or VCS, to its geeky friends, was definitely the modish man of the match, the Binatone was cheaper. (*For more, please see* **TV Games**.)

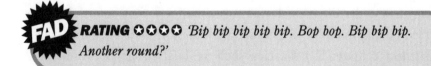

FAD **RATING** ✪✪✪✪ *'Bip bip bip bip bip. Bop bop. Bip bip bip. Another round?'*

The Aubergine

Once upon a time the ordinary people of Britain did dine on corned beef and boiled potatoes. Tea-time on Friday nights was pork pies and crisps. 'Afters' could range from the full sponge pudding and warm custard to bread and condensed milk. When Little Britain became more health conscious, fried bacon and sausages may have given way to grilled bacon and sausages but we kept the fish and chips. In the winter you couldn't beat a good stew. For this, you bought something called 'stewing steak'. Bung in a dumpling, get a result. Toad in the hole – liberally doused with lumpy gravy – was good for generations, as was shepherd's pie. Black pudding, Scotch egg, roast on Sunday. This is the food that made Britain great. Then it happened.

In waltzed the aubergine.

It's not the eggplant's fault. It thought we were leading it on – after all, there we were listening to Nana Mouskouri and Demis Roussos like butter wouldn't melt. We'd bought our **hostess trolleys**. We sang along to 'Shaddap You Face' and 'Que Sera Sera'. We were giving out all the signals. Britain was ripe for an invasion. Once the moussaka had got its sweaty feet under the table, it was only a matter of time before the cows started getting in on the act. Steak and kidney pie was ousted in favour of suspect continental delicacies such as 'beef stroganoff' and 'boeuf bourgignon'. This, as we now know, is stew, but then, as we tentatively sipped our liebfraumilch (*see* **Black Tower**), a whole world of continental promise seemed to open up before us like the Danube delta (*see* **Trivial Pursuit**) and beckon us to a world where Serge Gainsbourg and Jane Birkin had better sex on a record than we could even imagine.

Staying at home was the best option. You couldn't risk an evening out at a Berni Inn or a Beefeater for fear of coming face to face with the 'Black Forest Gâteau', with its insouciant *mélange* of Gallic and Teutonic evils. From there it was only a short gamine hop to the profiterole. We couldn't spell any of it, but what could that matter? What fed the imagination fed the bank accounts of those who flogged this fancy foreign food. The author remembers one Cornish pub offering this choux-based effort as the appealingly Freudian 'Profit Rolls'. Would there be no end to it? Even **yoghurt** – once satisfactorily subdued into a strawberry-flavoured mush – was jumping on the bandwagon by going 'live'. Before we knew where we were, the cheese box had turned itself into a smorgasbord, ham had repackaged itself as Parma ham, the cracker had calcified into the **French toast** and – the final nail – gravy became *jus*.

Such things reflect the aspirations of the masses. There was a time when Britain dreamed of a place called 'The Continent'. A kaleidoscopic land of diverse, yet oddly homogenous culture. And all of it was better than our own. Why shouldn't we enjoy something more interesting and complicated than the fishcake?

With hindsight it is hard to imagine that there was ever a time before the tiramisu, unthinkable that such welcome culinary diversification was ever a fad. But not everyone agrees that the humble aubergine is to blame for the trend. Leading eggplant apologist Nicholas Clee, author of *Don't Sweat The Aubergine* (Short Books, 2005) explains:

When Elizabeth David wrote *Mediterranean Food* in the early 1950s, the aubergines, courgettes, peppers and even garlic she described were exotic to, and mostly unobtainable by, British domestic cooks. It was only in the 1960s and 1970s that they began to appear in the shops. However, the fancy food that people started to want to cook didn't use those ingredients very much: the fashion then was for

Robert Carrier-style, butter- and cream-rich dishes learned from classic French cuisine. Then, in the early eighties, there was nouvelle cuisine, in which the sauces were refined and reduced, as were the portions. In reaction, we turned to heartier, Mediterranean cooking; that was when the aubergine came into its own. So I feel that you are maligning the aubergine, which, even when served as 'aubergine caviar', is unpretentious, versatile, and delicious.

The joke of it all is that in the new glorious European Union, imported culture works both ways. Now, as the French happily tuck into their McCain frozen pizza, we are stuck with their *foie gras*. Let's give it back, this book says – what's good for the goose is good for the gander.

FAD **RATING** ✪✪✪ *'Eggplant belongs to the nightshade family, which includes the poisonous Jimson weed and Belladonna. The eggplant itself contains toxins that can cause illness.'*

Babycham

It's like this: big, booming Barry White lookalikes would *not* love a Babycham. None of them. The author doesn't mean to cast aspersions, the gentleman in question was merely being gallant. But the fact was that the old Babycham image really did need a makeover.

Invented in the late forties by Francis Showering, this rather insubstantial sparkling perry – or pear cider if you prefer – was first shipped nationally out of Shepton Mallet near Wells in 1952. Aimed at women, the logo was a fawn, or more specifically a baby chamois deer. Just as cute as the fairer sex. The inspired advertising hookline was 'I'd love a Babycham.'

Thirty odd years later and lasses were drinking pints like everyone else, classy women drank 'a glass of dry white German wine please' (*see* **Black Tower**) and Babycham had gone the way of Pomagne – sixth prize in the Church Hall raffle or last dregs in the office Secret Santa. Something needed to be done.

And so it came to pass that advertising 'creatives' launched a valiant bid to place this pear-based rudeness directly into the funky **Yuppie** wine bars that were starting to spring up. That the woman who asked for it was greeted with disbelief was a measure of the depths to which our deer-related beverage had sunk. But lo, a black man did like it. That gave it disco credibility. Babycham, now owned by Allied-Lyons, wanted you to understand this: 'We know it's been very low rent for decades, but we've now decided it's hip to drink fermented pear juice again because we haven't been selling any. So off you go and buy some of the stuff we've made loads of.' Instantly everyone in the bar was downing it like orchards were going out of fashion, tossing their **Filofaxes®** in the air and partying their high-octane careers away.

But we weren't buying it. Eventually Allied-Lyons became Gaymers in a management buy-out and dropped the deer. Deers were not disco. A better choice might have been to drop the name. What is it, champagne for babies? Babycham earns its place in the fad hall of fame because it embodies the doomed advertising craze for trying to make mundane comestibles seem chic and exotic simply by telling us they are. Ferrero Rocher, Piat D'Or (*see* **Black Tower**), Gold Blend (*see* **Instant Coffee**) – even **milk**. In the search for class, only the mass-produced will do.

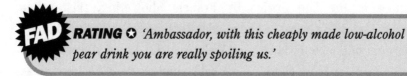

FAD RATING ✪ *'Ambassador, with this cheaply made low-alcohol pear drink you are really spoiling us.'*

HOW TO START A CRAZE

Keep your ear to the ground

Martin Lindstrom, brand marketing consultant to the likes of Coca-Cola®, is adamant that children are the decision makers or major influencing factors in the brand choices adults make. Frank Hornby made his first tentative **Meccano** structure to please his kids. When they and their friends started liking it he knew what to do next. The same thing happened with Richard James and his **Slinky®** spring. When Tibor Laczi observed kids in Budapest playing with **Rubik's Cube**, the dollar signs lit up. Listen to what the kids are doing and talking about. Once you get an idea, trust your hunch. Your next million is in their lunchbox.

The Barbie® Doll

In truth, dear Barbie® should not take up too much of our time here. Created in 1959 by Ruth Handler, one of the original founders of the now giant Mattel toy company, our beloved breast-wielding bimbo is the bestselling doll toy of all time and has become a household name through steady patronage, thus disqualifying her from any list of mere ephemera. But in a world of toys dominated by men, it's interesting that this rather idealized vision of the female form should have been created by a woman and mother.

Named after her daughter, er, Barbie, Barbie® was originally intended for the teenage market and boasted a rather improbable hourglass figure. It is as hard to imagine any thirteen-year-old girl living up to Barbie's® bouncy 36–18–38 physique as it is to imagine any thirteen-year-old girl actually playing with dolls. Consequently, Barbie® found her true home with pre-school and pre-teen girls, a rather more impressionable group. The vitriol directed at Barbie's® predominantly WASP-ish looks over the years (though note: nineties Barbie® Starlight Splendour was black) is matched only by many parents' contempt at the values she seems to promote.

Oddly, though, Barbie's® long-time beau, Ken, was based on Handler's son – Ken. So in fact Barbie® and Ken are brother and sister. Risqué even for *Knotts Landing*. This news comes as something of a deal-breaker to the author's niece, now a London PR. But while the revelation of Barbie® and Ken's true relationship has shattered a number of long-held beliefs, she remains adamant that she never felt bullied by the doll's appearance.

> When I was eleven or twelve, the age I sort of gave it up, I never really gave my body shape any thought at all. Later I remember thinking Barbie® had a funny figure, but I never envied it. I definitely aspired to her lifestyle though, she was cool and could do whatever she wanted, but I never wanted her to get married because that would make her too old. There was also Karen. I called her Karen. I cut her hair and she became Bad Barbie® because she had bad hair. My favourite Barbie® was called Rachel, long before *Friends* came along. But I think all their surnames were Wakefield, to tie in with the Sweet Valley Twins.

Note: 'sort of' gave it up. Say what you will about Barbie®, but no one ever got cluster-bombed doing their nails. Surely no country in history ever got occupied, subjugated and razed to the ground by lobotomized teams of all-American air-heads... The success of Barbie® was a huge driver in rival Hasbro's gamble on boy-toy GI Joe. In the UK, Joe became **Action Man**.

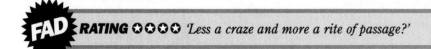

FAD **RATING** ✪✪✪✪ *'Less a craze and more a rite of passage?'*

The Barn Dance

'Take your partners by the hand... and watch them flail to the banjo beat.' The organized release of endorphins never took such an unwelcome form as the eighties 'barn dance'. American Western-style square dancing was a UK fad in the fifties, while the similar invention of line dancing was to take off in a big way in the nineties, with the help of emetic hits such as Billy Ray Cyrus's 'Achy Breaky Heart' and novelty bands such as Steps, a kind of Stetson-toting Abba. But such commercial exploits have no real place in the 'barn dance' of yesteryear.

The barn dance was of course the same sort of thing, but unique in that all barn dances were organized by committees. Your local PTA was the worst offender. In order to raise funds for slates and chalk (*see* **The Etch A Sketch**®) the idea was hatched that people would pay to make idiots of themselves in a predetermined manner, while some kind of band and 'caller' would have to be paid too. What was left would be handed over to the school library fund or similar. What a waste of time and money. A simple whip-round, say a fiver each, followed by early adjournment back home where you belonged would have solved that cash conundrum. But it was not to be. The barn dance took hold.

The formal folk dance, of course, is not something the author can safely mock; in fact his own ill-fated attempts are well documented (see *The Magic Spring* by Richard Lewis, 2005, ISBN 1843543079) but this was not the genuine article. The barn dance was ersatz folk dance at its worst: a hokey hoe-down, a countrified confection, an unpalatable pot pourri of traditions, all flavoured with the obligatory waist coat and neckerchief attire of TV's *Alias Smith & Jones* and *The Virginian*. Why, when the British were so unwilling to give any credibility to their own folk-dance traditions, did they think such retro lolloping would be OK as long as they were dressed as cowboys? Did they think they could just slip it by unnoticed? The fact that the Americans themselves are really not at all sure where we found this unsavoury convention should have given pause for thought, but no, we two-stepped on, foisting this hay-based affront on to school kids, office parties and anywhere else a committee could be found. Here are some common phrases associated with a barn dance: 'Come on,' 'It'll be fun,' and 'I'd rather eat my own fingers.'

While they flourished in the eighties, barn dances have been sighted well into the following decade. But lest a misunderstanding occur, let the author set it out clearly. There is nothing wrong with dancing. But the dance is not the issue. The issue is the barn. It's just wrong – morally wrong.

FAD **RATING** ✪ *'And promenade...'*

ELEVEN DANCE ERRORS

1. **The Lambada**
2. **The Body Pop**
3. **The Line Dance**
4. **The Breakdance**
5. **The Double Dutch**
6. **The Macarena**
7. **The Shag**
8. **The Hand Jive**
9. **The Conga**
10. **The Frug**
11. **The Pogo**

The Bean Bag

The chief defect of the bean bag as an item of furniture is that it is not filled with beans. Instead it is invariably filled with cheap polystyrene balls that escape through gaps in the zip and appear in random locations in the author's living room. The other problem with the polystyrene ball as a filling solution is that prolonged pressure from, say, a behind will cause the filling to compact to unacceptable levels, necessitating constant refills from a stall in Shepherds Bush market.

FAD Fact Marketers have found that so-called 'pester-power' increases in inverse proportion to the amount of time parents spend with their children. There are 1.5 million single-parent families in the UK.

When full, the bean bag operates as a kind of sub-standard pouffe, neither one thing nor the other. When the 'beans' are fully compacted the behind is generally separated from the floor by an amalgam of approximately 1mm of fabric and polystyrene. In tests, the zone of comfort between too full and too compacted was found to last 1.5 days. And that's scientific fact.

An auxiliary drawback of the bean bag as furniture is that the author's dog will use it as an unofficial latrine, causing the author to set fire to the bag for environmental reasons. As furniture, the bean bag is a failure. As an activity, however, it has achieved moderate success as the **Hacky Sack**®.

FAD RATING ✪ *'Buy a chair, you hippy.'*

The Beanie Baby

This was a collectible soft toy manufactured in the early nineties by US company Ty Inc. Each different Beanie Baby – following the formula set out by the **Cabbage Patch Kid**® guru Xavier Roberts, who in turn was very probably influenced by the **Kewpie** phenomenon – carried a tag with its name and birthday. Despite the toys being soft and cute, a vicious collecting craze broke out on both sides of the Atlantic, the flames fanned by McDonalds' insistence on licensing the toys for its Happy Meal range. In McDonald's on Oxford Street, London, the author witnessed a grown woman slap another woman's child for being served the toy she wanted ahead of her.

FAD Fact In the run up to Christmas 2001, 80 per cent of UK television advertisements were aimed at children. (Pine & Nash)

Among the new Beanie toys is 'Hero USA' the bear. He is dressed in an American army camouflage jacket and his motto is: 'We all pray/when day is done/that freedom comes/to everyone!' Or how about M.C. Beanie, the bear with the Mastercard-branded nose, whose own personal rhyme suggests his new friend take out a Mastercard. That we are a damaged species is not in question. The question is, how did we do it to ourselves?

FAD RATING ✪✪✪ *'Parents, we may also send surveys to your child.'*

The Betamax Video

The rise and fall of Sony's delightful Betamax video format, the first to achieve widespread use, is a lesson from which Apple Computer should have learned by now. Smaller and more compact than the rival VHS cassette format developed by JVC, Betamax originally offered a more reliable picture quality, better sound via Sony's 'Beta Hi-Fi' and more responsive transport. It also took up far less space. For a time, when home video-cassette recorders, or VCRs, were a relatively new phenomenon, Betamax was considered the superior format in every sense. Aspirant acquirers of gadgetry would tote the name like a badge of honour: 'Well, it's kind of you to offer to lend me *The Evil Dead*, but we run Betamax at our house,' was the kind of damning, throwaway line that would mark out the Beta Man as an Alpha Male (*see* **Evel Knievel**), a creature of elevated knowledge and taste, a higher earner by extension, one of life's winners (*see* **The Yuppie**). The kind of man that hits his KPIs (*see* **Eleven Key Corporate Issues**) and could, one imagined, easily beat you in a fist fight.

But he was laughing on the other side of his face a few years later. Take a trip to the video-rental club in the eighties and you would see that the Betamax shelf was ever diminishing in size and range, while the giant, clattering VHS tapes were taking over the store. The problem, as Sony co-founder Akio Morita later admitted, had been in Sony's 'inability' – or was it proprietary reluctance – to license their format to other manufacturers. JVC had done this early on; with more and more companies marketing their tapes and VCRs under licence, the VHS format hit the tipping point and came to dominate the industry.

The technical superiority of Betamax is demonstrated by the fact that, while the home-video market adopted VHS as standard, the television and video industry stuck with Betamax and Betacam for decades, really only fully giving way when digital video reached the required standard. Now that DV and DVD are viable realities, both old video formats have been consigned to the dustbin of history.

In the face of such competition, Sony eventually conceded defeat and began manufacturing VHS products and, while it continued to make a few Beta lines for the Japanese market, here too it eventually had to admit failure. While its heyday had long been over, Beta finally died in 2002, when Sony reluctantly switched off the life support and laid a wreath.

But if you're feeling a sudden rush of warm nostalgia for the vintage format, you could log on to one of the internet chat rooms dedicated to Betamax love. These are strange and frightening places, where people – men, the author is guessing – converse in product codes and strings of numbers designed to intimidate and confuse 'newbies'. The format may have died, but the chest-puffing lives on.

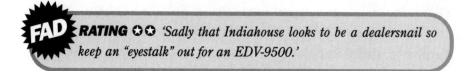

FAD RATING ✪✪ *'Sadly that Indiahouse looks to be a dealersnail so keep an "eyestalk" out for an EDV-9500.'*

'The Birdy Song'

The best possible application for The Tweets' eighties dance craze 'The Birdy Song' was discovered in 2004 by the Chinese authorities in Hong Kong. They used it as the theme tune to a series of grave radio warnings about the dangers of bird flu, which had successfully migrated to humans and was killing them to death. It worked very well, as radio listeners, who were subjected to the broadcasts over two years, had long come to associate the chirpy electronic melody with spasmodic convulsions and a desire to die.

 RATING ✪✪✪ *'With a little bit of this and a little bit of that...'*

ELEVEN FAD ADJECTIVES

1. **Bad** *adj.* – good
2. **Bling bling** *adj.* – booyakasha *qv.*
3. **Booyakasha** *adj.* – bad *qv.*
4. **Cosmic** *adj.* – gravy *qv.*
5. **Cruddy** *adj.* – minging *qv.*
6. **Gravy** *adj.* – groovy *qv.*
7. **Groovy** *adj.* – cosmic *qv.*
8. **Minging** *adj.* – cruddy *qv.*
9. **Safe** *adj.* – sweet
10. **Wicked** *adj.* – safe *qv.*
11. **Wizard** *adj.* – wicked *qv.*

Black Tower, Blue Nun, etc

'Sometimes you want something easy, something casual, something fresh…' But you have no idea what that might be, so you chicken out and buy Black Tower. This, the Nescafé of white wines (*see* **Instant Coffee**), offered a clearly branded solution to the grape-ignorant plonk-seeker, which was in fact 90 per cent of the market. Alas, because of the extreme snobbery now attached to giving and 'appreciating fine wines' – and the aspirant nature of 90 per cent of the market – Black Tower is now condemned to join its natural stablemates Blue Nun and Mateus Rosé in the bucket marked 'reduced for lone drinkers'. Or is it?

There is an initial sense in branding wine. The punter knows what he is going to get. It's safe and not actively offensive. But that will only get you so far. What wine-makers fail to realize is that the act of branding wine with anything other than a discreet château label renders it instantly unsuitable for giving, due to the embarrassment factor, thus cutting out that 90 per cent of the market again.

There was a time when no British citizen, other than one or two émigré publishers, could tell the difference between a Pinot and a Pineau, and we were glad of any help we could get in choosing alcoholic drinks. Such brands seemed dashingly sophisticated and continental, shining out like a golden stepping stone to a better life. Today Woking, tomorrow Venezia. But now, thanks to cheap snobbery mentors such as the bestselling Malcolm Gluck, we are all experts on the supermarket aisle and the branded wine has become unspeakably 'non-u'. Hardly the thing to take back to our suburban homes. Cheaper travel and communication has allowed Lord Belborough and Chippy Minton alike to find out for themselves that the French certainly do not 'adore le Piat D'Or', nor have they ever heard of it. Even perky flat-top peddler Paul Masson, once the modish Californian number-one seed, has now gone the way of all brands. Nowadays, anything bearing the legend Liebfraumilch (not literally 'Lovely Lady-Milk') has been sent to Coventry in favour of anything bearing the legend Chardonnay (eighties singer of 'Smooth Operator'). But in the view of this book, given the precedent, the brash antipodean favourite Blossom Hill is frankly on borrowed time.

THAT WAS THE YEAR...
Pre-war Toy Crazes

c. 1600 Hoop-twisting craze sweeps England.

1759 Roller skates invented. Swiftly put away.

1903 Crayons. Those wild Edwardians.

1908 Hornby bangs out Meccano.

1909 The Kewpie Doll enthrals mawkish America.

If only. The facts prove the author wrong, even as he writes. French vineyards, saddled with mountains of unsold *Vins de Pays d'Origine Contrôlée*, sporting the labels of distinguished if obscure châteaux, have recently been forced to sell off their finely crafted export produce for car fuel as foreign punters in their millions eschew the quality viniculture of generations in favour of branded Australian plonk. Oh well.

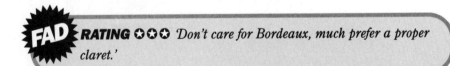

FAD **RATING** ✪✪✪ *'Don't care for Bordeaux, much prefer a proper claret.'*

The Blakey

Once you had attached this crescent-shaped shoe-support to your sole, you could preen about, clacking the heels of your tatty shoes for effect. In the past people repaired their heels with tin tacks. Then companies such as Blakey sold pre-shaped apparatus. Worn for effect by many, Blakeys were often banned by schools for causing (deliberate) damage to floors. 'Would you walk about like that at home?'

That was in the days before the great shoe-repair depression, during which cobblers were forced to diversify into key-cutting to carve out a living. Now, of course, shoes are made to fall apart; in many instances the only thing holding them together is their brand label. And when the world peeks through the bottom, we just buy a new pair.

FAD **RATING** ✪ ✪ ✪ *'Ee, look at me seggity boots!'*

The BMX Bike

The concept of bicycle moto-cross differed greatly from real moto-cross, the rough-country motorbike sport. BMX was about doing special moves on a bike designed and bought for the purpose. BMX bikes had straight forks and horizontal pegs coming out of the wheels, to aid in the gravity-defying freestyle tricks that people insisted were not silly, such as 'double-pegging'. But the BMX was an advance on the skateboard in that it was at least a proper mode of transport. Sort of. Until you went down a hill. Lack of gears meant your legs went round very fast indeed and the low-slung nature of the frame meant that tall people looked like giant spiders when they sat on their BMX. A great bike for jumping on building sites, in the days before parents sued for accident compensation, the BMX soon disappeared from the streets and was reclaimed by the sporting types who invented it, probably much to their glee.

FAD **RATING** ✪✪✪ *'I ride street and park.'*

The Body

The early nineties saw the rise to prominence of the leotard as a viable female undergarment. Vest and pants all in one, the 'body' offered one design factor that set it apart from gymnasium attire: the poppered gusset, for speed-toileting. Some say the breast-flattening former swimming costume was as fundamentally unsexy as the **leg-warmer** or the ski-pant. But do not underestimate the ticklish sense of anticipation garnered by that promising 'pop-pop' sound.

 FAD **RATING ✪** *'Let me slip into something less comfortable.'*

HOW TO START A CRAZE

Sell something that already exists

The Frisbee®, the Yo-Yo®, Jacks, the Hula-Hoop®, Pogs. No one dreamed up anything new here. What Knerr and Melin of Wham-O did with the hoop-twirling craze was simple. They were very very quick. A friend tipped them off that it was happening already in a low-key way. They simply found something they could patent – a cheap plastic-hoop design – something they could trademark – the Hula-Hoop® – and the rest was advertising. They pulled off the same trick with the Frisbee®. Donald Duncan's slogan, 'if it isn't a Duncan, it isn't a real Yo-Yo® top,' claimed the ancient 'bandalore' toy for one man. If people are going to do something anyway, they might as well do it your way.

The Budgie

Statistically, both you and your granny are less likely to own a budgie these days. It seems hard to imagine – in our age of vegetarianism, free speech and sandals – but there was a point in time when you simply couldn't move for cuttlefish bones.

The word 'budgerigar' comes from the native Australian *'betcherrygah'*, meaning 'good food'. Which is true if the alternative is wombat and lamingtons. In their native Australia, wild budgies gather in massive billowing flocks, free as the day they were hatched, until they are caught in a net and sold to an old woman for money. Their natural plumage is light green, but selective breeding has caused budgies to mutate into a variety of colours pleasing to the collector, including mostly blue. First noted by a colonist in the eighteenth century, the budgerigar has become the most popular cage bird of all time. If you were playing Trapped Bird **Top Trumps**, for example, the budgie would be a prize card and would probably beat the parrot, the canary, the minah, the cockatiel and the finch on a number of counts.

Some might suggest that budgie-keeping has fallen from favour because of the cruelty involved in trapping a winged creature in a tiny cage and never giving it a proper worm. But in fact a budgie should never be given a worm. They are vegetarians and prefer a mix of seeds, green leaves and fruit. Budgies fed on worm will soon die – perhaps another reason for the decline. Budgie enthusiasts are clear about correct feeding: 'Budgerigars should not be fed biscuit or cake as they make the budgerigar fat,' says one breeder. Quite.

The keeping of birds is now viewed as ignorant and immoral by a growing number of people in many countries; the keeping of exotic birds, more so, as a bird designed to hatch on the Australian plains and fly thousands of miles in its eight-year life really doesn't belong in a cage in Cleethorpes. Those of us tempted to put this, the smallest of the parakeet family, into our living room as a kind of living, tweeting ornament now tend to feel shamed out of it, however much we might secretly long to stroke its shiny feathers, sing it music-hall songs and feed it Viscount biscuits and Guinness.

If you want to look at a bird, open the curtains. While writing this entry the author has spotted a jay, a thrush, several starlings, a robin, an unidentified warbler and, earlier this morning while walking along the river, he saw a family of tufted ducks, twelve coots, some Canada geese, moorhens and mallards, a yellowhammer, two mute swans, a heron and two cormorants. In Wild Bird **Top Trumps**, that would beat a budgie hands down. This said, you might also spot a budgie in your garden. The creature is hardy enough to live outside all year round and you can't help but whoop with encouragement at those who have defiantly flown the cage. If you own a budgie, know that one day it will seek its freedom. A **Tamagotchi**, however, will never leave you.

FAD Fact In recent studies, pre-school children knew the difference between television programmes and advertising, but thought they were watching public service announcements. (Pine & Nash)

FAD RATING ✪✪ *'Why won't it speak?' 'Because it hates you.'*

The Bungee

'I cannot imagine it. It is crazy,' bungee-jump operator Georg Hoedle told the *Sonntags Zeitung* newspaper in his native Switzerland. 'We went over our safety guidelines painstakingly after the Saxetenbach accident, in which 21 people drowned. Every staff member is safety conscious right down to his fingertips. And now this.' Mr Hoedle, owner of the Adventure World action-holiday company, was talking to reporters about the tragic fate of a 22-year-old American, who had just leapt 100 metres to his death on an elasticated rope provided by Adventure World. Mr Hoedle admitted that there had been two cords in the cable car from which the man had plummeted – one for the 100-metre jump and another for a 180-metre jump – but could not confirm which had been used when the man's head collided with the ground at full speed. 'We don't know anything,' he said.

In the olden days there was the bungee. It was a short length of elasticated flex with hooks on either end. Your dad used it to trap items on his roof rack. When it was not being used for this purpose it hung on a hook in the garage or shed. And that's bungee history. Then, on 10 October 1982, something happened. The following day, *The Times* reported it thus:

'A man leapt 170 foot from the Clifton suspension bridge in Bristol yesterday using an elasticated rope. He bounced like a **Yo-Yo** twice before freeing himself and disappearing.'

According to the report, bridge toll staff who witnessed the scene called the police immediately, but 'neither the jumper nor his accomplices' were to be seen. There was speculation that they may have made away in a speedboat. Accomplices? Police? In 1982, the only person who performed feats such as the one *The Times* recounted with such relish was James Bond. Perhaps suspecting this was a story about diamond smuggling or international espionage, our journal of record dished it up as national news.

It only seems naive in retrospect. Nowadays, the craze for bungee-jumping, which blossomed in the nineties into both 'extreme' sport and ubiquitous sideshow, is so well known that it only makes the news with stories like that of Mr Hoedle. He's not the only one whose career in bungee provision took a dive. In June 2001 a 22-year-old woman died in the same way after leaping from a French viaduct. The organizer in this case admitted an 'error' with the elasticity of the cord.

You might think it was relatively simple. The principle of bungee-jumping is this. You leap. The cord stretches, stretches, stretches, then recoils. You are pulled back up into the air to experience something called a 'rush'. For this to work, the cord in its flaccid state must be much, much shorter than the distance from platform to ground to allow it to reach its full extension and still clear the Tarmac. Otherwise the jumper will instead experience something called 'death'. You might think this sort of thing goes beyond elementary physics and becomes simple common sense. But what role would common sense have in bungee-jumping? Common sense would stay at home. Indeed common sense had clearly stayed at home in 1997, when the *Washington Post* reported the sad tale of fast-food worker Eric Barcia, who decided to bungee-jump 70 foot from a railway bridge. Mr Barcia had accordingly constructed his own 70-foot bungee cord for this specific purpose. Those two numbers again...

Tales of death by bungee abound. That's because people often die by bungee. The reader may choose to decide that evolution alone is in play here, that nature is simply regulating itself in the only way it knows. In this respect, bungee-jumping is the best of crazes, as it allows people to experience lemming-like behaviour at its most literal and elemental.

FAD **RATING ✪✪✪** *'I'm flying I'm flying I'm...'*

Buzz Lightyear

Parents want to please their kids. But the big toy-manufacturers had passed up the opportunity to make *Toy Story*'s space-ace hero, as they felt the film would flop (*see* **Star Wars**). The task fell to an obscure Canadian firm, which struggled to meet demand. With supplies on the thin side and Buzz mania raging, competition for the toy was rife. There was fighting in the aisles and not everyone could afford the £26.99 price tag. Shaun Markey thought

FAD Fact Some psychologists believe children do not learn to be sceptical about television advertising until between the ages of seven and nine. But research has found that children display loyalty to brands from as young as two years old.
(Pine & Nash)

he had got away with stealing his from Woolworth's in Hereford. Police gave chase, but lost him when he hid motionless behind a hedge. Markey kept silent as the sniffer dogs prowled, but not the toy, whose speech programs were activated by motion sensors. 'Buzz Lightyear, permission to engage,' the hero space-man cried into the night. 'If it hadn't been for Buzz Lightyear I would definitely have escaped,' Markey told the *Daily Mail*.

FAD RATING ✪✪✪✪ *To infinity and beyond.'*

The Cabbage Patch Kid®

'One day, a young boy named Xavier Roberts wandered into a magic cabbage patch hidden behind a beautiful waterfall. He discovered busy little Bunnybees® sprinkling cabbages with magic crystals. Suddenly, all sorts of different kids and babies peeked out of the cabbages! Each one had his or her own special look, personality, name and birthday. "I'll call you the Cabbage Patch Kids®!" he said, as everyone cheered.

'Xavier fell in love with the 'Kids™ and built Babyland General® Hospital just for them. It's a safe, happy place to live and play until someone like you...' finds them stuffed into a cardboard box and piled high on a shelf at Toys R Us, price-marked, barcoded and traded for money like so much meat.

So runs the 'folklore' tale peddled as the 'legend' of the Cabbage Patch Kids®. More or less. The real ending has each child 'adopted' in glowing soft focus, amid a cloud of beneficent Bunnybees®. It's easy to adopt one of these kids. There are no forms to fill in, no criminal-record checks and no social worker will call. All you have to do is hand over the 'adoption fee' – formerly known as recommended retail price – to the oik behind the till.

The first problem with this story is that it is lazy. So lazy, in fact, that it verges on the contemptuous. A risibly unimaginative pastiche of Walt Disney schmaltz, it bears all the hallmarks of something written not *for* children but *at* them. Why is everyone cheering?

The second problem is that Xavier Roberts is real. The fact that the progenitor of this craze contrives to write a fairy tale in which he is the hero tells us a little something about where he is coming from. Not a young boy, exactly, but a canny quiltcraft student who, in 1977, came up with the 'marketing concept' of adoptable people with birth certificates, perhaps after reading of the phenomenal success of the **Kewpie Doll**. Babyland General® was a real place, staffed by bogus carers in uniform, who adopted the 'Kids™ right out of their simulated beds. Roberts, who founded the 'Original Appalachian Artworks' company with some friends to manufacture the dolls, found that punters were willing to pay quite high prices for his hand-made 'Little People' dolls. Actually, Roberts didn't like them to be called 'dolls' – they were real children, as anyone could see, by the puffy cheeks, close, deep-set eyes and woollen hair. Despite utmost ugliness the dolls appealed to those of us who like doilies, cosies, cross-stitch and other homespun arts and crafts (*see* **Macramé**), which, it turns out, is an awful lot of us. In 1982 Roberts signed a licensing deal with the toy company Coleco, which ushered in the Cabbage Patch name and mass-produced the quilted kids for mass 'adoption'.

The adoption was not just a coy gimmick. In sending back the adoption papers to Coleco for a phoney certificate, children and adult collectors were giving away valuable information about themselves for use by the marketing department.

Doll-seekers regularly slept outside toyshops for the right to fight each other for the fast-selling 'Kids™. They were highly collectible, you see, because each was unique, just like a real child. Except they wouldn't fill their nappies or walk under a bus. Coleco used its marketing muscle to ensure a 'Kid™ went up into space in a highly publicized NASA shuttle mission. Christopher [cough] Xavier became the first Cabbage Patch Kid® in space. Now there's history. As popular with adults as with children, original hand-made dolls now regularly sell on the second-hand market for upwards of £200. Sorry, that word is taboo. They do not sell. They adopt. They do not resell, they readopt.

There is nothing intrinsically wrong with these toys, they brought happiness to millions, not the least of whom was Xavier Roberts. The real problem with this mawkish confection of a product is that so many people bought into it. The adoption schtick was central to the success of the Cabbage Patch Kids® brand. Children and adults alike just loved it. But are we really so emotionally impoverished that this trademarked sentimentality-lite can push all our buttons to the tune of 65 million units – sorry, 'Kids™ – in eight years?

And how were we repaid for our love? In 1996, *The Mirror* reported that a child had unwittingly donated part of her body to a greedy Cabbage Patch® doll. 'The Snack Time Kid, which is only supposed to "eat" plastic French fries and other fake food, clamped its jaws on her scalp and pulled her hair out by the roots.' The story alleged that **Barbie**® marketers, Mattel, who now market the 'Kids™, had received ten such hair-eating complaints in the US.

It's nice to make soft toys and these did no one any harm beyond the supermarket stampedes and a few reported scalpings, and the Snack Time Kid was never sold in the UK. They're soft, for the most part non-violent, unthreatening dolls. It could be so much worse. But the success of Roberts' marketing ploy is a sad indictment of our emotional priorities. If we want to pay £200 for the buzz of adopting something, why don't we adopt something that is genuinely alive, at least today? As the landfill sites spill over with unwanted hair-eating toys, there are conservation centres the world over who would be glad of our money.

FAD RATING ✪✪✪✪✪ *'Stop lecturing me, you hypocrite. You bought a My Little Pony.'*

The Care Bear

According to the Which Care Bear Are You? quiz, the author of this book is Cheer Bear. This means he is the 'Care Bear cheerleader'. His 'spunky' personality and optimism lifts everyone's spirit. Though he wants everyone to be happy, he stands his ground on issues he feels strongly about and this can bring disunity among his friends. Despite this, he is a true believer in working together. It also means he is pink and has a rainbow on his belly, but that's not for here.

Had he answered the questionnaire differently he could have been Bedtime Bear ('usually asleep on the job'), Birthday Bear ('happy-go-lucky personality makes you vulnerable to cheap tricks'), Friend Bear ('sometimes you worry about your friends' problems so much you forget about your own responsibilities'), Funshine Bear ('filled with unlimited energy'), Good Luck Bear ('everything will turn out just great'), Love-a-lot Bear ('everyone considers you the sweetest person they know'), Tenderheart Bear ('power to command attention'), Wish Bear ('The dreamer of the group') or, heaven forbid, Grumpy Bear. Grumpy Bear is always complaining about something, but 'people like him anyways because he is mysteriously charming and cute when mad.'

Which Care Bear are you, dear reader? Come on, think.

It's always a comfort for consumers when a toy contains its chief instruction in its name. *Care* for your *bear*. *Care* about getting a *bear*, who *cares*. For you. At no point let your imagination take *care* of your *bear* needs. Do not invent your own name for your *bear*. Who *cares* about such random, unbranded *bears*? Our *bears* have been *care*fully programmed with preselected personalities, names and stories by American Greetings. Because AG *cares*. About you and your *bears*. Do not engage

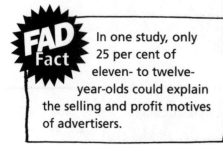

in creative play. Repeatedly act out scenes from our two-season TV series on ABC America, our syndicated TV series and our smash-hit feature film *The Care Bears Movie* and its three sequels. Or take inspiration from the 45 million Care Bears books, comics, colouring and activity books we have *care*fully published at you. Do as we say.

Hey, parents. Don't you *care* about your children? Don't you *care* that they don't have the right *bears*? Don't teach them that 'Ring o' Roses' rubbish. Sing the Care Bears songs we made up for them, such as 'Nobody *Cares* Like a *Bear*'. That's it. Now we own the whole learning process, your child will grow up *caring* about our *bears*. When it is old enough to *care* for children of its own, what *bear* will it choose? That's right. The Care Bear. Because American Greetings *cares*. Especially about the money it has made from 40 million Care Bear 'units' sold between 1983 and 1987 alone. Ah, children are so easy to manipulate. It's a piece of cake, a lovely piece of **Strawberry Shortcake**. Hold on. Now *there's* an idea.

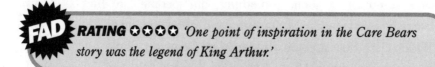

FAD **RATING ✪✪✪✪** *'One point of inspiration in the Care Bears story was the legend of King Arthur.'*

The CB Radio

Breaker one-nine. Hey, good buddy, took my big mack down the big slab to Big-D, got the bears on my back all the way, know what I'm sayin'? So I got the pedal to the metal tryin' to beat the bushes an' all, not sure of my twenty but I think I lost them. So I pull in for a coke stop at this choke 'n' puke and I'm sitting there in the beaver trap, chewin' the cud when this alligator station starts breakin'. Now I ain't sayin' I'm no fog-lifter or boast toastie, but this breaker dude comes on with his Benton Harbor Lunchbox, ain't getting' nothing but beer tone outta that rig, copy? Yeah that's a big ten-four. Gotta split now, Big Daddy on my back, catch ya on the flip-flop. Eighty-eights around the house an' all the good numbers, down an' on the side, jus' copyin' the mail, good buddy.*

And so on.

The Citizens Band radio was the brainchild of a Toronto-born wireless enthusiast called Al Gross (1918–2000). As a child in the 1920s, Gross was captivated, one day out on the great lakes, by the sounds made by a steamboat's telegraph. 'I got up to the top deck and I came near the radio room and I heard the noise of the spark transmitter,' he told the *Institute* magazine. His father bought him a **crystal set** radio and Gross was away. He discovered the amateur radio (or ham radio) band, found a local operator and asked the man to teach him. By the age of twelve Gross had his own workshop, built from junkyard scrap.

In adolescence, Gross decided to focus on creating a stable two-way communication device, and in 1938 his prototype, which he called the 'walkie-talkie', attracted the attention of the US Office of Strategic Services.

The OSS recruited Gross and, throughout the Second World War, the inventor developed an enhanced walkie-talkie system for military ground-to-air communications. Its broadcasts were impossible to intercept by enemy surveillance and the device remained classified until 1976.

After the war, Gross formed his own company, the Citizens Radio Corporation and developed two-way radio for personal use, selling to coast-guards and farmers. In 1948 Gross successfully lobbied the US Federal Communications Committee (FCC) and gained approval for his sets to be used on the newly developed Citizens Band airwaves.

Sadly, Gross was a man ahead of the zeitgeist. By the time his inventions took off, his patents had long-since expired. He had also invented the radio pager, back in 1949, but by the time the bleeper had been embraced by the world's drug-dealers, gangsters and middle managers, Gross was no longer profiting.

By the early seventies, the Citizens Band had found a niche with American truckers, who developed a singular slang (*see* above *and* below). America was in the grip of an oil crisis at that time, and draconian speed restrictions had been introduced in a bid to save fuel. Truckers disliked this, hence the constant need to tell their 'good buddies' about any smokeys (police) and speed traps there might be lurking.

Cult interest in the CB was at a high when Hal Needham's slang-ridden 1977 trucker film, *Smokey and the Bandit,* brought it firmly into the public domain, as renegade haulage-contractor Burt Reynolds outwitted caricature southern sheriffs by cunning use of the Citizens Band. Sam Peckinpah's *Convoy* brought the point home the following year, and the two movies, with their tales of under-the-counter fellowship, effectively popularized the CB radio worldwide and glamorized it as a tool for the rebellious and cool. It was your gateway to the sub-culture. Users had 'handles' or pseudonyms. Hey, we could be anyone!

Fast-forward to Cradley Heath, England, 1982. In a small terraced house in Scrivens Close, socially challenged fourteen-year-old and newcomer to the CB hobby Robert Skeetes has just 'gone live' with his own illegal rig, made from a Fray Bentos tin and cheese-grater. Let's tune in and hear the 'bleedover' from that bodacious CB chat in full:

'Breaker, breaker…'

'A-right. What's your handle then?'

'The Exterminator.'

'No because you can't be called "The Exterminator" because you know Nick Preet, he's already called it. Come back?'

'Oh, right. Ten four, mate.'

'You can't say *mate*, you've got to say *good buddy*. Are you new or sommut?'

'Oh yeah. Soz.'

(30 seconds' radio silence)

'So, what kind of rig you got then?'

'Fray Bentos tin and cheese-grater.'

'No because that's rubbish because you know my cousin, he's got the Maplin Hobbymatic and that's well bostin, copy?'

'Piss off.'

'No because you're not allowed to swear on CB because that's *profanity*.'

And there you have it. The CB was never legal in the UK, which boosted its appeal to the average adolescent. Sadly, the conversations did not really merit the risk. This cruel anticlimax, however, was more than compensated for by the boom in mobile telephones, which was waiting just around the corner. Al Gross was ultimately behind this too, having invented the technology that made cellular telephony possible. Portable phones could reach people more than five miles away, people you actually knew and liked, while the socially challenged now have internet chatrooms. But that's a whole other fad, slang and rulebook. Despite being obsolete, the CB radio still exists. Aside from those US truckers who continue to find it professionally useful, the medium is now chiefly the domain of amateur broadcast enthusiasts and gadget collectors. Or, as one proud user put it: 'CB is still a leading hobby.'

Mr Gross had a slightly different take when, shortly before he died, he told reporters: 'If I still had the patents on my inventions, Bill Gates would have to stand aside for me.'

* **Translation**: Breaker one-nine. (*Sorry to butt in but…*) Hey, good buddy (*we have never met*), took my big mack down the big slab to Big-D (*I was driving my articulated lorry down the freeway towards the large Texas city of Dallas*), got the bears on my back all the way (*some hairy homosexuals appeared to be mounting me [surely, the police were chasing me? Ed.]*), know what I'm sayin' (*because I was breaking the speed limit by going at 50 miles an hour*)? So I got the pedal to the metal tryin' to beat the bushes an' all (*so I accelerated to try to evade arrest*), not sure of my twenty (*I had forgotten my A–Z*) but I think I lost them. So I pull in for a coke stop (*short rest*) at this choke 'n' puke (*'at your Moto service station'*) and I'm sitting there in the beaver trap (*lorry [vulg.]*), chewin' the cud when this alligator station (*loudmouthed individual*) starts breakin' (*talking over me*). Now I ain't sayin' I'm no fog-lifter or boast toastie (*I don't pretend to be fascinating company*), but this breaker dude comes on with his Benton Harbor Lunchbox (*Fray Bentos tin and cheese-grater*), ain't getting' nothing but beer tone outta that rig, copy? (*The sound quality of his inferior CB radio was not up to my standards, thus I win.*) Yeah that's a big ten-four. (*I agree with whatever you just said.*) Gotta split now, Big Daddy (*the FCC*) is on my back (*for using more than my legally allotted talk-time*), catch ya on the flip-flop (*I'll call you again on my return journey, if you can wait that long*). Eighty-eights around the house an' all the good numbers (*best regards*), down an' on the side (*I'm going to stop talking but, for your information, I will keep the speaker on*),

jus' copyin' the mail (*and listen to everybody else's conversations*), good buddy (*relative stranger*).

FAD RATING ✪✪✪✪ *'Ten-four on that choke 'n' puke.'*

SEE THE JOIN

The CB Radio + The Magic Eye™ = Morris Dance

The common factor in this grisly equation is one Sir Charles Wheatstone (1802–75). The British physicist experimented with electricity, optics and acoustics, and his forays into the former led him to invent and develop the telegraph. He was also the first scientist to create a three-dimensional image from two flat images viewed from different perspectives: the stereoscope. In 1844, inspired to perfect the breed of portable 'free' reed instruments of which the harmonica was the humble father, he patented the concertina. I think we both know where this is going…

In the early twentieth century a Canadian called Al Gross was inspired to create the talkie-Talkie radio after hearing the sounds from a steamboat's telegraph. This became the mode by which people could hold two-way radio conversations over the US 'Citizen's Band' during the seventies. Meanwhile, the Hungarian-born US optics expert Béla Julesz had developed his random-dot stereogram from Wheatstone's early work on spatial perception. This formed the basis for the algorithm behind the Magic Eye™ puzzles of the eighties.

In 1899, the English composer Cecil Sharp was so overwhelmed by the sounds of rustic country dances coming from a concertina played by William Kimber of the Headington Quarry Morris that he vowed to revive the waning dance tradition and integrate it fully into the nation's cultural heritage. His efforts spurred a widespread craze for country dancing around the turn of the last century and helped to create the revived, concertina-toting Morris we see today. All in all this gives us a fully-fledged fad hat-trick from the talented Sir Charles.

The Chad

The original British 'Chad' was a picture of a man peeping over a wall and asking the perennial question, 'Wot no… ?' Widely believed to have been originated in 1938 by the cartoonist George Chatterton, Chad enjoyed a long freelance career as a graffito, commenting on topical socioeconomic issues. Wot no meat? Wot no justice? Wot no jobs? Wot no booze? However, in the second half of the twentieth century, the UK's version of America's 'Kilroy was here' suffered a slow decline. There is no apparent reason for this, but Chad lovers can take heart from the fact that the word has recently found new employment as the minute disc of card punched out of an American voting slip during the 'counting' process. Dimpled chads are on offer, along with pregnant chads, while the now infamous 'dangling chad' was blamed for vote-counting 'errors' in the 2000 US election: a political scandal that has become known as 'Chadgate'.

FAD **RATING** ✪✪✪ *'Wot no democracy?'*

The Chemistry Set

Aunty's Christmas present today. Tomorrow's iron filing stuck in your toe.

Perform simple experiments at home, such as making stink bombs and spilling the potassium permanganate over the carpet to create an indelible purple stain. Watch and document Daddy's facial expressions, repeatedly over time.

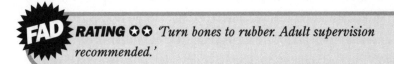

FAD *RATING* ✪✪ *'Turn bones to rubber. Adult supervision recommended.'*

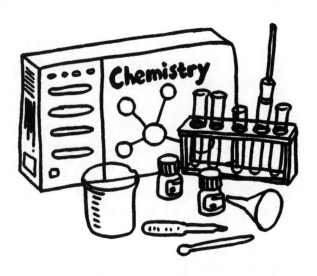

Chintz, chucking out one's

In 1996 the advertising agency St Luke's came up with the slogan 'Chuck out your chintz' as a way to browbeat the British into updating their interior décor at Ingvar Kamprad's Ikea chain. Despite the campaign being 'much praised' by the industry, by 2002 the fifty-year-old Swedish retailer had severed its links with the agency and taken its advertising contract in-house. Reports vary. It's not that the British dislike having their taste criticized. But as the popularity of the brutal makeover show *What Not To Wear* has shown, we like our critics to be home-grown.

There is something about being invaded by Scandinavians that sits uneasily with the Britannic race memory. The idea of being chastised by someone whose name contains an 'ø' has us raising the drawbridge and reaching for the mead. Some say the campaign was an 'advertising disaster' that caused British consumers to avoid the giant home-furnishings warehouses in droves. But, looking at the queues for meatballs and berry sauce on the average Saturday, the author is not convinced. We can't transform our living spaces fast enough. In 2000, 230 million people got rid of their flying ducks via the chain's portals worldwide, no doubt aided by the deluge of home-improvement shows on television – not only a UK phenomenon. In justifying its move away from St Luke's, Ikea said: 'The brief was to tackle the issue of British homeowners' conservatism. Six years on and that battle is won.' Yes, but there's no need to rub our noses in it. We island races can be tetchy.

FAD **RATING ✪✪✪** *'You have been assimilated.'*

Clothkits

The enterprising Lewes-based company Clothkits Knitwear, now sadly defunct and sorely missed, sold flat pieces of fabric, printed with shapes. What happened was that your mum then cut out the shapes, sewed them up into a stripy T-shirt or stripy pinafore dress and made you wear the result as your actual clothes. A generation of urban children thus faced a hostile world dressed as Amish settlers. The company also served a very useful purpose in allowing parents to save money while indulging in the seventies craze for soft crafts (*see* **Macramé**). It was a make-your-own rag-doll kit. And that rag doll was you.

FAD **RATING** ✪✪ *'You'll grow into it.'*

The Comedy Tie

Offices in the early nineties were immeasurably brightened by the use of comedy ties by male middle-managers and other minor executives. Toy elephants, the Simpsons, Sylvester and Tweety-Pie, Wicked Willy. Not only was it really, really funny but it was also a biting post-modern comment on corporate conformity.

In truth, we are to beware of men whose idea of levelling a serious challenge to the reigning authority is to wear a tasteless tie. The statement is clear: 'I might turn up on time every day and perform my duties like an unquestioning drone, but I'm still well mad, me, eh?' This is not how revolutions are won. As a result of their bold stance on this and other issues, such as the amusing anatomical photocopy, all wearers have now been promoted laterally to improbably named positions behind glass partitions, where they are free to play with their **executive toys** and devise company policy on **dress-down Friday** without affecting the bottom line.

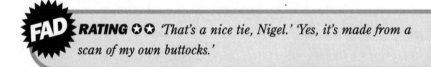

FAD **RATING ✪✪** *'That's a nice tie, Nigel.' 'Yes, it's made from a scan of my own buttocks.'*

Commando comics

Boys who played with **Action Man** or built **Airfix Kits** of tanks and fighter planes were also wont to read *Commando* comic. While girls were given pink and purple comics called things like *Twinkle* which focused on love, friendship and bracelets (*see* **The Friendship Bracelet**), boys were offered in 1961 this small format mini-book about killing by DC Thomson, who also brought you *The Beano* and *The Dandy*. Filled with ultra-real line drawings of anguished squaddies meeting their bloody end in a swamp or being blown to smithereens by a grenade, and all the rage for a certain time, the comic's chief accomplishment was in fact to teach a whole generation of schoolboys to say, 'Die, pig-dog,' and *'Gott im Himmel!'* Lest we forget, eh?

 **FAD RATING ✪✪** *'Schnell, schnell.'*

Crimped Hair

You could make your hair look simultaneously like a crinkle-cut chip and Dougal out of the *Magic Roundabout* by simple application of the crimper. What you did, you took a clump of your hair and singed it between the two hot, ribbed sides of what was basically a small electric **Sandwich Toaster**. Possibilities were numerous, such as the crimped fringe and ponytail combination. When you had done the whole lot you became Crystal Tipps and frightened suitors away. For this reason the crimped hair, but a passing fashion in normal circles, found its true and lasting home with the Goth during the eighties and can still be seen in parts of Cornwall.

 FAD RATING ✪✪ *'That's how Siouxsie Sioux does it...'*

The Crystal Set

Instead of spending good money on a proper radio, why not laboriously construct this gimcrack half-measure? All you needed was a coil of wire, a crystal diode, a slide contact, a long wire 'antenna' dangling out of the window and a soldering iron, and you were all set to almost hear approximately one radio station. Why bother? Well, as the Crystal Set Society will tell you, building a working radio from scratch is a worthwhile and great learning activity. How do you think the first radios were made, eh?

 FAD **RATING ✪** *'Fffffft, bzzzzz, parp, ffffft, breaker one-nine...'*

ELEVEN MORE FAD ADJECTIVES

1. **Bobbins** *adj.* – rubbish
2. **Shite** *adj.* – wack
3. **Wack** *adj.* – bobbins
4. **Naff** *adj.* – shite
5. **Pukka** *adj.* – safe *qv.*
6. **Sound** *adj.* – pukka
7. **Crazy** *adj.* – groovy *qv.*
8. **Capital** *adj. (C19th only)* – sound *qv.*
9. **Happening** *adj.* – slammin'
10. **Swinging** *adj.* – happening *qv.*
11. **WYSIWYG** *adj.* – What You Get Is Bobbins Software

Cup-a-Soup®

Never underestimate the money to be made from selling people things they already have. It worked in 1800 when Spencer Perceval's Tory government privatized England's common ground. More importantly, it worked in the twenties for the **Yo-Yo**®. Here's another example: soup. Bachelor had been selling tinned soup for aeons before they decided that opening a can and heating up the contents simply wasn't instant enough. No, the thing to do would be to sell the public dehydrated soup. Tip in the powder, pour on the boiling water. Done. Yes, I know it tastes bad, but people are lazy. They'll drink sump oil rather than make their own dinner. So – now we have a luminous gloop that tastes like crisp flavouring. How to sell it? Tell people they don't have time for stuff. 'You're too busy to make dinner, you live a hectic life because you're important, you're at your desk all day, you need instant soup. Buy it. Thank you.'

Gosh, they're right. I *am* important. Instead of taking a well-earned, unpaid break this lunchtime I'll stay at my desk with my **executive toy**, donate a free hour of work to my employer and drink soup that tastes of crisp flavouring. If that's not a measure of my importance I'd like to know what is.

Bachelor's Cup-a-Soup® is now owned in the UK by Van de Burgh Foods, a subsidiary of Unilever, the world's third largest food manufacturer. While the adverts tell you, 'You always get a hug from a Bachelor's mug,' some parents' websites allege you'd be a mug to drink it.

For example, the author has just got outside of a cup 'a' 'Creamy Broccoli and Cauliflower'. It's good news for his blood-sugar level but bad news for vegetable fans. Broccoli is vaguely present at 3 per cent. Cauliflower is more of a trace element at 1.3 per cent. Where the product majors, however, is in the provision of carbohydrates: glucose syrup solids, glucose syrup and plain old sucrose figure high on the list, along with salt, flavour enhancers (more salts), spices and cheap bulking-agent maize starch.

Now the marketing. In the US, Cup-a-Soup is sold under the Lipton brand. At www.cupasoup.com you can find instructions for beating the '3 p.m. slump' at your desk. Basically this involves drinking Cup-a-Soup. There is a picture of a man, galvanized and reanimated. In an instant. Sugar will do this, yes.

There was a time when anything instant was *de rigueur*. **Instant coffee**, instant mash. Such things spoke to us of a brave new post-war world, a modern world, where technology, **Tupperware** and astronaut food would lead us out of depression and into the light. Now, of course, we have *seen* the light. We now know that instant soup has virtually no nutritional value and tastes of crisp flavouring. Life's hugs should be more exciting than that.

FAD **RATING ✪✪** *'Soup of the day is Cup-a-Soup, Sir, crisp-flavouring flavour. Would you like to see the wine menu? I can recommend the Black Tower.'*

The Deely Bopper

Ostensibly fake antennae for non-insects, the so-called 'deely bopper' consisted of a plastic hair-band with a pair of perpendicular springs on the ends of which were attached, for no reason, chunky hearts, stars or other shapes. The wearer could, thus kitted out, pass himself or herself off as any six-legged creature and gain entry to insect events, clubs and societies. Insect life was all the rage in the early eighties and nary a youngster was to be seen on the high street or out clubbing without his or her insect feelers. Happy times, sadly missed.

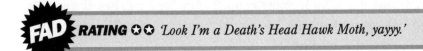

FAD RATING ✪✪ *'Look I'm a Death's Head Hawk Moth, yayyy.'*

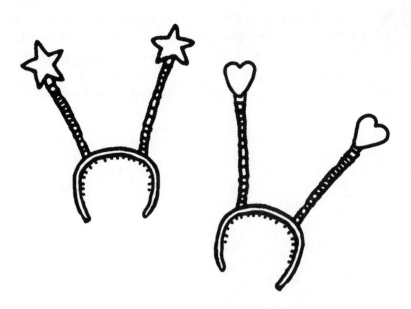

Designer Stubble

Back in the seventeenth century the unbearded man was looked upon as sinister. Bearded men were both mature and virile, while the cleanshaven were callow, vain and probably treacherous. Those were the days. Now things have gone to the dogs. As the author's favourite newspaper, the *Workington Times and Star*, points out, while musing on the first episode of the Lone Ranger: 'Back then the baddies wore black and hadn't shaved for a couple of days.' Facial growth became a synonym for mad, bad and dangerous to know.

It was probably Serge Gainsbourg, the prolific, provocative French singer-songwriter and lover of women, who first made intermediate chinwear fashionable, albeit in France (*see* **French Toast**). His unkempt look was scrupulously cultivated, but the venerable old roué only had one hit in the UK: not enough to change British face habits. The UK next saw the fuzz phenomenon on the lower half of Bjorn Borg's head but again, Borg being from a longboat, the budding fashion suffered somewhat from Ikea Syndrome (*see* **Chintz, chucking out one's**). What was needed was a home-grown figurehead, someone to carry the fuzzy-face torch for Britain. And who better than our own George Michael to set the trend? Following the success of Michael's early work during the eighties with the duo known as Wham!, chinwear became acceptable and began to appeal to **The Yuppie**.

THAT WAS THE YEAR...
Pre-other-war Toy Crazes

1919 The Pogo-Stick first put forward as mode of transport.

1925 Hornby trains chuff out of the siding.

1929 Duncan Yo-Yos® 'sleep' for the first time.

1930 Mickey Mouse dolls: the first licensed toys.

1931 Scrabble invented by jobless man.

1936 Monopoly invented in America.

However, there is a crucial difference between the version of the style that the author sports, which is called 'Forgetting To Shave' (FTS), and the version that concerns us here: designer stubble. Where FTS is patchy and wont to fluctuate from day to day, designer stubble is uniform fuzz, kept to a regulation 0.5 mm with specially designed clippers and worn with pride, along with an expensive suit and open-necked shirt. It's casual masculinity for the razorially challenged, for those who resist the tyranny of the daily shave and don't care what you or anyone else thinks. It is a good fad, which this book applauds. Fight the good fight, men. This fad is not recommended for women.

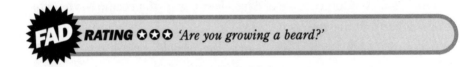

FAD **RATING** ✪ ✪ ✪ *'Are you growing a beard?'*

The Devil Banger

Also known as the 'Fun Snap'. Tiny bags of paper resembling albino tadpoles, filled with evil rocks. The evil rocks were, in fact, grains of sand coated with a gossamer of impact-sensitive silver fulminate (*see* **The Chemistry Set**), or possibly the cheaper nitrogen triiodide. You threw them at the ground from multi-storey car parks, into the path of oncoming pedestrians. They went 'snap'. You had fun. Hence the name. Boxes contained fifty 'pieces', as if they were chewing gum. Chewing your Fun Snaps, however, was a mistake.

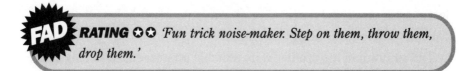

FAD **RATING** ✪✪ *'Fun trick noise-maker. Step on them, throw them, drop them.'*

The Digital Watch

The first digital watch to fall across the Fads & Crazes radar entered the author's house in 1976, on the wrist of a neighbour's adolescent boy. Roughly the size of a Fabergé egg or Tunnock's Teacake, the watch had digits made of large red light-emitting diodes (LED). To conserve battery power this function was switched off by default and had to be manually activated by pushing a button. That way, you had to really, really want to know the time. No furtive peeking for the proud digital-watch owner – indeed the simple action of finding out the hour became as ostentatious as the device itself. 'What time is it? I don't know, let me just consult my *digital* watch. Give me a minute. It works best in the dark. Do you want to turn the light off a sec?'

The author and his brother were suitably impressed, especially as the author himself was not to be allowed a watch at all until he could tell the time, some years thence. But what they didn't know was that their neighbour was *so* six years ago. The watchmaker Hamilton had released the Pulsar, the first ever digital electronic watch, as long ago as 1970. A mere two years later Seiko and Longines both developed liquid crystal displays (LCD) for digital watches, bringing clarity and better energy efficiency.

But we are not concerned here with innovation, only with mass phenomena. It was to be a few more years before digital watches really took off. Soon middle managers had giant Casio calculators strapped to their wrists, which they took pains to activate with the nib of a **PaperMate® Replay**. But the inherent naffness of the digital watch was soon to cause its fall from fad grace. The bitter truth was that no one really cared what the time was in Singapore. There was never any real need for the stopwatch facility, apart from allowing games teachers a fleeting illusion of superiority on the athletics track. Before long the digital watch simply became too cheap to be trendy. Technology advances so quickly that it would take a full- blown wrist-held recording studio to bring the electronic watch back into vogue.

Some think the rot began in the late seventies, when the writer Douglas Adams published *The Hitchhiker's Guide to the Galaxy*. The foreword teased that the inhabitants of earth were so primitive they still thought digital watches were 'a pretty neat idea'. But this encyclopaedia can reveal that the phasing out of the digital watch was in fact a conspiracy by the combined watch-repair employees of Timpsons and John Lewis. Too many of them were on long-term sick leave due to depression. Something had to be done. There are only so many lithium batteries a trained clocksmith can replace before he starts to see black. So many special tiny instruments, so little call for the loving removal of dust with matchstick and Blu-tack®. It's all hush-hush, but the CIA, Dodi Fayed and Rolex were involved.

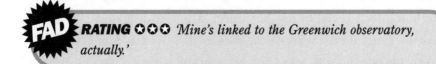

FAD **RATING ✪✪✪** *'Mine's linked to the Greenwich observatory, actually.'*

The Dinky Toy

FEATURING CORGI, MATCHBOX AND HOT WHEELS

SUPERFAD British train-set chief Frank **Hornby** had already made a success of **Meccano** construction kits when, in 1933, he branched into miniature cars. A year later the dinky little die-cast vehicles acquired the brand name to match. Hornby's range of mini-vehicles chugged happily across our floors unchallenged until 1953, when fellow compatriots Leslie and Rodney Smith (no relation) formed Lesney Products, acquired die-cast expert Jack O'Dell and launched their 'Matchbox' range of tiny cars. Well, not cars exactly. The first Matchbox toys were in fact a dumper, a road-roller, a tractor and a cement-mixer. Despite their tiny size, Lesney Matchbox cars boasted a stunning attention to detail, while the bounciness of their suspension was a tactile thrill. The author was known to spend hours simply dropping Matchbox cars on the table and watching them bounce. Read what you will into this.

A more direct aesthetic challenge to the Dinky came in 1956, when the British company Mettoy, who would later bring you the **Space Hopper**, launched a rival brand of toy car: Corgi. The Corgi models had actual windows. From there on it was car wars all the way (*see* **Star Wars**).

What can you do with a toy car? You can roll it, race it, swap it, smash it. You can even loop it around a yellow plastic track, a kind of poor man's **slot-car racing**. Or you can keep it mint in its box as a collectible investment. Getting die-cast car toys was an end in itself for some, and building a 'collection' by 'collecting' them from the shop via the medium of paying for them was a proper hobby. What you then did with them was up to you, but simply displaying them was an option. The author's favourite was Matchbox, for its size and for its price, which increased the likelihood of netting one on a trip to the newsagents with Granny.

Despite tough competition from Corgi, Dinky die-cast models continued to fill our hearts with joy until 1979, when the much bought and sold Meccano company called in the receivers and shut up shop. Now you really do have to 'collect' them. Be prepared, though, to pay very silly amounts of money. Corgi became Corgi Classics when Mettoy was sold to its management, and those miniature wheels continue to roll on.

Matchbox meanwhile was facing challenges of its own in the tiny cars market. Receivership bounced the die-cast dealer from Universal to Tyco, where it began to square up to opposition from **Barbie**® bosses Mattel. The sleeker, funkier Hot Wheels range by Mattel appeared in 1968 and continued to bludgeon Matchbox into submission. Today the Matchbox brand still exists, but under the ownership of Mattel – and it's Hot Wheels that today's kids see in the shops.

None of which means anything, of course, to anyone other than the misty-eyed nostalgia lover. Hot Wheels are pretty neat, but they don't come in the little yellow matchbox the author knew and loved. Stupidly, the author smashed up all his toy cars in a rite of passage. Had he not, he could be rich on profit by now. Even so, the author's brother will remember his Corgi James Bond Aston Martin for ever, while the author will remain sentimentally attached to his beloved Corgi Batmobile and his cherished Matchbox 'Hairy Hustler', over which the pair of them fought bitterly for many years, and which was eventually mashed to a pulp with a tent mallet. Happy days.

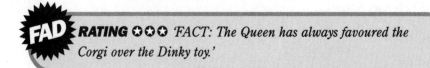

FAD **RATING** ✪✪✪ *'FACT: The Queen has always favoured the Corgi over the Dinky toy.'*

ELEVEN GREAT CAR-STICKERS

1. **Baby on board.**
   And that's why I'm driving at 90 mph.

2. **My other car is a Porsche.**
   Plus, my other brain works.

3. **Don't follow me, I'm lost too.**
   I also wear a comedy tie to work.

4. **I slow down for horses.**
   I also slow down for no reason.

5. **Nuclear Power? No thanks.**
   Do I want to hear about your beliefs? No thanks.

6. **I've Seen the Lions at Longleat.**
   And they saw you coming.

7. **Greenpeace.**
   I'm not actually in it.

8. **Windsurfers do it standing up.**
   Look at me, I do sport and have sex.

9. **Darren . . . . Sharon.**
   No one cares who you are.

10. **Old taxidermists never die, they just get stuffed.**
    Etc etc etc.

11. **Jesus Saves.**
    But why won't he save us from car-stickers?

Dress-Down Friday

Company bosses had long known that employees tended to slow down on Fridays. The giddy anticipation of the fleeting, momentary freedom of the oncoming weekend tends to bring on a dangerous, light-hearted torpor. Workers prevaricate: 'He's in a meeting, we'll have to get back to you on that one.' Why bother returning calls that can wait until Monday? Why rush the job that lands on your desk? Avoid it for long enough and it will become next week's problem. Employees tend to make more jokes on Friday. They are less inclined to take management directives seriously. The smell of the weekend fills them with an unseemly bravado that, frankly, borders on insolence and insubordination. A favourite time for calling in sick, Friday is a flimsy non-day.

Bosses knew they couldn't do anything about Friday Syndrome, short of moving to a four-day week. And that would only give rise to Thursday Syndrome. But what really got under their skins was the terrifying notion that their hired drones might not be fully subdued. So they put their heads together. They consulted management gurus, who told them, 'Every threat is an opportunity.' What was needed, they concluded, was a way to own, manage and contain Friday Syndrome – turn it around and extract from it some kind of business benefit. The result of this was Dress-Down Friday.

One way of maintaining the illusion of control over an employee is to note down what the employee is doing anyway, and then make it an obligation, a target or a personal-development goal. Employees were duly told that they were to dress 'casually' on Fridays. Casualness was thus formalized. And owned. However, there had to be limits. The thing had to be contained. You couldn't have people turning up in any old filthy

T-shirt and sandals: they might come to believe they were independent, free-thinking individuals. And when an employee realizes he or she is an individual, he or she will cease to be a 'team player' (*see* **The Team-Building Weekend**). So the proviso was added that clothes be 'casual yet professional'. This caused no end of problems, with employees, unsure of what to wear, turning up in clothes that were deemed 'inappropriate' for work. Too casual, in fact. Many organizations found they had to define 'casual' and, according to one management consultancy, a general rule of thumb was that 'casual' excluded: denim; sportswear, including trainers; T-shirt; sweatshirts; Lycra; and shorts. This pretty much excludes everyone's casual wear. So desk drones who had previously been used to wearing business suits during the week and jogging suits at the weekend suddenly had to go out and buy chinos and Ben Sherman shirts in order to dress casually formally. There was a further complication. Many bosses felt that their clients would not have faith in their abilities if they were not wearing a tie. So employees who wore casual dress on Fridays were normally obliged to keep a suit standing by, just in case.

But that was only Stage One: 'subjugation'. Stage Two's objective was to claw back some business benefit. This is where the genius came in. Where possible, employees were made to pay for the right to buy extra clothes. What? Well, nothing is free in this world, and they need to learn. So employers deducted a nominal sum each week from employees' salaries in return for the 'right' not to wear a tie. But you didn't keep the money: that would only encourage mutiny. So you gave their money away to charity. No one would dare complain about that. So their Friday idleness became your charity tax-dodge, which you then publicized as a virtue in the trade press and local papers: free publicity that would generate measurable revenue. God, we are geniuses. And the beauty is that none of the idiots ever figured out what we were up to. That's why we are the bosses and they are *so* not. Bu-wa-ha-ha-ha-ha.

But then a curious thing happened. With the explosion of hip, young 'dotcom' companies came a new race of nominally rich CEOs in the Jeff Bezos vein, who wore chinos and casual shirts *all the time*. Suddenly old-school managers were forced to come face to face with the idea that it might just be possible to run a successful business without a tie on. Companies didn't want to look as though they were old-fashioned and slow to react. So, around the time that every business in the world launched expensive websites with no real purpose, many offices moved into casual wear as the rule. Tie-wearing has become such a novelty that it is now being suggested that 'dress-up Friday' could become a reality.

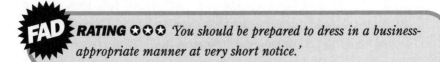

FAD RATING ✪✪✪ *'You should be prepared to dress in a business-appropriate manner at very short notice.'*

ELEVEN KEY CORPORATE ISSUES

1. **Going forward** – no longer going backwards.
2. **Forecast** – random figure, doodle or pocket fluff.
3. **Strategy** – we are going to put on a blindfold and throw a dart (*see* **Executive Toys**).
4. **Pre-tax profit** – loss.
5. **Bullish** – no longer strictly making a loss.
6. **Key** – universal adjective. Can be added to any key word or phrase to enhance key message e.g., 'synergistic solutions are absolutely key to our core strategy,' 'you've raised some key issues,' and 'key performance indicator' (KPI). When used correctly, it should be possible to remove the word 'key' from the sentence without altering the grammar or key meaning.
7. **Enhance (1)** – increase, e.g., 'key synergies will result in enhanced Q3 profits.'

   Enhance (2) – decrease, e.g., enhance supplier relations = reduce their margins.

   Enhance (3) – completely ruin, e.g., changing our core brand 'Royal Mail' to 'Consignia' will enhance our reputation as a key player in the logistics industry.
8. **Incentivize** – threaten.
9. **Appraisal** – bollocking.
10. **Major contribution** – we've sacked him.
11. **Pension plan** – that's the plan, anyway.

Dungeons and Dragons

At last: a team game for loners. Dungeons and Dragons is the name of the orc-heavy multi-player game launched in 1974 by Chicago-born entrepreneur Gary Gygax and various legally disputed pals. No doubt they were heavily influenced by the elf-ridden landscapes conjured by J. R. R. Tolkien in his *Lord of the Rings* (*see* **Harry Potter**) and by their own experiences of war-gaming clubs. But the name soon became a despised umbrella term for the hobby of fantasy role-play-gaming, or FRP, as its finicky devotees called it.

The premise, as first proposed by Gygax, was that a number of players sit around a table directing the actions of their own invented characters, as they navigate their way though a 'dungeon' or landscape generated by another player, who assumes the role and title of Dungeon Master or 'DM'. This player is also guardian of the rule book: a hefty tome full of tables laying down everything from weapon strengths to gods and eating habits. With this minimal structure in place, the players and the DM basically make the game up as they go along, limited only by their imagination within the confines of the D&D world.

One of Gygax's innovations was a range of multisided dice, capable of generating numbers in various ranges from 1–3 to 1–20. The outcome of various interactive encounters, such as combat and pillaging, was determined by a combination of the players' vital statistics

FAD Fact

A MORI poll found that 84 per cent of British parents thought companies targeted their children too much. According to the National Family & Parenting Institute, which commissioned the research, parents feel uninformed about the effects on their children of internet and text-message marketing.

and the number generated from one of these so-called 'D3's or 'D20's.

Gripping stuff. Or, at least, it could be, depending on who you were playing with. Since this was a game for bookish intellectuals and people who loved facts and lists, finding a group of four like-minded friends could sometimes be a cruel challenge. That's where hobby conventions came in very handy. Enthusiasts from all over the country could meet in poorly ventilated rooms and keep their coats on while pretending to be virile, popular or successful. They could reinforce this image of themselves while playing via the use of die-cast figurines, which they would laboriously paint with Humbrol enamel paints (*see* **The Airfix Kit**) and keep in a tobacco tin along with their D9s and their D10s.

Such was the success and omnipresence of D&D that lovers of the activity swiftly tired of the game itself. It became rather infra-dig 'around the hobby', so much so that many refused to acknowledge the term 'DM', showing their contempt by using the term 'GM' for 'Game Master'. FRP fans turned instead to the myriad rival games that had sprung up in the wake of Gygax, such as the Samurai combat game Bushido, or Call of Cthulu, based on the occult mystery novels of H. P. Lovecraft.

This latter game did much to perpetuate the fallacious notion that FRP players were actually involved in a sinister sect. This misapprehension was probably aided by a BBC news report in 1985 that described the then blossoming hobby as 'somewhere between a game and a cult'. A cult game is what they probably meant to say.

Another useful spin-off for the stubborn stay-at-home was the postal gaming sub-hobby. This activity centred on a number of amateur fanzines, with names like *Lokasenna* (ed. Brian Dolton) and *Demon's Drawl* (ed. Nick Edwards), which published ongoing games, notably the European war game Diplomacy, which subscribers could join, sending moves to the magazine and reading the outcome each time it went to press. This meant a person could play and effectively socialize with other contrary fact-collectors without ever having to leave his bedroom or bedsit.

Predictably, there was great scope for cross-hobby pollination. Apart from the obvious connection with sci-fi hobbies such as *Doctor Who* and *Star Trek* appreciation, as a general rule, those who were actively involved in the promotion and consumption of real ale and the propagation of folk-rock music by the likes of Jethro Tull and Fairport Convention could also be found at the FRP 'hobbymeets' discussing the merits of jointly developing a universal logarithm for generating the reaction of elves to orc attack while downing the Smiles Best and singing, 'Indicate the way to my abode,' to the tune of 'Show Me The Way To Go Home'. They could also be relied upon to write up the discussion at length in their fanzine, which they would publish alongside the latest news of Gygax's tumultuous business relationships, an unfavourable review of a bestselling game and some research on feudal Iceland.

The craze slipped off the radar for about a decade, but shows signs of heating up again, helped by the high sales of fantasy novels, comics and accompanying games prompted by the success of movie versions of *The Lord of the Rings*. In the meantime, the arrival of the internet in every home and library, as well as the expectation that games happen on a screen, has now given such interactive pursuits an entirely different interface. What is even more astonishing is that this time around, girls are playing too. It's just possible that nevermore will liberally acned boys sit around a table sipping cocoa, listening to Richard Thompson and saying, 'My cleric roars, "Begone from here in the name of all that is holy and just or be smote by my battle axe", D10.'

FAD RATING ✪✪✪✪ *'Actually, I think you'll find a D10 may only be used for knives, scimitars, swords and scalpels – the heavy weapon series including axes, bludgeons, battering rams and rocks calls for the D12.'*

The Eight-Track Cartridge

Program one: Promotion and endorsement by Ford Motors in the early seventies lent eight-track the critical mass that enabled the bulbous, clunking tape-format to get a foothold. Developed by committee, a motley band that included tape-makers Ampex and music-peddlers RCA, this revolutionary plug 'n' play cartridge offered a neat solution to music fun with magnetic tape. Prior to the eight-track, tape came on giant reels, which the user insinuated across the playback head and spooled on to a blank. This was considered to be fine for home use but clearly impractical in a car, unless you wanted to end up dead in a ditch. The eight-track eliminated this problem and thus was widely lionized as the audio format to end all others.

Program two: The tape in an eight-track is a continuous loop, divided along its length into eight channels, or rather, four sets of two. Playing two channels at a time to achieve stereo, the head would physically jump across the width of the tape with each new 'program' of music, divided by a splice, giving the sonorous clunk lovers of the format so enjoy. As long as you also love those four programs, you really are in heaven for, left to its own devices, the loop will repeat endlessly until you die in a ditch.

Program three: But timing is everything. Had this enterprising consortium waited just a while, they would have been able to invest their money in the cassette format that was soon to be developed by Philips. The neat, compact cassette offered a number of advantages over the enormous, paperback-sized eight-track, especially as a format for in-car entertainment. Apart from physical size, the stereo cassette had no need of a moveable tape head, which allowed for cheaper hardware, was less inclined to spool up, tangle and concertina inside its body, and your listening enjoyment was not limited to four programs, only by the length of each spool of tape. Cassette tapes had no splice between programs, since they had no programs, so they would not break at the join like an eight-track tape. In addition, there was less chance with a cassette of cross-talk from the tracks caused by misalignment of the head. Less chance, not no chance, although the fading-out associated with eight-track pressure pads was somewhat diminished by the cassette. Still, there were plus points to the older format: two eight-track cassettes that have recently come into the author's orbit include an offering by The Seekers and 'The Lustful Sex Life Of A Perverted Nympho Housewife'.

Program four: Some have claimed the eight-track was the **Betamax video** of the audio world, but this is not quite true. Betamax was a superior format trampled by its lesser rival VHS due to a lack of business acumen by Sony. The eight-track was simply made obsolete by better technology, earning its place in this book by dint of its cult collectibility. The Betamax of audio is surely the Minidisc, again from Sony (*see* **The Walkman**). When the much-vaunted recordable disk hit the shops, the end of cassettes was predicted. This did happen, but it was actually the inferior but virtually shareable MP3 that finished them off. How long can the adorable Minidisc now hold its own?

Program five: I'm sorry, this is physically impossible. Please go back to the drawing-board.

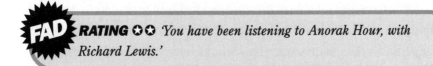

FAD **RATING** ✪✪ *You have been listening to Anorak Hour, with Richard Lewis.'*

The Etch A Sketch®

In a book full of ephemera, what could be more apposite than an article about an enduring, iconic machine dedicated to the making of non-permanent images? The Etch A Sketch® was once a fad gadget, but clearly inscription and erasure has a long and distinguished pedigree. Before we begin, let us place our glorious red friend in context.

First there was the sand and finger, a method favoured by Ancient Egyptians, Greek mathematicians and, on occasion, Jesus of Nazareth. The finger, of course, could be substituted for a stick or sharp stone as required. It seems likely that this technique for the creation and deletion of pictograms, numeric equations and writing ran concurrently for some time with the stylus and papyrus option favoured by the Romans. The latter, being essentially a form of engraving, had one drawback: if you were unhappy with what you had committed to papyrus it was more or less tough luck. Going back to the drawing-board meant getting out some more papyrus. Sand was a lot cheaper.

With the advent of ink and paper the problem showed no signs of abating. There was no real way to replicate the rubbing-out of sand-drawn lines until the carbon graphite pencil was well established. Graphite drawing is an English invention that followed the disinterment of a large quantity of graphite in Borrowdale in Cumbria in the mid sixteenth century. Despite this invention, the inferior but less labour-intensive technology of slate on slate carried on, in some cases well into the twentieth century. One of the reasons for this may well have been the fact that a hand rubbed over graphite markings will indeed tend to smudge and erase your work. This would have been evident from the outset, and yet the first commercial erasers don't show themselves until the mid nineteenth century.

In the mid twentieth century, both permanent ink on paper and erasable graphite on paper were fully fledged inscription basics when the French inventor Arthur Granjean emerged from his basement flushed from his own eureka moment (*see* **Pac-Man**). He had succeeded in creating · a machine that simultaneously made creative line-drawing both less permanent and more difficult. With the help of his box-like wonder, would-be artists would now have to overcome severe motor- function challenges in order to make the most rudimentary marks that, once achieved, could disappear again with the slightest tremor. Granjean was excited. He would surely become a wealthy man.

Granjean's *Écran Magique* – or Magic Screen – used the hitherto unexplored medium of stylus with aluminium powder and plastic beads. The mixture was applied to the back of a glass screen to create a grey tablet or 'slate' enclosed in a frame. The stylus was navigated by two knobs, one for vertical movement and one to send it horizontally. As it travelled through the mixture, the stylus left a black line in its wake, which could be wiped out with a flick of the wrist. When shaken, the powder was dispersed across the pane once more, effectively erasing your work. As the knobs went only up and down or from side to side, to create a curve, skilful dual-control action was required.

Drawing is a talent. You either have it or you don't. Now, those who thought they could draw well were challenged to think again. Drawing with a Magic Screen was the art equivalent of rubbing your belly with one hand and patting your head with the other. You had to train your two hands to act independently of one another, while simultaneously engaging your left brain for the technical functions and your right brain for the art.

In 1959, 400 years after the invention of the pencil, Granjean took his miniaturized sandpit to the Nuremburg International Toy Exhibition. There it was snapped up by representatives of the American company Ohio Arts. Under their stewardship the Magic Screen became the Etch A Sketch®, the cumbersome red nonsense we know and love. First brought to market in 1960, the toy was still doing good business two decades later, when its appeal began a slow decline.

But why would Etch A Sketch® catch on when a pencil and paper does a far better job? Well, the answer is threefold. People enjoy a challenge: the same craze-making principle that drove sales of **Magic Eye™** and **Rubik's Cube** puzzles worked for the Etch A Sketch®. Secondly, a paper and pencil is a bit like schoolwork, while a chubby red plastic thing is clearly a toy. Lastly, it really was 'magic'. Why would that work exactly, turning a knob to make a line? In the days before computer graphics such a thing did indeed make a person look on in wonder.

There was something else too. The people who could draw well with a paper and pencil were not necessarily the same people who drew well on the Etch A Sketch®, employing as it did rather different skills. Forward planning, or at least problem-solving on your feet, was needed, as once the line had started you could not effectively 'lift' your stylus off the slate to break up a line. The unique talents needed to create good art on the Etch A Sketch® gave the little red menace a cultish status, resulting in the formation of the Etch A Sketch® Club.

Now, in the era of scanning, digital-image manipulation and computer drawing-packages, the Etch A Sketch® can look a little primitive. However, while the craze has slipped away, sales of the lumpish red box are trickling on, with several updates and advancements offered from the manufacturers. One of these includes a CD-Rom version, rather defeating the purpose. It is not specified whether the delete key will suffice in this instance, or whether the entire computer must be shaken to wipe away the powder…

 RATING ✪✪✪✪ *'It's a car, it's a car. With square wheels.'*

ELEVEN FAD NOUNS

1. **Alcopop** *n.* – bobbins drink
2. **Crew** *n.* – gang *qv.*
3. **Posse** *n.* – crew *qv.*
4. **Gang** *n.* – posse *qv.*
5. **Daddio** *n.* – dude *qv.*
6. **Dude** *n.* – cat *qv.*
7. **Cat** *n.* – daddio *qv.* As in 'This one goes out to all you cats in the proctology unit.'
8. **Mover** *n.* – shaker *qv.*
9. **Shaker** *n.* – maker e.g., Shakermaker®
10. **Loser** *n.* neither mover nor shaker *qv.*
11. **Chav** *n.* – naff dude *qv.*

Evel Knievel

Many men flirt with danger. Knievel shagged it to within an inch of his own life. Irresponsibility never looked so good. He didn't just defy death, he swore in its face like the fearless orphan he was. No wonder he took off. But what goes up must come down. As no one knew better than him, it's a question of when.

Montana-born alpha male Robert 'Evel' Knievel was the proud owner of the original Death Wish. No one quite wanted to expire, mutilated, in a blaze of heroic glory quite as much as Evel and no one wanted to be more like Evel than all boys in the seventies. 'Motorbike Daredevil.' Motor, bike, dare, devil. What a seductively appealing combination of words. How much cooler could a person be?

As a young copper-miner, Knievel was not content to extract metal from stone, possibly with his teeth (not confirmed) – he was also a prodigious semi-professional sportsman, taking an active business interest in skiing and hockey, although he was keen on any physical activity, especially if there was a chance he might get hurt. His pursuit of injury led him to join the US army, but it obviously wasn't dangerous enough, so he got into the elk-hunting business – clearly another excuse to get in the way of bullets. Then came the bikes. He had been interested in bike jumping ever since he was a kid, and sustained his first motorbike-related injury in a race in 1962. Later he ran Honda dealerships and offered a sizeable discount to anyone who could beat him at arm-wrestling. All this before the age of twenty-five. With so much still to prove, Knievel launched his daredevil career in 1965, at the tender age of twenty-seven.

And how the world followed it.

The basic premise was to take off into the air on a motorbike and land a really long time later. How much later was in theory determined by the amount of cars, buses, Pepsi-Cola trucks (think sponsorship), live rattlesnakes and dragster racers he could clear. Unless he crashed and burned. That was the risk he took. And the more risks he took, the more we loved him. A career that had seen him barely squeaking by to begin with blossomed into a multimillion-dollar business, the spoils of which he spent as recklessly as he earned them.

When vehicles and serpents seemed tame, Knievel turned to canyon-clearing, his chief aim being the Grand Canyon. He couldn't get permission, so he bought his own, Idaho's Snake River Canyon, and made plans to jump it in a specially designed 'Sky Cycle'. This was not such a great plan. Despite his lack of faith in his or the Sky Cycle's ability, he made the jump out of a sense either of macho pride or misplaced obligation to his fans. He missed and parachuted hundreds of feet to the river below, where he narrowly escaped being engulfed by the great flood. This was to be a turning point. Knievel had failed us, all of us who were living vicarious fantasy lives through his stunts. We realized there was a limit to his prowess. Our interest waned. In any case there were rivals on the scene: the improbably named Doug Danger and the UK's own Eddie Kidd.

Our love of Knievel was given gratification and indeed in no small part manufactured by the range of toys and accessories marketed by Ideal (*see* **Rubik's Cube**) in the seventies. Such ownable classics as the Evel Knievel Stunt Cycle, the Evel Knievel Scramble Van, as well as various action figures, were helped into our grubby hands by feature films such as, er, *Evel Knievel* and *Viva Knievel*. If you want to buy these toys today, be prepared to pay serious money. A mint, boxed 1973 Stunt Cycle will fetch upwards of £300. Peripheral items from wristwatches through pinball games to radios were also branded with the Knievel message, but his influence spread wider. For this writer's money, the ultimate expression of Knievel mania was the **Raleigh Chopper**. Falling off a bike never felt so good.

These days the former jump star focuses on painting and charity work. Is there nothing he can't do? He also broke the world record for the number of bones broken in one body: thirty-five. Now, if that is not something to aspire to, we'd like to know what is.

FAD **RATING ✪✪✪** *'For sale: Canyon Sky Cycle, mint condition, never played with.'*

The Executive Toy

Will I be promoted to my level of incompetence? Shake the 8-ball: 'Signs point to yes.' I feel floored by an overarching sense of powerlessness; what should I do? Spin the wheel, roll the die: 'Call a meeting.' Phew. That's better.

The addition of the prefix 'Executive' to an otherwise vacuous proposition has long found favour with the anxious, aspiring climber. The Executive Home, for example, is a way for, say, Mr Peter Principle of London to buy a cardboard box in Hayward's Heath with a defective combination boiler and three square feet of Executive Scrubland without wanting to put his head in the Executive Oven (not supplied). Likewise, the Executive Washroom is a cheap way to achieve smugness during routine micturition. The Executive Hotel Suite allows canny hoteliers to charge double for an ordinary room with a swivel chair behind the table, or 'desk'.

Such marketing ploys tickle the status anxiety of the Senior Meetings Co-ordinator into the spasm of purchase. In essence, and happily so, use of the Executive prefix is a way of mocking the stupid while making money, and the formula finds its zenith in the executive toy, which this book applauds. Let's have more of them. For the executive toy acts as a kind of office semaphore. See it on the desk of your immediate boss and the chances are that, keeping your nose clean, you'll be promoted above him while he is fiddling with his pit and pendulum. See the toy on the desk of your employee and you know to keep the flounder where he is. There is a tidy symmetry here.

Clacking balls, magnetic art, stress-relievers... While the genre emerged in the sixties, enjoying modest yet steady patronage during the seventies, the craze proper began and ended in the eighties, during

Margaret Thatcher's reign and the **Yuppie** boom. During this period the range of futile desktop gewgaws was greatly expanded to include something for everyone. From the humble gonk of the stationery supervisor to the 'living' sand sculpture of the middle manager, the tat industry enjoyed a brief but delicious boom. As long as the price and the chrome content were high, it mattered not what the product was. The gyroscope. Billiards in a Box. Pin art.

But the essence of the executive-toy phenomenon was distilled in the form of Newton's Cradle. This series of five swinging chromium balls suspended by string exploits Isaac Newton's law of equal and opposite action and reaction, a principle of physics sometimes known as elastic collision, and thus confers upon its owner a mild patina of pseudo-scientific prowess. It makes the owner feel clever and important. It is also known as 'Newton's Balls', thus neatly summing up its office value.

If corporate ball-swinging is too Freudian for you, consider the 'anti-gravity' globe. An ordinary globe, held up by science alone (i.e. magnets). Look at me. My world is so small. See me make it spin. The desktop fountain, far from marking us out as peaceable oases of reason, will serve only to remind us how trapped we have become, while the Zen Rock Garden, which claims to help 'clear the mind of the chaos associated with everyday business life… all while sitting at your desk', is essentially a sandpit. If you yearn to play in sand you have already been promoted way too high. If your business life is truly in chaos you are no good at it. Quit your job and become a gardener.

The pick of the crop, though, is the Executive Decision-Maker. It comes in various forms, from the simple wooden die, or dartboard, to the deluxe casino-effect roulette wheel. Give it a spin and see the nihilistic fruitlessness of your daily decisions play out before you. Buy, sell, fire, go to lunch, play golf, leave early, stay late. Do as it says. For the irony here is that, if you actually have one of these, you would do well to trust its judgement above your own.

While today, in the brave new millennium, the office trinket is still very much at large, at one end of the scale it has acquired an ironic edge, a knowing, kitsch appeal: the clockwork walking sushi, for example. At the other extreme it marks out the dinosaur, the has-been, the bygone relic waiting for his pension: the Newton's Balls. Modern middle-managers with unfocused designs on that glass-fronted office now prefer the Palmtop computer, a kind of very expensive **Filofax**, which comes with its own cradle. The Newton's Cradle alone can no longer convince its owner of his significance. The genre has become a cliché and the craze is over. But there is, however, room for a renaissance of the 'Executive' prefix fad as a means to improve the desirability – and therefore the price – of unappealing items. Novelty pens out, marketing department – here are a few ideas for as yet untapped bounty:

Executive Colostomy. Executive Sombrero. Executive Pilchards. Executive Pontypridd. Executive Cider. Executive Belgium. Executive Pay-Cut. Executive Crack Cocaine. Executive Scotch Egg. Executive Cock-Fighting. Executive Shake 'n' Vac. Executive Crisps. Executive Pension.

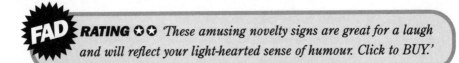

FAD > **RATING** ✪✪ *These amusing novelty signs are great for a laugh and will reflect your light-hearted sense of humour. Click to BUY.'*

Fido Dido

This ubiquitous cartoon character with vertical hair first appeared in 1985 as an illustration by Susan Rose. Developed by Joanna Ferrone and controlled by R M Licensing, the surfing, skateboarding, soda-drinking all-American slacker went on to become a worldwide hit, his image gracing everything from underwear to hygienic wet-wipes. Slogans included, 'We are all in this together,' and 'Just Cool: That's my brand.' Indeed. Those were probably the coolest hygienic wet-wipes on the market.

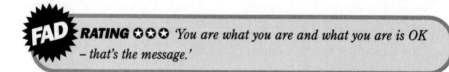

FAD **RATING ✪✪✪** *'You are what you are and what you are is OK – that's the message.'*

The Filofax®

The Filofax® personal organizer first reared its head in the closing years of the First World War. A neat, simple development of the diary, the organizer used loose-leaf pages, ring-bound in a leather wallet. This meant users could tailor it to suit their own needs, removing – perhaps – the imperial-to-metric conversion tables, the calendar of Christian holidays and the list of British monarchs in favour of a week-per-page planner and address book, plus some pink sheets for doodling. It was a great business idea, allowing the makers to sell not just one item, but unlimited items. And only their own official items, as nothing else would fit in the binder. Everything from moussaka recipes (*see* **The Aubergine**) to travel guides could be purchased and hooked into one's Filofax®, creating a veritable file o' facts. Ha ha. A one-stop shop for all your data needs.

However, in spite of its ingenuity, the Filofax® did not really take off in Britain until the eighties, with the advent of **The Yuppie**. A decade before e-mails, two decades before the palmtop-computer explosion, this device – which even had 'fax' in the name – sounded pretty zippy. If you needed an organizer, it showed you had a life worth organizing. It meant you had two things: meetings and contacts. So businesspersons who wanted to show the world they both moved and shaked, wielded and toted their Filofaxes® like the keys to the City. How hectic things must be. Hell, you were so busy buying and selling money and drinking champagne that you would never remember the trivial things, like birthdays, without your leather friend.

'Have you seen my Filofax®?' cried Colin, the only gay/middle class person in TV's Albert Square, repeatedly and with mounting anxiety. 'It's a small leather booklet...' He was met with eyes raised to heaven by the salt-of-the-earth denizens of Walford. For the world divided into two classes: the Filo-haves and the Filo-havenots. If you were a Filo-havenot, it meant you were plain folk and you liked how you were. Filo-haves were to be mocked, derided and possibly attacked. Thus the hapless midget ringbinder came to symbolize all that was ostentatious, pretentious and self-regarding about the chief beneficiaries of Margaret Thatcher's polarized society.

Nowadays such people have the PDA, or personal digital assistant. This is the self-aggrandizing generic name for the 'Palm Pilot' (which is also, the author is given to believe, an entry-level service available from cheap Kings Cross ladyboys). Given this development, the humble Filofax swiftly became the domain of teachers and grannies. But could it swing back into vogue? Those who carry PDAs know that when the battery runs out, all its appointments and contacts are irretrievably lost, along with any spreadsheets they might have been fiddling with. This can only be remedied by laborious backing-up on a desktop computer, a process requiring cables, cradles, at least one crash of the computer and about thirty minutes. Those who carry PDAs know that in the time it takes you to point the plastic stylus at enough letters to make a word appear, a Filofaxer armed with a **PaperMate® Replay** could have written a thesis on status anxiety, rubbed it all out and had time left for a mocaccino (*see* **Silly Coffee**). Or perhaps not. To keep pace with technology and keep its place in the corporate market, Filofax, now owned by the Letts group, is developing digital 'paper' for use with electronic pens that will 'interface' with Outlook Express. There may be trouble ahead.

FAD **RATING ✪✪✪** *'Clear your Filofax and get out.'*

Fimo®, *coating everything with*

The great thing about Eberhard Faber's Fimo® patent polymer clay (try saying this with two **scented erasers** in your mouth) was that you could bake it hard in your own oven in only half an hour (*see* **The Shrinky Dink**®). There was no need for a glaze firing, as it came pre-coloured and with patient kneading of colours you could achieve any desired shade. And there was no need to get messy with wheels and slurry, as it was entirely malleable, like plasticine. In short, it was a boon for any home-based amateur craftsperson (*see* **Macramé**) who felt intimidated by actual pottery. That was also its chief drawback.

There is in life a definite limit to the number of zany-coloured, fingerprint-heavy, coated Zippo lighters, tobacco tins and poorly executed fridge-magnets to which a person can be exposed before the medical term known as FAD, or Fimo® Affective Disorder, sets in. Symptoms range from the stifled wince to stamping, breaking and cackling.

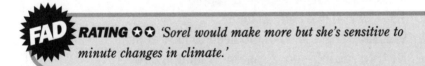

FAD **RATING ✪✪** *'Sorel would make more but she's sensitive to minute changes in climate.'*

The Fingerless Glove

This quintessential piece of eighties apparel served no useful purpose whatsoever. The fingerless glove failed to provide any tangible warmth, for obvious reasons, while simultaneously preventing any form of manual dexterity. Marginally more silly than the **snood**, a shade more practical than the **leg-warmer**, the garment has as many advocates as it has detractors. But the author suspects these people also wear socks with individual toes.

 RATING ✪✪ *'Ha, ha, you look like Steptoe.' 'Who's Steptoe?'*

ELEVEN FAD EXPRESSIONS

1. **Yah** – yes, if speaker is Yuppie
2. **Ciao** – goodbye, if speaker is Yuppie
3. **Yo** – look at me, I am an idiot
4. **Wassaa** – I am an idiot, no need to look at me
5. **Nothin' doin'** – no, if speaker is idiot, *qv.* yo
6. **Crivens** – crikey
7. **Lorks-a-mercy** – blimey O'Reilly
8. **Wassuuup** – wassaa *qv.*
9. **Yah** – yes, if speaker is Sloane Ranger
10. **Check-it** – yo *qv.*
11. **Not** – what I just said is untrue, e.g., 'I enjoyed your last book about Morris Dancing. *Not.*'

The Flared Trouser

Wide as you can at the bottom, high as you can at the belt part, number of buttons critical. If you couldn't find a pair wide enough, you could always split them up the side and sew in a triangle, preferably in a garish fabric. The decade that brought us the flares in a big way at its outset also turned in on itself in **punk** rebellion at its end. Consequently, the eighties were characterized by intense flare-hatred. Any trouser that didn't actually taper to a 5 mm slit was ridiculed as being 'flarey nice'.

In the nineties, when society's attitudes towards fashion became more permissive, the flare made a sneaky comeback. They were still silly, however, as could be evidenced by the fact that they drooped all over the ground, picking up mud and moisture that leaked up the leg in glorious chromatography (*see* **The Chemistry Set**). During the flare's seventies heyday, when everyone from the tartan-loving Bay City Rollers to the mud-loving Mud were sporting them for a generation, the bell bottom's chief use was in catching itself between the spokes of your **Raleigh Chopper** and causing you to fall off without even having to reach for the gear stick. Modern, millennial flares have been crossbred (*see* **The Budgie**) with the low-slung hipster to create a ladies' leisure trouser that is mostly on the ground, affording not just a visible panty line but visible whole pants. Out and proud, that's the way. This book applauds all silly trousers. Time for a lederhosen revival?

FAD **RATING** ✪✪✪✪ *'Where d'you get they, Flarefax House?'*

Fluorescent items

The early eighties craze for dressing in fluorescent socks, preferably made from towelling (*see* **The Sweat Band**), was possibly a side effect of the hit movie *Tron*. Thankfully defunct, this craze for reflectivity has left us one item of lasting use: the highlighter pen. Where would 3M's humble yet intrusive Post-It note be without this office essential?

 RATING ✪ *'At least I won't get knocked down at the ankles.'*

Footbag

See The Hacky Sack®.

French Toast

During the seventies the British discovered that adding the word 'French' to an otherwise prosaic item would lend it a veneer of sophistication. If it could work for 'dressing', it could surely work for toast. Here was another great example of the fundamental marketing rule that your best money is made selling people what they already have. Toast, for example, that most British of delicacies, is the easiest thing to make. You just slam your bread under the grill until it is done to your liking. We should have been content with this, but clever people sold us toasters. Nowadays no one puts their bread under the grill.

As with toasters, so with toast. Pre-toasted bread was a dry and unpalatable proposition until it became 'French Toast'. We didn't know any better – we were only just getting our heads around the **aubergine**. 'Is that how they do it on *the continent*, then?' we mumbled, buying pack after pack of brittle, compacted sawdust.

What we didn't know was that true French Toast is as American as **Strawberry Shortcake**. First created in 1724 by Joseph French at his roadside tavern in Albany, New York State, this hedonistic breakfast dish should, perhaps, in the interests of good punctuation, have been called 'French's Toast'. However, he called it simply 'French Toast'. In America, French Toast is a decadent delicacy with limitless possibilities. To make it, you want to mix the following in a bowl: 6 eggs, 6 tbsp milk, ½ tsp salt and pepper to taste, a few drops of vanilla essence. That's enough mixture to soak nicely into twelve slices of crusty white bread. When they're fully dunked, take them out and fry them quickly in hot butter until lightly crisp. Serve warm and add a topping of your choice. The author favours maple syrup, but you could just as easily go for cream, chocolate sauce, jam, honey or custard.

That's what French Toast ought to be. Sadly, the British were sold slices of desiccated chipboard, which they were led to believe had once been a baguette. Ultimately, though, the marketers lost this game, as they had previously with French Guyana (who wants to go *there* on holiday?), the French Letter (give me a Dutch Cap any day) and French Leave, which we discovered wasn't really proper leave at all. And we soon found out that so-called 'French Polish' had nothing to do with Poland but, like the inedible toast, was simply a thin patina of glossy continental chic.

FAD **RATING ✪** *'New from Inland Revenue: It's French Self-Assessment.'*

HOW TO START A CRAZE

Make it a sport

The success of genuine, organically developed sports such as surfing, skating and skateboarding gives us a superb example on which to draw. If we can only capture that wave and ride on its back… Donald Duncan sponsored Yo-Yo®-spinning competitions. Wham-O founded sport associations to propagate both Frisbee® and Footbag, two 'sports' in which the prime playing piece is a trademarked property. Sports people are fantastically evangelistic – and healthy too. And newspapers dedicate a third of their pages to sports. It's a goldmine. Setting the sporting world loose to spread the good news with your product works in much the same way as licensing your property: other people do the publicity for you, while you sit back and count the receipts. Imagine what the blanket magazine- and newspaper-coverage of 'extreme' sports such as snowboarding did for the peddlers of boards, clothes and accessories.

The Friendship Bracelet

You made it from threads of coloured cotton. You wove it lovingly. You gave it to someone you liked as a token of your esteem and goodwill. Your friend undertook to wear it at all times as a permanent physical reminder of your everlasting devotion, your badge of ownership, your unflinching control of their every thought and action, and when it unravelled in the sea it meant your friend hated you.

The joy of the friendship bracelet was in choosing from the haberdashery department in John Lewis the colours that would best suit the object of your affections. The joy of the friendship bracelet was in the loving, careful attention you gave to weaving its intricate lattice patterns. Time is a wonderful gift, perhaps the most valuable gift you can offer a friend, and to devote your spare hours to the creation of this permanent tattoo or brand, this tag or label, this badge of proprietary pride, this mark of Abraham, this – no, sorry, it's not happening. If you want handicraft, try **Fimo**®.

 RATING ✪✪ *'I'll wear it for ever until I take it off.'*

The Frisbee®

SUPERFAD Have you ever walked along a beach and chanced upon the lid from a tin of paint, washed up on the high-tide line? Have you then picked it up and flung it into the wind, remarking upon what a great Frisbee® it makes? Have you then noticed that, unlike the Frisbee®, the tin lid often tends to list and veer, drop like a stone and land on its edge? With a few minor modifications, surely such a lid could really be made to fly. This is pretty much how the Frisbee® was invented.

But first: pies. In 1871, William Russell Frisbie, the son of a Connecticut grist miller, got a job managing the Bridgeport branch of the Olds Baking Company. He subsequently bought the bakery and renamed it the Frisbie Pie Company.

Frisbie's company manufactured tinned pies and cookies, which sold widely, the proud name 'Frisbie' embossed on the lids. The pies found favour with students at the nearby universities of Yale and Harvard, and it was not long before these youthful consumers discovered the joys of launching Frisbie pie-lids at each other. The low-key pastime of 'Frisbie-ing' might well have stayed this way had a Second World War veteran called Walter Frederick Morrison not returned from the Nazi Stalag 13 prison to an America obsessed with UFOs from outer space.

In 1948, Morrison, bent on exploiting this sidereal enthusiasm, started work on a plastic flying saucer that would incorporate a number of aerodynamic improvements on the paint-tin lids he threw about as a youth. Morrison, the son of an inventor, understood how the difference between high-pressure areas formed above a flying lid and low-pressure pockets below gave the discs lift. He also understood the principle of angular momentum, or the way that spinning the disc would give it stability and allow it to fly, the same way a spinning top or bicycle in motion can stand upright.

Morrison's first attempt, imaginatively named 'The Flyin' Saucer', was not a great success. It used spoilers to give extra lift, but Morrison put them on backwards, so the disc would really only work with left-handed players. One of his more successful innovations was the 'Morrison Slope', the curved outer ring of the disc. The eventual result of this tinkering, in 1951, was the 'Pluto Platter', a kind of plastic flying saucer with a raised cabin, which Morrison patented and attempted to sell.

Fast-forward to 1955, and Wham-O, a new toy company run by Californian whiz-kids 'Spud' Melin and Richard Knerr (only in America can you find names like these), was already enjoying success with its **Hula-Hoop**® when the partners saw Morrison's Pluto Platter on the beach. Morrison, accustomed to flogging his Platters on the streets, was duly seduced, rights were bought, and production began in 1957. But 'Pluto Platter' was not the name for the game. What *was* a Pluto Platter? Was it some sort of cooked-meat selection? The Platter was not an immediate success in California and clearly a more catchy name was called for. On a marketing sojourn to the Ivy League universities, Knerr

apparently chanced upon the Frisbie tin-lid phenomenon and borrowed the name. A year after the Frisbee® was launched into the wind, never to fall again, the Frisbie Baking Company of Connecticut went out of business, never to bake again. This is, perhaps, a coincidence.

The newly named Frisbee® really took off. What gave the fad-gadget extra lift was a stroke of marketing genius from Wham-O. They pushed Frisbee® heavily as a new sport. Tricks, rules, rudiments and league tables. It's a winning combination, and one that, once unleashed, will gain an angular momentum all its own, keeping the product afloat without much effort on the part of its creators. Frisbee® Tennis, Frisbee® Golf, Frisbee® Baseball: such games put a new spin on favourite ball games and caught the imagination of the masses: both the punters and the pundits.

The first 'pro' Frisbee® model was launched by Wham-O in 1964. The designer was Ed Headrick, who improved upon Morrison's aerodynamics. Headrick, who eventually became CEO of Wham-O, also created the game of Disc Golf in 1976. The sport, propagated and regulated by the Disc Golf Association, Inc.® (founder: E. Headrick), now has around 2 million players. There is also 'Folf', Ultimate Frisbee® and 'Guts'. Such things snowball: Wham-O shifted an impressive 100 million flying discs before selling the rights to toy-giant Mattel.

Frisbee®, like Biro, Hoover and **Yo-Yo**®, is a trademark that has gone beyond its own branding to become a generic household-name. While the craze has settled and the Frisbee® – or the millions of Frisbee® clones with names such as Flying Disc, Super Disc, Super Flying Disc or Discbee – have become part of our lives, we can safely say the mania achieved its acme in 1968, when the US Navy invested $400,000 in a Frisbee®-launching machine, for military use. Look out, Osama.

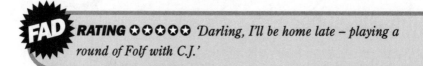

FAD **RATING** ✪✪✪✪✪ *'Darling, I'll be home late – playing a round of Folf with C.J.'*

The Furby®

Intelligent, fluffy yet curiously brittle and unyielding virtual animal designed by Dave Hampton of Sounds Amazing – who was influenced by the **Tamagotchi** and Richard Levy. A record seller (43 million in two years), the beast could communicate and interact with other **Furbies**® – a trick to make you buy more than one – and spoke its own language. It could be taught English, and doting owners swore that their **Furbies**® were alive, alerting them to burglaries, fires and other coincidences. Despite the plush, because of its hard plastic core it ranks as the single most uncuddly fluffy toy on the market. But for more on the Furby® and its imitators, including the slew of millennial robot-dogs, see the full entry on **The Virtual Pet**.

FAD **RATING ✪✪✪** *'Why won't he lick me?'*

The Global Hypercolour T-Shirt

The sartorial equivalent of the dental disclosing tablet, this piece of eighties attire used humiliation as its unique selling-point. The cutting-edge technology made the fabric change its colour according to heat. So let's be clear: it was clothing designed to show everyone else where you were sweating (*see* **The Aubergine**). How proud you were to step out in your funky new top. How chagrined you subsequently became when everyone pointed and laughed at your sticky crevices. Frankly, not the world's best 'pulling top'.

 **RATING** ✪✪ *'Nice pits, love.'*

The Hacky Sack®

The Hacky Sack® is not, as the author first thought, burlap storage for spare journalists. It's a **bean bag** and a registered trademark.

The author was first introduced to the Hacky Sack® in a London park, where a circle of people were attempting to keep a small beanbag in the air with their feet. The author was invited to 'join the hack' and subsequently 'hack the sack'. This, he was told, was a non-competitive game of co-operation and goodwill. There was something a shade pious about the way this group talked about their sport, and the codified language was not helping. Fearing immediate induction into a cult, the author made other plans. Had he, however, 'hacked the sack', he would have discovered a game of skill and patience known as 'Footbag' and most probably hurt his instep.

Footbag was invented in Oregon City, USA, in 1972. John Stalberger was recovering from knee surgery and taking a constitutional walk when he ran into Mike Marshall, who was fiddling with a homemade bean bag. The two began kicking it about together and thought their co-operative, non-competitive game of 'hack the sack' was so mellow and unheavy that it really ought to be exploited immediately for personal profit. They developed their bean bag and trademarked it the 'Hacky Sack'®. They also coined the term 'footbag' for the sport.

Footbag may have helped Stalberger's knee, but it couldn't

> **FAD Fact**
>
> Children between the ages of nine and ten receive an average of £3.65 a week in pocket money. Our eleven- to fourteen-year-olds receive £7. At fifteen and sixteen, children get around £13. Their combined spending-power was worth £2.7 billion in 2002. (NFPI)

help Marshall's heart. Three years after this fateful meeting, Marshall had a coronary seizure and died. Stalberger continued to carry the Hacky Sack® torch, forming the National Hacky Sack® Association. He then sold the rights to Wham-O, **Frisbee®** manufacturers to the world, which continued to promote both the product and the sport, something for which the company had a remarkable aptitude.

There are now various 'footbag' sports, including Footbag Net, a kind of cross between bag volleyball and bean badminton. Only with feet. There is also Footbag Freestyle. This is something else entirely, which causes its exponents to perform choreographed routines composed of complex tricks to music. The various sports now have a regulating body, the International Footbag Committee, which imposes 'official' rules on players, creates artificial hierarchies and gives footwear advice.

It's easy to mock, but footbag is a serious sport that can inspire almost spiritual devotion in its fans, as American footbag enthusiast Dan Ednie here explains: 'When I first saw Brian McKenzie on the 1999 world championships, I was almost overcome with not only sheer amazement but also respect. This was a respect I had only ever attributed to a select group of political figures – Mandela, Gandhi, Lenin – a handful of philosophers – Kant, Phittskennypipe, Hyanthes and Nietzsche – and of course the Jedi. The particular move that was really embedded in my mind, the one that gave Brian that supernatural effect, was a Baily Paradox Blender. The Blender, the Möbius, P.S. Whirl and so many Dexy Down-Time moves share the elements of supreme agility, speed, strength, and the most perfect, almost instinctive technique and ability with the light-sabre movements of the **Star Wars** Jedi.'

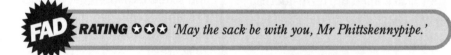

FAD **RATING ✪✪✪** *'May the sack be with you, Mr Phittskennypipe.'*

Harry Potter

SUPERFAD There are two tiers to the worldwide phenomenon that is Harry Potter: the author and her books. Starting with the former, it's not hard to see how first-time writer Joanne 'J.K.' Rowling captured the imagination of the media and the hearts of the masses. The folklore has it that this impoverished single mother regularly hunkered down in an Edinburgh café, where the heating was free, and wrote the children's book that would change not only her life, but the face of children's publishing: a comfortably familiar fantasy-story about a budding wizard called Harry Potter. Even allowing for the exaggerations of the press, it's a classic rags-to-riches story, and one that also embodies the universal fantasy: achieving fame and fortune from publishing that novel you've been meaning to sit down and write.

The first novel, *Harry Potter and the Philosopher's Stone*, was acquired for Bloomsbury in 1996 by Barry Cunningham, who paid the writer a very modest four-figure sum. Rowling kept the wolf from her door with the aid of a grant from the Scottish Arts Council. The book was published the following year and won the Nestlé Smarties Gold Award for the nine-to-eleven-years age-group. The publicity this engendered gave a huge boost to sales, recognized in the form of the industry prize for Children's Book of the Year at the 1998 British Book Awards. When the follow-up, *The Chamber of Secrets*, was published in July 1998, the work was done. It went straight to number one in the former BookTrack bestseller list, while further awards followed. Harry Fever began in earnest, and Bloomsbury showed itself more than equal to the challenge.

Besides the obvious benefits to Rowling and her publisher, Harry Fever had a positive knock-on effect for booksellers. Suddenly people who never went into bookshops were queuing at the counter, picking up all kinds of things as they waited. That is, if they hadn't gone to the supermarket, petrol station or Chinese takeaway first. Harry Potter books went on sale everywhere that tills lived.

Other writers benefited too: firstly, veteran children's authors such as Philip Pullman and Jacqueline Wilson. As parents desperately searched for something to keep their kids reading, Pullman's intelligent fantasy novels and Wilson's empathy fit the bill perfectly. Secondly, unpublished children's writers gained as Bloomsbury's rivals scrambled to sign up the next J.K. Rowling. Would it be American upstart 'Lemony Snickett' (aka Daniel Handler) or self-effacing Irish writer Eoin Colfer? Would it be loquacious bearded man Philip Ardagh or 'Zizou Corder', the pseudonym for the mother-and-daughter team which made all the papers when it transpired the mother looked a bit like J.K.? New Rowlings could be anywhere, and such writers suddenly found themselves to be the toast of the town, giving a fillip to the whole trade.

J.K. Rowling was not the first writer to publish a book along the lines of *Harry Potter and the Philosopher's Stone*. She will certainly not be the last. So why did Harry fly so high so soon? Senior executives at Bloomsbury are famously tight-lipped on the secrets of their success. Like Coca-Cola® with its special recipe, Bloomsbury people guard their secret with a steadfast loyalty bordering on cultishness. Even when caught with their guard down in a bar at three in the morning, directors tend to smile benignly and change the subject. Good for them. The truth is that there is no secret formula for a bestseller. But finding itself with one on its hands, Bloomsbury was agile and canny enough as a company to make quick decisions and act swiftly.

The first book was bought because Cunningham thought it was good. But Bloomsbury could not have predicted the extent to which this would convert into sales. What is certain is that the publisher was smart enough to capitalize fully on that early success. Adept at exploiting the publicity prospects, Bloomsbury ensured that subsequent novels were shrouded in carefully manufactured mystery, the launch dates turned into high-profile, must-see events with ever more draconian non-disclosure provisos to the trade and newspapers. Such paranoid secrecy begets intrigue, and such intrigue begets column inches, and column inches beget Harry Fever.

As a craze, Harry has it all. There is the compulsion to collect the set. There is anticipation, competition and fashion. Possibly for the first time ever, reading a book, not simply owning it, was a trendy playground craze. The craze, as well as the writing, appeals to both children and adults, while the publicity machine has gathered its own momentum, with journalists competing for coverage, battling for the Harry story that will put their paper or news channel ahead of the rest. But unlike other fad collectibles such as, say Pokémon cards, the product delivers on its promise. It's a whole book – with a beginning, a middle and, well, where will it end?

Bloomsbury need in fact do very little now to perpetuate the mania. The pressure, sadly, falls upon Rowling herself. While she has set a limit on the number of books she will write, when she actually pens the 'final' one, the pressure upon her to continue will be enormous. There is hardly an aspect of her personality or private life that has not been paraded in the media. Her personal fortune is a matter of public record, and now this rather shy mum and writer is under pressure to act as a kind of Princess Diana substitute, dispensing goodwill and charity to all and sundry in a series of designer frocks, when she would probably prefer to crawl under a rock in her jogging pants and eat Pringles.

She has had to weather some unseemly criticism of her 'unremarkable' writing with good grace, lest she seem ungrateful for her millions. But such jealous nay-sayers miss the point of Harry Potter. It's simple stuff, told with the art that conceals art. The same appealing mix of fantasy and clearly demarcated forces of good and evil that helped

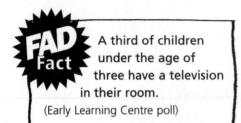

Star Wars reach global status also pushed Harry Potter to the top, revitalized children's publishing and bookselling and ensured a successful rebirth of Tolkien's previously moribund *Lord of the Rings* trilogy. But unlike Tolkien, Rowling is not challenging or daunting to read, her language is not so dense that the kids don't understand, and indeed her very lack of writerly pretension in general give her work and private life a homely charm that only adds to the brew. Her characters mature and have emotional experiences that Hobbits never did. Add in the well-made feature films and the endless merchandising, the rights to much of which Bloomsbury cannily bought back a few years ago, and it's not hard to see why some are sick of the sight of Harry Potter.

But spare a thought for J.K. Despite her obvious affection for her characters, she's probably more sick of it than anyone knows. At book five Rowling was already displaying a reluctance to jump through the media hoops; it's possible that the last thing she wants is to live through the whole circus again. But as this author writes, the world is eagerly awaiting book six, *The Half-Blood Prince*. For the time being at least, the world seems unwilling to let Ms Rowling rest in peace. All of us who have made an easy buck on the back of her 'mediocre' typing – well, we need her unique talents too much to let it lie.

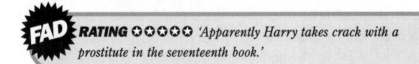

FAD *RATING* ✪✪✪✪✪ *'Apparently Harry takes crack with a prostitute in the seventeenth book.'*

Hello Kitty

Cat-based accessory craze marketed by Japanese **Tamagotchi** moguls Bandai, under licence from something called Sanrio. The idea was simply to come up with a picture of a little cat, with a bow or flower in its 'hair', write the words 'Hello Kitty' under it and then put this whole logo on to anything you could, as long as it was pink. Targeted at little girls, Hello Kitty was also very popular with young women who wanted to look like little girls for kitsch or other reasons. There was also a cursory range of toys, such as the Hello Kitty deluxe playset, but they didn't really do anything: basically someone had done a doodle and sold it all over the world (*see* **The Pokémon**). Other Japanese favourites in this vein include the equally indecipherable 'Afro Ken': a dog with a range of rainbow-coloured Afro haircuts (*see* **The Perm**).

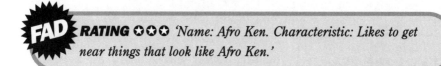

FAD **RATING** ✪✪✪ *'Name: Afro Ken. Characteristic: Likes to get near things that look like Afro Ken.'*

The Hornby Train Set

British **Meccano** inventor Frank Hornby released his first model train set in 1920, a clockwork effort inspired by advances in German toy production. Five years later his first electric set sparked into life from the mains, transforming into a 6-volt system in 1929. By 1938 mass-production techniques had advanced to such a degree that further miniaturization was possible. Thus Meccano developed the seminal 'Dublo', or double 'o' gauge railway, we know and love, sparking off a more accessible craze for the train-set hobby. While recession forced Meccano to sell out to Triang in the sixties, the Hornby brand was retained to become synonymous with model train sets.

The Hornby train set, along with its apparatus, is a classic toy, both an ongoing concern and an antique collectible, yet it is none the less subject to little pockets of fad-like activity, peaks and troughs in its wider popularity outside the modelling hobby. The author's own ascent into Hornby heaven was in fact the result of **pester power** engendered by a school teacher who happened to have a spare catalogue and used it as a bizarre psychological carrot to promote harder work and better behaviour. Reeking of B.O. from his plaid jacket, this demonic pedagogue would creep up behind a troublesome child, dangle the catalogue, and say, 'Wouldn't you love to have one of these?' Suitably galvanized by the promise of a gift, the child would then buck his

---

THAT WAS THE YEAR...
Post-war Toy Crazes

1943 The Slinky®.

1949 Lego makes first bricks.

1951 *Muffin the Mule*.

1952 Mr Potato Head®.
The Matchbox car.

1956 Scalex plugs into the mains.
Scalextric is born.

1959 Barbie® struts forth.

ideas up for a whole term, at the end of which bitter disappointment would force him to initiate the nag-factor, a hideous descent that, in the case of the author, resulted in the acquisition of an LNER 'steam' locomotive with cargo carriages. For the teacher it worked a treat: better results while the parent footed the bill. Little coteries of Hornby owners sprung up like mushrooms across that class of 1981, but it was not long before we realized that a model train simply goes round and round and round and that's it. Hardly **Star Wars**.

The true joy of this hobby is better harnessed by adults, as it lies in the modelling, the designing, the adding, the collecting and the making. None of these things appealed to the child author, who had only to come within smelling distance of plaster of Paris or papier mâché to break out into full-blown fight-or-flight syndrome (*see* **The Airfix Kit**). The model trains, however, remain a marvel of design, beautiful things to own and never play with.

FAD **RATING ✪✪✪✪** *'Can I have a go, Dad?'*

The Hostess Trolley

The subjugation of womankind in the home during the Demis Roussos years was given a perambulatory slant (*see* **The Maternity Smock**) in the shape of the 'hostess trolley'. It was not enough simply to have your husband's colleagues, fellow golfers or boss round for a bit of **aubergine** bake and Black Forest gateau, washed down with a dashingly continental German white wine (*see* **Black Tower**). No – to achieve the correct

---

GREAT BETTYS IN HISTORY

Betty James

Betty rescued James Industries Inc. from massive debts caused by her husband's donations to a spiritual group and helped secure the future of his invention: the **Slinky**®. When Richard James made waves by slinking off to Bolivia, leaving his family and business in order to serve God, Betty did not buckle or warp. Instead, she soldiered on. Under her auspices the high-mass, low-tension coiled spring we know and love enjoyed many innovations and walked downstairs right into the history books. She turned the fortunes of the company around and successfully managed the sale of this singular and newly profitable toy empire to a company called Poof, ensuring financial security for her six children (although they were already grown up by then). Hooray for Betty.

impact, the whole ensemble should be wheeled in on a hostess trolley by the little lady herself, the plates perhaps kept warm by tea-lights. It gave the impression that one was in fact in a rather exclusive restaurant, in which Her Indoors was both cook and waitress. The roles and boundaries were clearly defined: there were no 'host trolleys'.

For those households who could not afford a hostess trolley, there was always TV's *The Generation Game*, in whose final conveyor-belt memory game a person could actually stand the chance of winning one for free, week after week.

Nowadays, since the dawn of the 'New Man' (Nigel Slater) and even the 'New Lad' (Jamie Oliver), men can't wait to cook. It's no longer a case of deigning to 'slam in the lamb' of a Sunday – real men don't feel properly masculine unless they can bang out a Thai green curry and baked plantain, their virility measured by the quantity (in hundredweight) of cloves of garlic they shove in the pot. And while the hostess trolley of yore would wobble out from that mysterious room where wives and Bovril were stored, its contents fully formed, the recent deluge of flamboyant, self-promoting male television-chefs has prompted today's men to build themselves 'performance kitchens', in which to show off their culinary prowess. Look at me, look at me, I'm *so* boiling this egg.

FAD **RATING ✪✪** *'Pukka.'*

The Hula-Hoop®

We are not talking about crisps. The concept of playing with hoops is as old as the hoop. The Ancient Greeks favoured hoop-twirling around the waist as a weight-loss exercise. In Egypt they made them from vines. The seventeenth-century English blamed the activity for a spate of coronary seizures, possibly giving rise to the more sedate occupation of hoop and stick. But this is hardly relevant. The 'Hula-Hoop'®craze of the late fifties that we all remember was formulated and controlled by Richard Knerr and Arthur 'Spud' Melin of America's Wham-O toy company.

Wham-O was not the world's most original innovator. Where its talent lay was in anticipating trends, taking punts on hunches and understanding and manipulating markets. In 1957 Knerr and Melin were tipped off about hoop-twirling in Australia by a visiting friend. While most of us would probably say, 'Really? How fascinating,' and turn back to our colour supplement, Knerr and Melin sprung into action. Their agility paid dividends. Very quickly they had designed a brand-new, lightweight hoop of hollow Marlex – a revolutionary plastic recently developed by Philips petroleum – and trademarked the name 'Hula-Hoop'®. Less than a year later, in 1958, they had a product to take to market. This they did with some considerable aplomb, selling 25 million Hula-Hoops® in the first two months of trading. The international orders soon flooded in.

But could supply meet demand? Police protection was needed by the manager of the State store in Torun, Poland, when 'hoop-happy buyers' stormed the premises, desperate for purchases, *The Times* reported in 1959. The story demonstrates the speed with which the craze swept the globe. In fairness, these were not Wham-O hoops but likenesses produced by state co-operatives and independent workshops.

You have to admire anyone who can convince the world to make like idiots, wiggling a hoop on their hips. But as they say, you can't fool all of the people all of the time. Keeping a Hula-Hoop® hip-bound is not especially easy, and even when you are successful it is a highly dubious achievement. 'Look, look, I'm doing it!' 'Ah. So you are.' The novelty soon wears off. The decline began after only a year. Did Wham-O care? Not really. Knerr and Melin had already made a stunning $45 million in profit when the craze began to fade, and in any case, by 1958 they were already on to the **Frisbee®**.

Though the original Hula-Hoop® craze was short-lived, it made a lasting impression and numerous comebacks in the decades that followed. In 1973 the current incarnation of this fad was still fresh enough for snack manufacturer KP to feel confident using the name for its new hoop-shaped potato snack. The author has found the Hula-Hoop® to be one of the most frequently and fondly remembered crazes. When kids grow up and have kids of their own, they tend to seek out the toys, games and books they remember from their own childhood. This may account for the fact that, in 2005, Wham-O – independent once again after being rescued from the clutches of toy giant Mattel – is still selling its original hoop.

If this has rekindled your hoop affections and you feel like a bit of hip fun, you could do worse than take tuition from Lori Lynn Loreli, the 1973 World Hula-Hoop® champion. You may have seen her on Japanese TV's *Cook-a-doodle-doo*. According to the blurb on her instructional video, her personal best is a whopping fifteen hoops – beat it if you dare – and her secrets could be yours for $14.95.

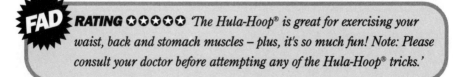

FAD ✮ **RATING** ✪✪✪✪✪ *The Hula-Hoop® is great for exercising your waist, back and stomach muscles – plus, it's so much fun! Note: Please consult your doctor before attempting any of the Hula-Hoop® tricks.'*

Instant Coffee

Dairylea peddlers Kraft (*see* **Milk**), along with Nestlé, who are responsible for the welfare of the Milky Bar Kid, dominate the market for instant 'coffee'. The former sells under the brands Birds, Kenco, Maxwell House and Café Hag, while the latter holds the top spot with Blend 37, Gold Blend, Alta Rica and of course plain old Nescafé. Through soap-opera adverts in which a smug couple seduce each other over a series of Gold Blend-based encounters, Nestlé did a good job of convincing us that this dehydrated, thin-tasting forgery of a drink was coffee.

This sly prestidigitation was based on the assumption that everyone thought it was really convoluted and difficult to make coffee, real coffee: some arcane and laborious process involving precariously balanced filters or Heath Robinson machines that went 'plop plop plop' just like the man in the adverts. But in fact coffee is really, really easy to make, as everyone found out. What's more, with the arrival of the rival nineties craze for **silly coffee** from America and the subsequent realization that Britain could have its own 'café culture', albeit imported, no one wanted to be seen getting outside of a mug of Mellow Birds, and now only the Queen drinks the stuff – out of **Tupperware**.

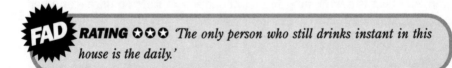 **FAD** **RATING ✪✪✪** *'The only person who still drinks instant in this house is the daily.'*

Jacks

The unfathomable yet involving game of jacks is not so much a fad but one of a select band of über-crazes, such as **marbles**, and **skipping**. Über-crazes (that's the scientific term) occur when a classic game enjoys discrete pockets of fad activity over many centuries, picking up endless variants and local idiosyncrasies along the way. Such activities, soaring beyond the limited clutches of capitalist marketeers, move on from the shifting sands of mere ephemera and enter the green and pleasant realm of folklore, their manifold reincarnations imitating the life-force itself, endlessly renewing.

Jacks is the most enduring and common name for the ancient game of fivestones or knucklebones. A game that evolved out of the land, at its most elemental, fivestones requires just that: five small stones. The player holds them in the palm and throws them into the air, catching as many as possible on the back of the hand, scoring a point for each. What the player then did was limited only by the imagination. Throwing the caught stones up again while snatching the remainder is but one option. You could perhaps take advantage of the time during which the stones are airborne to slip the others behind your ear and quickly eat a biscuit before they land, or bounce a ball while touching your nose as many times as you can with your free hand. The possibilities, and hence the game's appeal, are as limitless as the different types of pebble. But you needn't use stones.

Where there are cloven-hooved creatures, such as in Hell or Wales, there are astragalus, or knucklebones. These smooth, small oblong bones work themselves free from the ankles of a rotting sheep carcass and, once severely disinfected, fumigated and quarantined, are ideal as playing pieces, adding an element of competitive collecting fun.

The earliest written reference to '*pentalitha*', or fivestones, comes from the second century CE and appears in Pollux's *Onomasticon*. Even then, stones and knucklebones were interchangeable. But illustrations show the game being played as far back as 5 BCE.

In England, variants such as creepmouse and toodles have enjoyed passing success, as have spansies, fingers, pantysnicket and squelm (note: the last two are made up). The French played it too, as *Les Osselets*, although, typically, they insisted on kissing the bones.

Entrepreneurs over the years have been able to kickstart not a few mini-crazes – and make a few bob – by banging out attractively packaged sets. Various materials have been used in the manufacture of substitute knucklebones. According to the folklorists Iona and Peter Opie, who have published an engaging history of the game, terracotta, onyx, ivory, brass, lead and gold have all been used. But eventually manufacturers began to cast the familiar six-footed metal stars we know today. Numerous names have been applied to these pieces, such as 'dibs', 'snobs', 'bobbers' and 'hucklebones'. But jacks will for ever be the strange, rule-defying game played with five curious metal pieces and a bouncy-ball.

FAD **RATING** ✪ ✪ ✪ ✪ ✪ *'What's the ball for again?'*

The Kewpie Doll

The mother of all collectible dolls was devised in 1909 by Rose O'Neill. What started as an illustrated poetry column in the *Ladies Home Journal* soon evolved into paper dolls, then ceramic dolls, then... a deluge of Kewpie-branded merchandise. Although the product was not actually patented until 1935, what makes O'Neill herself the mother of all such doll toys is that she gave each of her emetic little sods a name and personality: a trick countless toy manufacturers have tried to pull off time and again, from the **Cabbage Patch Kid®**, to **Trolls**, to **Strawberry Shortcake**, to **Care Bears**, to **My Little Pony**, to **Beanie Babies** to **Pokémon**... to... well, there really is no end to it, nor will there ever be until the world ends.

FAD **RATING ✪✪✪✪** *'Cute, but naked.'*

Klackers

The sound of 1971 was klick klack, klick klack all day long. Possibly the most irritating toy of all time, these LOUD plastic balls on string bounced off one another in your very hand, in the manner of elastic collision (*see* **The Executive Toy**). Once this was acknowledged, the only thing you could actually do with a pair of Klackers was go klick klack, klick klack all day long. No wonder parents were so keen to get on their children's **Space Hoppers**, which also gripped the nation that year, and bounce off into the distance. Klackers were officially banned from all schools for health and safety reasons, i.e., 'If I hear that thing one more time I will harm you.' Klackers, or imitations thereof, have enjoyed sporadic patronage over the decades but never have they been successfully revived as a craze. Big shame.

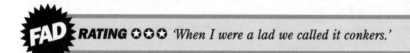

FAD · **RATING** ✪✪✪ *'When I were a lad we called it conkers.'*

Lego

The word is a household name, theme parks bear its legend. But the acrylonitrile butadiene styrene building bricks we hold so dear started life as wooden stepladders. The Lego company was formed in 1932 by Ole Kirk Christiansen, a Danish carpenter. Formed from the Danish words '*leg*' and '*godt*', meaning 'play well', the company made ladders, ironing boards and wooden toys. The first plastic bricks appeared in Denmark in 1949, under the name 'Automatic Binding Bricks', and are identifiable by the lack of cylindrical infrastructure inside the brick. Later, in 1958, the studs and tubes were added and patented, giving the more secure join that Lego calls 'clutch power'. By 1960, when a fire prompted Lego to drop wooden toys from its inventory, the company had grown from six employees to 450. But it was not until the following decade that the concept of low-cost, pocket-money toys hit Lego. Small vehicles were sold as sets of bricks, wheels and other elements, with instructions on how to build them.

The author's own Lego lived in two Quality Street tins and contained elements from two generations of siblings. Thus some wheels had the smooth tyres of the sixties, some came on fat four-stud blocks, and many, many more came on the flat panels that landed with Space Lego in 1979. Space Lego, with satellite dishes, coloured 'light' bricks and space helmets, rejuvenated sales and took the toy into another dimension. This is the craze the author remembers.

In the wake of **Star Wars** and **Space Invaders**, Lego – never naff, like the stickle brick, or too egg-head, like **Meccano** – acquired a cool edge.

Lego's ability to market themes such as 'Technical Lego' as well as individual toys and loose bricks meant that a good-sized collection of Lego could include all sorts of peculiar pieces. Thus the author was able during summer months to construct scale models of the Radio One Roadshow van, complete with hinged front doors mounted with speakers, two circular swivels from an articulated space-buggy as the 'decks' and two taps from a Lego kitchen as the styli.

Influenced by the futuristic landscapes in *2000 AD* comic, the author and friends were also moved to construct elaborate Robo-repairers, vast salvage trucks with cranes, pulleys and vats full of 'reclaimed' junk that roamed the wasteland (the kerb) in search of stray stormtroopers or Princess Leias that might be passing.

Strange as it may seem now, this kind of creative play, promoting design, hand skills and, er, patience, is what has made Christiansen's Lego bricks last, while the repetitive recreation of scenes from a film offered by tie-in toys fades very quickly. The author was certainly still mucking about with Lego when the possibilities afforded by his **Star Wars** figures had long waned.

FAD **RATING** ✪✪✪✪ *'Pass me a sixer, I need a sixer.'*

Leg-Warmers

When girls were cold in the early eighties did they wear trousers? Hell, no. The thing to do was wear a ruffled mini-skirt with footless tights and leg-warmers. Leg warmers were simply the sleeves of a jumper, cut off and sold to credulous fashionistas. You stuck them on your legs, just above the suede ankle-boots, and rejoiced in sweaty legs. This ensemble was best topped off with an over-lacquered quiff and **snood**. All in all a perfectly sensible way to dress, unfairly mocked. Mothers and grandmothers rejoiced in the fact that something that was easy to knit was in fashion. Teenagers recoiled in horror at the thought. A home-knitted pair of leg-warmers? How stupid would that look?

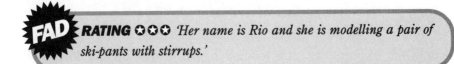 **FAD RATING ✪✪✪** *'Her name is Rio and she is modelling a pair of ski-pants with stirrups.'*

The Luncheon Voucher

One lunch-time in 1954, John Hack went for a bite to eat with a friend and was intrigued to see diners paying for their meals with a slip of paper. A discreet inquiry revealed that the restaurant had an agreement with a few local firms that wanted to subsidize their employees' meals but could not afford a canteen. The restaurant sent the collected vouchers back to their firms of origin, which then reimbursed the sum. Hack decided that a company that was prepared to take this clearing-house process off the hands of businesses could make money by levying a service charge. Luncheon vouchers were born the following year, when the government granted them exemption from National Insurance and offered a tax break of 15p per voucher.

Sadly for Hack, restaurants were slow to join the scheme, and it was not until a consortium of catering giants including Lyons and Forte bought the business that the voucher began to take off. By 1978 the luncheon voucher was part of British life. Very much so. In that very year Cynthia Payne hit the news after police raided her London house and

FAD Fact — HUNGARY

In the fifth century CE, the Hungarian tribes left the Urals and passed along the Volga and the Caspian Sea. These nomads wandered for several hundred years before they reached the Carpathian Basin, where they sat down and developed a language that resembles no other on Earth. A bit later, three separate Hungarians invented the Rubik's Cube, the Airfix Kit and the principle behind the Magic Eye™. And that's Hungarian history.

interrupted an organized sex party at which, according to the BBC, MPs, middle-aged and elderly barristers, journalists and police officers had exchanged their luncheon vouchers for sexual entertainment.

It may have been this unsavoury association that did for the luncheon voucher. Certainly it began a decline. The following year Margaret Thatcher came to power and began a regime of joyous capitalism in which workers stopped being workers and became consumers. They were encouraged to earn and spend their own money on whatever food they liked. The meal voucher was seen as a remnant of impecunious post-war rationing or a throwback to austere socialist rule. In this context, employers began to question why they should subsidize their workers' meals, travel and expenses. In 1999 the government removed the voucher's National Insurance exemption when it was discovered that some employers were abusing the system, avoiding NI contributions by paying employees very low wages and topping them up with vouchers and supermarket tokens. Although the Luncheon Voucher still exists and is accepted at a wide range of food outlets, it can be as difficult to spot with the naked eye as an organized sex party.

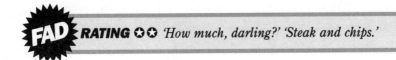

FAD **RATING ✪✪** *'How much, darling?' 'Steak and chips.'*

Macramé

The oriental fine art of macramé enables practitioners to achieve a Zen-like state by working with hemp. Follow the macramé way and make *anything* with knotted cord, from place mats and hanging baskets to fully operational computer workstations, ice-breakers and Tomahawk jet fighters (*see* **The Airfix Kit**). Keep away from naked flames, bright sunlight and damp. Common codes, ciphers and figures associated with macramé: 1mm (#20) 4 ply # jute, sinnet, picot. Common drawbacks associated with macramé: rot, mildew, fraying, combustion, ridicule. Some plus points: never waste money on store-bought raffia owls again.

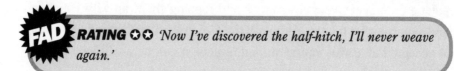

FAD **RATING** ✪✪ *'Now I've discovered the half-hitch, I'll never weave again.'*

The Magic Eye™

Suddenly, everyone was cross-eyed. The foremost benefit of the Magic Eye™ craze of the nineties lay in its ability to keep gullible people quiet and immobile for long periods of time while you stole cigarettes and/or cakes from under their nose. 'You've got to keep on staring at it until you see it, just keep looking – keep looking.'

Fools. What they were staring at was a page of squiggly patterns. What they were hoping for was the 'magic' of 3D vision. Opinion on technique varied from the unhelpful 'You've just got to stare at it' to the infuriatingly smug 'You've got to simultaneously look *at* it and *beyond* it'. But why? Why have you got to? The reward for your migraine-inducing efforts was the same page of squiggly patterns with the outline of a comedy dog floating in it.

But it had all begun so well. The original 'random dot stereogram' was developed by a Hungarian engineer (*see* **Rubik's Cube**) called Béla Julesz, in 1959. Prompted by the 1956 Soviet Union invasion of Hungary to resettle in America, Julesz got a job at AT&T Bell Laboratories, where his experiments with random number binary sequences led him to discover a way to test a person's ability to see in 3D.

The process is relatively simple. You take a selection of random dots. You outline a small section, say a circle, and shift them a little to one side. Then you put both together as a stereo pair and, as if by magic, the circle appears to float. Unless you can't see in 3D. If you can't see in 3D it would normally indicate that you are partially sighted, for to see the 3D image in the stereogram, you need good depth perception. And that comes from two healthy eyes diverging properly. The degree to which you fail to achieve this points to the degree to which you may need corrective treatment.

Julesz's rather altruistic creation was developed in 1991 by a group of American computer programmers and an artist, who patented their new full-colour, non-random technique and exploited it for commercial gain, syndicating strips in newspapers and magazines and selling the patterns as a series of posters, cards, books and other merchandise under the brand name Magic Eye™. They did well at this, ensuring a short-lived craze whose high point came during weekends, when all fathers could be seen with pages of the *Mail on Sunday* pressed to their bifocals for long periods of time. Hippies wallpapered their rooms with it. Men competed over 'divergence' times.

And that's why the craze worked: because some people are better at diverging than others. Those who finally saw the floating lump basked in a sense of achievement that lent a mild caché to the experience. Those who *couldn't* see the shapes desperately wanted to, in order to be part of that group. But what Baccei, Smith and Salkitsky of 'N. E. Thing Enterprises' failed to appreciate was that, if you *could* see it, you already had a much better and more stimulating 3D image in front of your face all the time, available 24/7 just by opening your eyes. The 'magic' of hurting your brain sort-of-seeing a 3D doggy adrift in a sea of purple dots could be enhanced a hundredfold by simply viewing a real doggy, who might lick you into the bargain. Patent that.

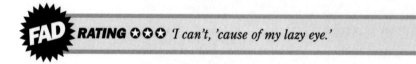

FAD **RATING ✪✪✪** *'I can't, 'cause of my lazy eye.'*

Male Strippers FEATURING THE CHIPPENDALES

Strippers used to be something men went to see. They were stored in seedy, stale-smelling rip-off joints in Soho and in the backstreets of your major towns and cities. The idea was that a man's one true – and shamefully secret – desire was to watch an unknown lady take off her frock and underclothes for money. This is a true fact, but one that men feel bad about. Real men inspire women to take their clothes off for free. Hence other men hid strippers and their clientele away in bad places where decent folk never went. They made it wrong, unlawful and not a little dirty.

Peter Stringfellow and his ilk did a reasonable job of updating the hobby by making it cleaner, shinier and very, very expensive. That way, men would come to believe that such an activity was only wrong if you were poor. Rich men deserved such things. Thus stripping acquired two levels, club class and economy.

Then the US entrepreneur Steve Banerjee turned the industry around by recruiting male bodybuilders as erotic dancers for ladies, naming his troupe of be-jockstrapped hunks The Chippendales. The idea of men on display for the titillation of women was such a novelty and such a refreshing reversal of stereotypes that the Chippendales worked. Very well. Women came in droves to watch these greased-up long-haired muscle-men bare all. This activity was as far removed from the seamy, under-the-counter world of female stripping as it was possible to be. It attracted all ages of women, who mostly laughed their heads off.

Some took it more seriously. According to the official history, Banerjee's original dancers worked for as little as $30 a night but supplemented their income by 'kissing' ladies in the audience for cash tips. The more interesting the 'kiss', the more they earned. However, this reversal of power in the sex- entertainment trade did quite a bit to loosen attitudes to sex and nudity on both sides of the Atlantic. In the wake of the Chippendales, hundreds of copycat troupes sprung up, such that male stripping is now part of life. Following the success of the British film *The Full Monty*, in which a bunch of average-looking unemployed blokes and cash-strapped tradesmen turn themselves into strippers to turn an honest coin, we now cannot move for ordinary men taking off their clothes. The nude-man charity calendar is now a fixture. Soon we will be sneaking into dark bars to watch naked people slowly put their trousers and cardigans on.

 RATING ✪✪✪ *'Get your kit on for the lassies.'*

Marbles

In Mansfield, Nottingham, on 29 January 1832, one John Lowe was convicted before magistrates sitting in Petty Sessions of 'playing at marbles on a Sunday'. He was reprimanded and ordered to pay costs. According to the *Nottingham Mercury*, which carried that story, he was the third that month. John Ivers and Joseph Dutton had already been banged to rights.

In February 1889 William Brogden, Chief Constable of the Borough of Great Yarmouth, gave notice that 'all boys and others obstructing the public thoroughfares of the Town, by... playing at marbles... will be summoned before the Magistrates and fined.'

In November 1924 *The Times* published a wry, yet plaintive editorial on the subject of marbles. A Lord Darling, it seems, had been in the midst of addressing a congregation of schoolboys on the subject of sports. He didn't much care for rugby football, which he considered 'muddy'. But marbles – marbles was *his* game, though he admitted it was 'somewhat despised at public schools'. Here he faltered, perhaps realizing where he was. The *Times* correspondent dryly noted that, having begun so well, Lord Darling abandoned 'the promising yet dangerous subject' of marbles in preference to some hastily uttered words of patriotism. 'The air of apology with which Lord Darling referred to it is evidence that it is dying,' the journalist wrote. 'Not much longer shall the language have a place for poppos and marididdles, for whinnies and glassies and for fine blood-alleys.'

Well, he needn't have worried. 'It sprang from Nature herself and didn't need to be invented.' Indeed. The game or games of marbles are so old that they even predate the marble. History shows that the urge to pitch one nut, knucklebone (*see* **Jacks**) or stone at another is as old as the nut, the knucklebone and the stone. The small children of Ancient Egypt found it perfectly natural to devise games out of pieces of the land, perhaps to work them a little to help them roll. Stone balls were found in Egyptian tombs, clay and glass spheres in Minoan Crete. Marbles were unearthed at the Roman forum and the British Museum has examples from Syria and Asia Minor.

The folklorists Iona and Peter Opie, who have compiled a detailed and colourful history, found that classic games such as castles, where one nut is pitched at a pile or pyramid, or ringy, where a nut is pitched at a ring of others, stretch across millennia from Roman times to urban England and persist more or less unchanged by the advent of shiny glass or ceramic balls. The simplest game of pitch and chase is recorded from the outset.

Other games, such as bagatelle and trunks, where marbles are rolled along a board in hopes of netting them in a hole, have been with us, it seems, since we were able to record them. And as long as marble-playing crazes have sprung up, others have sought to quell them.

What is it about the marble that so enchants us? A trip to the House of Marbles in Bovey Tracy, Somerset, will provide the answer. They are beautiful. In every form, from the dourest ball bearing to the most intricately patterned glass marble or painted alley, the sphere offers us so much. The very shape of our planet, the globe is at once terrestrial and preternatural. An object with no edges, brimming with potential energy, which simply asks to be played with, to be held in the hand, to be rolled and set in motion. It is not possible to set down a marble without it coming to life. It is not possible to hold one without wanting to watch it spin across the floor, catching the light and casting its glow upon the ground.

A bag of marbles is a bag of treasures and here of course lies the rub. Where is the point of marbles if you're not playing keepsies? What does that satisfying clack of glass on glass say to us, if not, 'Here is another gem, skilfully won and rightly ours.' Those who have railed against marbles have focused on the gambling. But that's the best bit.

Of course the grown-up author could simply buy a set of the most appealing little jewels and call it a day, but his original bag, the one that never left his side at the age of ten, was comprised of hard-won bounty. It was always useful to have a few biggies and a good supply of expendable cats-eyes, with their edible-looking swirl of coloured glass encased in a clear ball. More prized were the single-colour glass marbles that glowed deep ultramarine, warm orange and red or pale yellows like the sky. His schoolmates favoured 'alleys' – not in fact true alabaster marbles but glass 'chinas' painted in opaque colours. He was happy to sacrifice a few of these tiddlers for a good-coloured glassie. His secret weapon was an undefeated 'ball-bearian', whose weight and brute force rarely missed its target. And his most coveted prize was the china they called 'King Louis', a rich blue, white and red, rarer than any. By offering King Louis as bait, the author could count on upping the stakes and relieved many of his comrades of their most cherished petrol-coloured steelies before the royal china was stolen in a fit of jealous righteousness.

The worry, of course, would be that someone would catch you out on a technicality. Forgetting to call 'no ups' when the marble rolls off the kerb could leave you vulnerable. Your opponent could place the marble back up on the ledge, giving a clear shot. Similarly, stopping your marble from slipping down a drain without calling out 'stopsies' could forfeit you the game – although only a cad would take your stonesy on a stopsy. Or you might think you'd hit your target, only to hear a cry of 'clinks', meaning you only grazed the edge and thus you lose. In fact, over the aeons kids have devised unlimited get-outs and cheats masquerading as rules. 'Barricades' is the author's favourite. If you call 'barricades' you have the right to construct obstacles between your marble and the opponent's, such as a stick, a brick wall, house or icebreaker. 'Digsies' gives you the option to bore your marble down into the soil, allowing for a further call of 'clinks' should your opponent still manage to roll over the top of it. Such things can escalate. The author found it best to establish the rule-book before play. 'No nothings,' ensured a good clean fight, where a hit was a hit. It was still possible, however, that the loser might try to palm you off with an inferior marble, quickly calling 'no swapbacks' to attempt legal validation of his double-dealing.

Like jacks, marbles is an über-craze, a piece of folklore, a traditional and classic pastime, wont to blossom into mini-crazes at various points and places. Wherever such a craze blooms, people will always, curiously, try to keep it at bay. Teachers may ban it from the playground, Chief Constables may ban it from the streets. The Church may ban it on a Sunday. But, like May Day, marbles simply will not be silenced.

Of course, it's always possible to grow out of it. The author's marbling days ended with the move to secondary school. There the pupils gambled with real money, coins pitched across a stone slab. Marbles were for kids. But, contrary to the fears of the *Times* correspondent of 1924, so will they always be.

FAD ★ **RATING** ✪✪✪✪✪ *'Marbles out, smugglin's about.'*

The Matchbox Car

See The Dinky Toy.

The Maternity Smock

The notion of the pregnant woman as invalid has been a persuasive one for as long as this book cares to remember. But no amount of 'in your condition' platitudes can top the maternity smock for sheer depersonalization. Today's young women, weaned on All Saints and Madonna, may be surprised to learn that there was once a heady time when ladies 'in the family way' would drift around the suburbs in polyester tents resembling nothing so much as the Millets range of Stepford Wives.

Based loosely on the kind of garment favoured for use by those awaiting bowel surgery in hospital beds, the maternity smock was a clear sign to neighbours and passers-by. And the sign said: 'This female has now entered the phase of biological development known as maternity and must be kept in gestation conditions at all times. Her clothes and personal effects have been removed for this fragile reproductive stage. Once safely back at home, her duties with the **hostess trolley** over for the night, she will be placed back into the breeding pod for safekeeping. But for now she's got some shopping to do. 'I hope it's chips it's chips. I hope it's chips it's chips, la la la.'

The true purpose of the smock was to mask the unsightly lump of pregnancy: the diabolic stain of intercourse. But in fact it simply made women look like Moby Dick under a tarpaulin. The men who believed the physical evidence of gestation was something to be shamefully hidden behind swathes of the kind of fabric used chiefly for caravan curtains were of course the same men who were first to dish out the cigars and bask in macho glory after all the messy business was over. They were first in line for the 'Baby On Board' stickers, which they would stick on the rear windows of their cars, like flashing neon signs proclaiming, 'Not firing blanks, me.'

But men alone were not to blame for this phenomenon. Many women bought into the culture of sartorial subjugation, perhaps opting for comfort over appearance, or even believing that their new shape was unattractive. Perhaps they too believed that conception should be truly immaculate and any signs of sexual activity were to be swept under the rug. And this could be achieved quite simply by wearing the rug.

It was perhaps not until 1991, when the American actress and sex symbol Demi Moore caused outrage by posing naked and pregnant for the cover of *Vanity Fair* magazine, that the tide began to turn. Seven supermarket chains banned the US magazine from its shelves, but Moore was out and proud. 'Being pregnant is the sexiest thing in the world,' she declared.

Many men and women agreed, but it took longer for general attitudes to catch up. In 1998 MTV News reported on Tony Blair's G8 Summit 'rock' concert in Birmingham thus:

Two songs by All Saints were received coolly. The British press found the most notable thing about the performance to be the obviously pregnant state of the group's Melanie Blatt, who made no attempt to hide her budding belly with an above-the-navel short shirt.

Go, girl. But American attitudes were hardly more enlightened. The most recent high-profile woman to cause a storm across the pond was *Sale of the Century* host Nicky Buckley, who appeared in a state of ostentatious pregnancy on Channel 9. The display and backlash prompted the *Sun Herald* newspaper to launch a debate: 'Pregnancy – should it be shown off or shielded from view?' Buckley responded: 'They were saying that it's something that shouldn't be seen and I should be ashamed of myself. And to say that is to be ashamed of my baby, I guess, and I'm absolutely not.'

Slowly but surely, though, something has definitely shifted. Even the more conservative maternity-wear on offer from apparel merchants has moved on since the seventies. The author has trawled the World Wide Web in search of the retro maternity smocks of his youth – without much success. However, he is proud to announce, to all who still believe that pregnant women should look like Genghis Khan's living quarters, that the original patterns can still be purchased from Ruby Lane, as part of its 'Vintage Homemaker' range. Vintage homemaker! Doesn't that give you a warm scullery glow? It certainly makes this writer want to put a bun in the oven straight away.

FAD **RATING ✪✪✪** *'Mother-to-be in a pretty new fan-pleated smock with wide curved yoke and soft roll collar for ease and comfort. A wonderful adjustable skirt that will expand. Looks so slimming.'*

Meccano

At Osborne House on the Isle of Wight on 22 January 1901, Queen Victoria, the British monarch who had presided over sixty-four years of swingeing industrial and technological advances, died. By happy coincidence, the very same month saw the birth of Meccanics Made Easy, an innovative construction-toy system patented by Liverpudlian Frank **Hornby** and a fitting testament to the Victorian era.

Hornby, born in 1863 to Methodist parents, first hit upon the idea while constructing a toy crane for his children out of bolted metal plates. He thought the system could have potential, sought venture capital and formed a partnership to manufacture his idea.

The formula – kits of perforated tin plates with nuts and bolts to fasten them to one another, allowing the 'player' to create his (the kits were marketed at boys) own toy – was a new one, and it quickly caught the imagination of the masses. Hornby soon added gears to the portfolio of pieces, allowing for the construction of moving toys and automata. The joy of Meccanics Made Easy lay in its versatility and its broad appeal. Popular with both children and adults, the possibilities for model-making or for creative, instructive play, were virtually limitless.

The Meccano brand came in 1908, when Hornby bought out his silent partner and began exporting heavily. The company had already grown considerably, and when war broke out in 1914 the production lines did not stop. The twenties brought coloured metal plates and, a few years before the discovery of penicillin, a new Meccano magazine, encouraging enthusiasts to engage with the product and share ideas, and of course allowing Hornby to promote new designs direct to the market.

Hornby also employed a clever craze-making technique that

THAT MECCANO TIMELINE...

1901: Hornby patents tin construction kit *Meccanics Made Easy*.

1901: Queen Victoria pops Royal clogs (possibly not actual clogs).

1908: Hornby buys out Elliott and launches Meccano brand.

1908–1914: The nickel-plate years. Exports to Commonwealth.

1920: First Hornby trains marketed as construction kits.

1923: *Meccano* magazine launched. Horoscope not included.

1926: Coloured Meccano hits the shops.

1928: Penicillin discovered. Meccano sales not affected.

1931: Hornby elected Unionist MP for Everton.

1936: Hornby bows out due to death.

1939–1945: Meccano factory commandeered for war effort. Sadly, tanks too tiny.

1964: Lines Brothers acquire Meccano.

1970: Sets made smaller.

1971: Meccano and Dinky bought by Airfix.

1978: Set contents get complete makeover.

1979: Meccano calls in receivers.

1980: Factory demolished, *Pac-Man* launched.

anticipated the highly effective publicity stunts for the **Yo-Yo**®, the **Hula-Hoop**® and the **Frisbee**® which were to come decades later. His company sponsored model-making competitions, offering large sums of money that attracted a media buzz around his product. This brought the idea into the peripheral vision of people who might not have immediately jumped at the chance to make scale-model looms out of tin.

Why do we love Meccano so much? Firstly, it is an elegant and simple piece of design work. From a basic set of construction ingredients it is possible to build 3D models, fully working machines and automata. Its minimalist aesthetic belies a deep complexity, where the results are limited only by the imagination of the modeller. It's a cheap and easy way to build and to learn to build, deconstruct, design and redesign. Without adding anything to its basic pieces it has enough to keep children and adults busy for as long as their enthusiasm holds. On the minus side, you can only get it from France now.

FAD **RATING** ✪✪✪✪✪ *'Miniature Engineering For Boys.'*

HOW TO START A CRAZE

Make it interactive

Frank Hornby was no fool when he offered valuable cash prizes to the public if they won his Meccano model contests. Not only did he get the attention of the public, but it's a gift of a story to journalists. Thus the cycle continues. The rise of the internet and SMS text-messaging has made it easier than ever before to engage your market in interactive pursuits in a branded environment. Every toy or licensed property has its own website now. These are not only catalogues for the products you sell but genuinely engaging environments where your targets, especially children, can log in – important for capturing that valuable demographic information which you can then sell at 100% profit to other direct marketers – and play all day in the branded world you create for them. Once you have their details, you can send whatever you like, direct to your prospect. A text message, for example, inviting a child to text back to hear the latest on their favourite toy craze. Premium rate of course. We want to hear from you, text us now, calls cost… well, whatever you like. Chilling really.

The Metal-Detector

God works in mysterious ways. For example, once upon a time BCE, God told a 99-year-old man called Abram to cut off his foreskin and those of all his male descendants, change his name to Abraham and become the Jewish patriarch. In return, he got to keep the land of Canaan. Abram did it. It was a nice place.

More recently CE, in America, God told a lawyer called Charles Guiteau to shoot the president with a bullet from a gun. And Guiteau did it. It was 1881 and James *Abram* Garfield, the twentieth president of the United States, had been in office for 200 days and 199 nights. Guiteau pulled the trigger twice. The first bullet ricocheted off the president's arm, but the other lodged itself somewhere inside his body. The question was, where? Conscious, but wounded, the president was rushed to hospital which, in 1881, was not the safest place to be.

For a start, doctors had yet to acquire the habit of sterilization. The first doctor – a man called Bliss – jabbed his unwashed finger, followed by a non-sterilized spatula, into the wound. He failed to find the bullet, but did create a large cavity, which became infected. Then the army surgeon general had a go with *his* finger. He couldn't find the bullet either, so the navy surgeon general tried. This doctor pierced the president's liver and pronounced him as good as dead. But Garfield stubbornly refused to expire, so in a last stand the doctors called in leading telephone-inventor Alexander Graham Bell. Bell devised a machine to detect metal and passed it over the president as the injured statesman lay transfixed on the hospital bed. It bleeped. Eureka (*see* **Pac-Man**). Scalpels were raised. They cut into Garfield. They cut and cut right through him. Still no bullet – Bell had detected a spring in the hospital bed. Now the president died.

All you really need to know about the metal-detecting craze of the seventies is contained within this story, but the author feels compelled to add. In 1925 the German-born engineer Gerhard Fisher (*né* Fischer) developed the first hand-held metal-detector in Los Angeles, and this was the design that hit the consumer market in 1931. Fisher's first model showed a distinct improvement on Bell's, due to its portability, but alas no improvement on its powers of refined detection. All that bleeps is not gold and many a key-ring has since been disinterred in hopes of treasure.

But why hunt for buried treasure? Back in the fifties, the US government was paying citizens for uranium finds, and 'prospectors' hit the deserts with portable Geiger counters. The government eventually stopped paying for uranium, but the prospectors had the technology bug. To stay afloat, the Geiger-counter manufacturers switched to making metal-detectors, and those prospectors headed for the wasteland again in search of silver and gold.

But the metal-detecting hobby began to register on the author's Craze-o-meter™ during the late seventies, especially from about 1977 to 1980, when no British beach, alive with rockpooling kids and sunbathing mums, was complete without a lone male – or 'detectorist' – panning the sand for buried booty.

This peak has two possible causes, says the Council for British Archaeology (CBA). Firstly, advances had been made in detector quality while the machines had become cheaper, which made the hobby more appealing to amateur prospectors. Secondly, the craze simply grew on its own momentum. It was an activity based on discovery of the unknown, with the added promise of treasure, a compelling reason to go forth and detect. Thirdly, it had gadget appeal, allowing the blokeish collector instinct to drive sales of detector upgrades. Fourthly, it allowed socially awkward men to get out among people without having to connect with them. As more people began detecting, so more valuable finds were made, which generated more publicity. This in turn attracted more to the hobby.

And a true 'hobby' it was. The first rule of hobbies is inventing rules for the hobby. At its peak there were around 180,000 known detectorists in the UK, many of them operating out of 400 different clubs and societies, all of which had strict criteria for entry. But despite the fact that detectors are now highly advanced and capable of discerning metal type and depth, most are now used by bona fide archeologists. In fact, the CBA reckons its opposition to amateur treasure-hunting may have done much to dampen the craze. The hobby declined rapidly in the early eighties, presumably when every ring-pull ever committed to the soil had been duly resurrected. The occasional weekend or holiday detectorists consigned their tools to car-boot sales, and those who were left followed the most fundamental rule of British leisure behaviour.

This rule states that when four or more individuals gather together in pursuit of a similar activity they shall form a committee. The National Council for Metal-Detecting is a membership group that promotes ethical practice among its detectorists. The normal route into the Council is via your local metal-detecting club. This ensures that that fundamental British hobby of forming and rising through pointless hierarchies lives on.

If this kind of toadying is not for you, consider joining the somewhat oxymoronic Federation of Independent Detectorists: a body which represents the interests of those maverick hobbyists who cannot or will not join a club.

It's at this point that the author's eyes begin to glaze over.

Metal-detecting didn't do the business for James Abram Garfield. He died from a massive heart attack due to blood poisoning after his doctors burrowed a two-foot crevice into his body with their dirty hands. Metal-detecting failed to help Charles Guiteau. Garfield's autopsy revealed that the bullet had lodged in a protective cyst inside his body and that he would have survived if the doctors had left him alone. Guiteau therefore argued that it was the doctors, not he, who had killed the president. But this did not wash with the authorities. They found Guiteau guilty of murder, executed him and stripped his flesh from its skeleton. Metal-detecting did not help the doctors: they billed the Senate for $85,000 and received only $10,000. But detecting certainly helped Gerhard Fisher, whose company is now one of the industry's leading players. And it's not too late for you. If God tells you to go metal-detecting, get your headphones on and get ready to stare at your feet. Why? Because you're worth it.

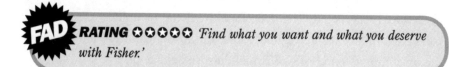

FAD *RATING* ✪✪✪✪✪ *Find what you want and what you deserve with Fisher.'*

THE METAL-DETECTOR WENT BLEEP AND I FOUND...

1. A Romano-British copper-alloy spatula handle in the shape of the goddess Minerva, dating from about 60–100 CE (Suffolk, 2003).

2. A medieval Flemish knife-plate in iron and copper alloy, depicting Saint Barbara, originally cast *c.* 1530 CE (Warwickshire, 2004).

3. A can (your back garden, all beaches, 1976–).

4. Iraqi weapons of mass destruction (Isle of Wight, 2056).

Milk

Oh, who were they trying to kid? They tried with Humphrey, the errant drinking-straw that was permanently sneaking up and trying to steal your pinta. This book says, 'Let him'. It was always warm and smelly by break time anyway. They tried with dancing milk-bottles and whistling milkmen. They tried with slogans, such as 'gotta lotta bottle' and 'drinka pinta milka day.' When that went sour they tried with two cute football-loving scouse boys who had been told by Liverpool's Ian Rush that if they didn't drink 'milchh' they'd only be good enough to play for Accrington Stanley. How tearfully they had us reaching for the gold-top.

In fact, prior to the deregulation of the UK milk market in 1994, the National Dairy Council produced extensive generic marketing of milk, cheese and cream in a bid to turn the consumption of a cow's private lady juice into a national craze. 'Eat dairy produce, because we've made too much,' is only one of the slogans I've just made up. But there were others. Leading British *fatwa* target Salman Rushdie will forever be remembered as the bestselling author of 'Fresh Cream Cakes: Naughty But Nice,' while milk adverts focused on alleged nutritional benefits. Oh, they tell you about the calcium, but they don't mention the gastro-intestinal complications. According to recent studies, only one-third of the world's population retains the ability to digest lactose (the sugar in milk) into adulthood. For the other two-thirds it's wind, cramps and diarrhoea. But will they provide a health warning on bottles? Not likely.

What's more, according to a recent memo from the NDC submitted to the UK Parliament's Select Committee on Agriculture, those ridiculous adverts actually worked. When they were stopped, consumption of dairy products, particularly 'liquid milk', fell. But instead of producing less according to demand or giving it to poor countries, such as Cornwall, production has continued and farmers are now begging the NDC to devise more silly ways to convince us to drink it (*see* **Yoghurt**).

But could anything be sillier than what happened in California? The US 'Got Milk?' campaign took a step into the absurd when the California Milk Processing Board convinced the Mayor of Biggs to change his town's name to 'Got Milk?, California'. The author is personally surprised more captains of industry and media moguls haven't seized this wonderful free-market opportunity to brand calcium intake. Could the promise of Virgin Milk draw punters? No, be reasonable. Milk will never be a craze and kids will do anything *but* eat a Dairylea.

 RATING ○ Nil. *'Liquid milk? Sorry, don't touch the stuff, but I have frozen some in my ice tray and plan to eat it later as a lozenge.'*

The Millennium Bug

Remember the Millennium Bug? All IT engineers do, for that is when they made their fortunes. The basic premise of this fear-based craze was that all computers the world over ran on internal clocks that would reset to zero at the turn of the millennium. What we did with this craze was whip up the scale of the problem from niggling aggravation to full-scale global disaster on the Triffid level. It wasn't just salaries that wouldn't be paid: credit cards would become invalid, records would disappear, medical equipment would fail. Everything, literally everything, would malfunction, spreading terror among the peoples of the 'developed' world. Aeroplanes would fall out of the sky, car-making robots would stalk car-owners. The sky would darken and fall on our heads. In the time it took worldwide business to make systems 'Y2K-compliant', the average IT engineer had become very rich indeed. For he or she knew the truth: there was no Millennium Bug. Nothing that wasn't easily fixed within seconds anyway. Certainly nothing to worry about. The author did nothing; the date came and went; his computer calendars kept pace: why wouldn't they? Nothing broke, nothing went bonkers. Perhaps one or two e-mails slipped through with the date 1904, but in fact that is nothing new, it happens all the time if you reset your computer and forget to set the calendar. The only tragedy was that journalists would have to write about boring politics again and IT directors would have to find new excuses to keep their budgets high. A few carefully engineered virus-scares would see to that, though.

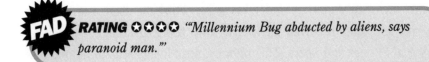

FAD **RATING ✪✪✪✪** *"Millennium Bug abducted by aliens, says paranoid man."*

Mr Potato Head®

Of the two joyous potato-based hobbies this book can offer (*see* **The Spud Gun**), George Lerner's Mr Potato Head® is perhaps the most creative. Or at least, he was to begin with. In 1952, when the world's first 100-per-cent-carbohydrate playmate was patented by Lerner, the product consisted entirely of plastic features and accessories. The idea was that the happy punter would then go and fetch a spare tuber and insert facial components, limbs, hats and – controversially – a pipe into self-made orifices in the potato itself. The possibilities were limitless, and the kit included enough spare pieces to make a couple or three potato friends. This, readers, is a fun thing to do, and Mr P. H. was a fun guy to have around.

By 1964, however, the party was over. Mr Potato Head® now came with a plastic body and pre-pierced orifices. Now there was only one place and one way to attach his lips. No matter how hard you tried, he always turned out the same. Once you'd built him, the only thing to do was pick off each of his features with your **pea-shooter**.

Curiously, this image makeover was precisely what was needed to kick-start PH's career in public life. In 1985 he received four postal votes in the mayoral election in Boise, Idaho. While this was not quite enough to secure office, people started to pay attention. In 1987, Mr Potato Head® gave up smoking under pressure from the American Cancer Society and later received an award from the President's Council on Physical Fitness and Sport. This phoney clean-living schtick helped him get a part in *Toy Story*, after which celebrity just went to his head. Like a crazed addict, hooked on fame, he started accepting any old offer that came his way, just to keep himself in the public eye. When the former fitness guru started advertising Burger King fries, the author stopped calling him. One hears on the grapevine that he got his own show on Fox Kids and that he's some kind of big shot in licensing and marketing these days – but he has no time for his old friends. The author hates to say it, but he's two-faced. We exchange Christmas cards, nothing more.

 RATING ✪✪✪ *'Hours of face-changing fun.'*

THAT WAS THE YEAR...
Toy Crazes of the Sixties and Seventies

1965 Corgi James Bond Aston Martin: the author smashed his. Now worth £700.

1966 Action Man: that moveable fighting 'man'.

1967 Spirograph®: fun with Biros.

1970 Rolf Harris Stylophone™: bleeping toy capable of musical note.

1971 Space Hoppers. Klackers. How we boinged. How we klacked.

1973 Mastermind: no relation, despite man in swivel chair.

1974 Magna Doodle: drawing made hard.

1975 *The Wombles*: the litter monitors from hell.

1976 Raw Power, the push-bike motorbike revver.

1977 Slime: instant clammy hands. Holly Hobbie dolls. Skateboards.

1978 *Star Wars*. Simon: he lit up, you threw him across the room. He stopped lighting up.

1979 Space Lego: see-through bricks.

My Little Pony

This is the kind of information the ruthless will try to use against you later in life. These craven blackmailers believe your guilt and shame will give them power over you. But they are wrong. It was a long time ago, and the author has moved on. But since we are here, there was a time in young adulthood when the author may have popped into the toyshop and purchased his very own My Little Pony, the blue one, called Bowtie, and kept it on his shelf. There's no defence really, he understands that. He was neither the sort of young man who hankers after a job in a hair salon, nor the type that is later revealed by reporters to have eaten some of his neighbours. Nor was he without alternative company. No, it was purely what Welsh politicians are now calling 'a moment of madness'. But for a short time – more or less until the mushrooms ran out – the author loved his MLP (as the collectors call it), and it glinted on his shelf in all its lurid beauty. The over-long groomable mane. The consistency of coloration. It may have looked more like a pantomime horse, but you could pet it and talk to it. You could fit it in your pocket.

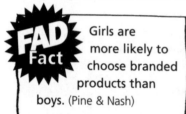

FAD Fact Girls are more likely to choose branded products than boys. (Pine & Nash)

The author never had the conviction to follow through and collect Lickety-Split, Butterscotch or any of the 'So-soft', 'The Beddy-Byes Eyes' or 'Double Fancy' range. Nor did he join the club and receive the 'magazine', which was in fact a thinly veiled catalogue for related Hasbro merchandise (*see* **Trivial Pursuit**). With hindsight he supposes his heart just wasn't in it. He believes he was a victim of media pressure. Each new range of toys was introduced by a series of animated TV specials, in which the benign Pegasi, seahorses and loveable dobbins would act out adventures and overcome evil, not-so-subtly worming their way into the romantic consciousness of little girls everywhere.

Had the author *been* a little girl, of course, this confession would not sound remotely perverse. But there you are. We live in a world of categories and conventions. One day, perhaps, such mule-harbourers will walk free and unjudged. Until then, Pony lovers take heart: MLP has become a highly collectible series of period pieces. If you are lucky enough to own one of the rarer Hasbro figurines, such as the mail-order Rapunzel model (never available in the shops), mint in its original packaging, it could fetch you up to $800 on eBay. Enough to pay for the first therapy session. Good luck, and happy hunting. The classic series was discontinued at the beginning of the nineties, ending the craze proper. But Hasbro has since bowed to pressure from 'investors' and released a 2003 set. The company has refused to confirm rumoured plans for a groomable New Labour series, My Little Tony. Shame.

FAD **RATING ✪✪✪** *'If your rudder runs aground or seaweed holds a grip (kelp)*
Count upon the Sea Ponies – they'll see you get help
Sea Ponies, Sea Ponies, simply signal SOS
Oh, yes!'

Pac-Man

Every great thinker, every great solver of problems, every forger of new roads, has one moment of blinding clarity. A glimpse beyond the horizon to a creative vision of a new future. A searing epiphany that changes the course of mankind and its history.

For the Greek mathematician Archimedes, so the popular legend goes, this moment came in a bath. When King Hieron asked his learned relative to find a way to prove that his crown was made of solid gold, the scientist put his great mind to work. For days and nights he wrestled without success and was eventually persuaded to take a break and have a bath. On entering the water and watching it rise around him, he is said to have seen, as if for the first time, the phenomenon of displacement. 'Eureka,' he cried – the Greek word for 'when a solid is partially or fully immersed in a fluid there is an upthrust on the solid equal to the volume of the fluid displaced.' An elegant language, Greek.

For Toru Iwatani, a young designer for the Japanese electronics company Namco, the fateful revelation came at a pizza restaurant. On cutting a single slice from his pizza, he observed, as if for the first time, that the remainder looked not unlike a giant, eating face. What he uttered at this point is not recorded, though it might have been *'pakupaku'*. This is the Japanese word for a mouth that flaps open and shut repeatedly. An elegant language, Japanese.

Iwatani returned to work galvanized by his vision of a giant cartoon pizza slice condemned to eat its way out of a maze of food. At that time the arcade game repertoire more or less amounted to Taito's hugely popular but monochrome **Space Invaders** and the various attempts to imitate it, such as *Asteroids, Missile Command* and Namco's own

Galaxian, the first arcade game to be released in colour. But Iwatani was thinking bigger. He wanted warmth, bold splashes of colour, a cartoon feel, better sounds and fewer explosions.

And so it came to pass. It proved too difficult to animate a pizza, so Iwatani compromised, bringing the sun out for a whole generation. He also unleashed those pesky ghosts. Red, pink, blue and orange, they chased our munching hero around his dot-filled labyrinth, bringing the threat of death on contact – until he swallowed a 'power pill', whereupon his foes became shadows of their former selves, spread out and fled. But here was Iwatani's genius: he gave them names. In English these troublemakers were called Blinky, Pinky, Inky and Clyde. Oh no, hold on. Those were just their 'nicknames'. Their real names were Shadow, Speedy, Bashful and Pokey. The names were a gift to the marketers of *Pac-Man*, for they allowed for the development of characters. And as merchandisers had learned with **Star Wars**, characters could be exploited endlessly. And so they were.

The year was 1980. The author remembers being dragged by a classmate some miles on foot to the nearest amusement arcade on the promise of something called '*Pac-Man*'. It seemed a good enough reason to go. It seemed the game was already a cult. It seemed the author might  just be left out of the zeitgeist if he didn't pull on his trainers immediately. With his 5p pieces in hand – those were the days – he marched solemnly up the hill where John Wesley had preached the Baptist faith to local miners, for his own conversion to the light and love of *Pac-Man*.

Namco didn't have to try hard.

Firstly, there was the ease of play. No stabbing at the 'fire' button until your wrist fell off. Skilful steering was all that was required. Then there were the tunes. How we whooped the first time we ate enough to be rewarded with a jaunty melody and animated interlude. The *waka-waka* soundtrack to our little Pac-friend's munching still rings in the author's head, as does the resigned, cartoonish sound that accompanied *Pac-Man*'s demise. Whoops, try again. Whoops, try again. Whoops, now pay me.

Pac-Man was perhaps the first arcade game to appeal directly to children, and its spaceship-free landscape helped it attract girls, so broadening the scope for mass, er, consumption. It was not long before Pac-habits emerged at school. No playground chase was complete without someone shouting a mocking '*waka-waka*'. At lunchtime, fish-paste sandwiches were removed from *Pac-Man* lunchboxes, while fellow pupils scratched furiously away at the silver panels on *Pac-Man* games cards. Want to ask a girl up the arcade? Simply lift the receiver on your *Pac-Man* telephone and make that call. Rebuffed like the small, stained boy you are? Why not drown your sorrows with some *Pac-Man* trading cards or lift your spirits with the official *Pac-Man* joke book? It went on and on. Then it stopped.

Suddenly the cocktail table *Pac-Man* game was no longer at the swimming pool. Arcades were full of *Super Mario*s and *Donkey Kong*s. Ultimately, *Pac-Man* stepped aside for the warmer platform games it had helped into being. A nation mourned. The world mourned. How could our loyal, yellow money-eating friend leave us like that? *Pac-Man* was novel, *Pac-Man* was sunny. *Pac-Man* was not *as* other games. Though technically it was surpassed in many ways, nothing that followed *Pac-Man* brought quite the same euphoric joy.

So there was really only one thing for it. *Pac-Man* is back. In response to lesser knock-off versions on the web and the constant hectoring from nostalgic punters of a certain age, Namco finally released its original *Pac-Man* game as a standalone unit that plugs direct into your TV. It's in the shops. Call in sick, go get those cherries.

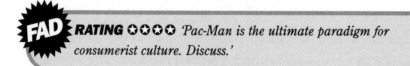

FAD **RATING** ✪✪✪✪ *'Pac-Man is the ultimate paradigm for consumerist culture. Discuss.'*

The PaperMate® Replay

The arrival of the first erasable ballpoint pen was a boon to schoolchildren and cheque-fraudsters. PaperMate's® hugely popular 'Replay' pen came in a range of delightful matt colours, including maroon and canary yellow (the author's personal favourite). Each boasted an inbuilt eraser (*see* **The Etch A Sketch®** *and* **The Scented Eraser**) suitable for biting off on Day One (*see* **The Pencil Top**). While the pen itself was a tactile thrill and an iconic piece of aesthetic design, the ink was neither. Not really a fluid so much as a volatile, flaky solid, the slug-trail left by your pen frankly couldn't leave the paper quickly enough. The eraser was hardly needed; you had only to look at the ink sideways and it was gone, leaving a papyrus-like indentation that cunningly defied over-writing. Which meant there was nothing to be gained by erasing. A generation reached for the Tippex.

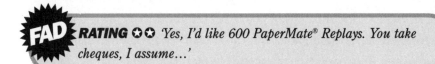

FAD **RATING ✪✪** *'Yes, I'd like 600 PaperMate® Replays. You take cheques, I assume...'*

The Parka

The ubiquitous parka anorak had numerous benefits. Mums, having filled their school-bound offspring with Ready Brek, could unleash them unto the winter chill safe in the knowledge that they were as well protected from the elements as any native Greenlander could be.

But there were other, more tangible rewards. Rig yourself out in the parka, and you would find that you had an enviable choice of pocket options, enabling you to transport all your **marbles**, at least one bag of Cola Cubes and an assortment of Fruit Polos, Victory Vs and Bazooka Joe (*see* **Eleven Fad Sweets**), plus the misplaced remains of a year's worth of the same, with ample room left over for your **pea-shooter** or **spud gun** and the collection of leaking pens that allowed you to observe in your coat fabric the phenomenon of chromatography, long before you even got a **chemistry set**.

Next there was the all-important fact that doing your hood up to its fullest, fur-lined extent allowed you to act out the part of Jawa in any **Star Wars**-based playground game. But the chief joy was that that same parka hood, when fully operational, effectively placed a metal tag and loop on the back of a person's head. This tag could be hooked with string or **skipping** rope, allowing you to walk the wearer on a lead.

 **FAD** **RATING** ✪✪ *'Heel, heel.'*

The Pea-Shooter

Much beloved of cartoonists working for comics such as *Whizzer and Chips*, the pea-shooter has been the weapon of choice for rambunctious boys since the dawn of the pea. Innocuous enough in itself, the pea-shooter is in fact an evolution of the altogether more sinister 'blow-pipe', which is used exclusively for launching poison darts at Victorian jungle-explorers or Tarzan. If it's a simple pea-model you're after, then appropriate apparatus can generally be bought by mail order from the back of comics, along with the complete stamp collection, which you unpack and put away in a cupboard, horns for your **Raleigh Chopper** that play the theme tune to *The Dukes of Hazzard* (*see* **Slot-Car Racing**) and x-ray spectacles that 'really work'.

A pea-shooter craze follows a distinct and consistent pattern. One boy acquires such a shooter and terrorizes his classmates for approximately one day, after which a full-scale war breaks out. Where a pea-shooter craze escalates, it is generally swiftly followed by a stringent ban and example-making suspensions from school.

More satisfying for classroom projectile-launching is the home-made zip-gun shooter, which can be constructed as follows. Remove the ink and head from a standard ballpoint pen or **PaperMate® Replay**, leaving a hollow pipe. Tear off a small strip of paper from your exercise book, or preferably your neighbour's special exercise book that was a risible Christmas present. Chew the paper for approximately three minutes until pulped *al dente*. Form into a ball with your tongue. Launch. The shooter can be converted into an innocent-looking pen at a moment's notice, helping the user to avoid identification and punishment. If brute force is the only way to win, consider launching **marbles** through a converted penny whistle (hacksaw and gaffer tape required).

 RATING ✪✪✪ *'No, because eating paper gives you worms.'*

The Perm

The official Year of the Perm, or 'permanent' wave, was 1975. But the queen of hairdos definitely out-reigned her welcome and only abdicated in parts of Cornwall at the turn of the millennium, when girls started oiling their hair flat with zig-zag partings. Ostensibly a ladies' fashion, the perm none the less received a macho endorsement when football hero Kevin Keegan 'sported' the style. Getting a perm was a one-way ticket. You see, it would grow out, causing the much-feared frizzy-ends style, which looked worse than the perm. The solution: another perm. Gah! Bad things about the perm: 1. the perforated plastic bag through which your hair was pulled seemingly by the roots and the pain this caused; 2. the smell of the perming 'fluid'; 3. the perm. Good things about the perm:

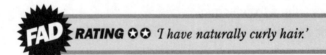

FAD **RATING ✪✪** *'I have naturally curly hair.'*

ELEVEN BAD HAIR DAYS

1. **The Mullet**
2. **The Wedge**
3. **The Perm**
4. **The Pudding Basin**
5. **The Mohican**
6. **The Pageboy**
7. **The Flick**
8. **The Rat's Tail**
9. **The Quiff**
10. **The Afro**
11. **The Wig**

The Pencil Top

Naked pencils were to be frowned upon. Naked pencils wouldn't do at all. What your pencil needed was a 'top'. The pencil top was any amusing, wacky creature or character (*see* **The Wacky WallWalker®**) with a 5-mm hole drilled in its rear, which you then attached to the end of your pencil for pencil fun. There were two activities related to the pencil top. One was collecting them. *Munch Bunch* pencil tops were a good idea. So were *Mr Men* pencil tops. The author is not aware of any other kind worth collecting, although readers' mileage may vary. The second activity involved stealing

FAD Fact Most children keep the television on while they do their homework. (ITC)

them. The fact that they lived on the end of pencils made them sitting ducks for misappropriation, and their wiggling, wriggling motion as the owner wrote made them as irresistible as a mouse to a cat.

Though disguised as a pointless decoration, the pencil top none the less served a useful function in preventing you from eating the end of your pencil, a far better solution than the, er, solution mothers used to daub on pencils and indeed fingernails to deter classroom munchies. A more welcome appliance, however, would have been the pencil bottom: any wacky character who slipped over the tip of your pencil and prevented you from doing any sums.

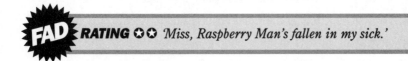

FAD RATING ✪✪ *'Miss, Raspberry Man's fallen in my sick.'*

BEHIND THE SCENES
Pester power

'Children, being vulnerable, are easily influenced by ads on television, and this activates "pester power", i.e. where the children harass their parents to purchase products they want. With the increase in number of working couples, the child's pester power becomes inversely proportional to the time available with parents. [The parents] might buy a product if it shows promise of satisfying or quietening [their children] temporarily. Considering the above, a marketer must try to develop a strategy which targets the kids and influences them totally...'

Strategy advice on <www.TheManageMentor.com>

In the run-up to Christmas 2002, 80 per cent of all television adverts in the United Kingdom were aimed at children. Half of British children have a television in their rooms by the age of six or seven, and most prefer to watch alone. A study by psychologists Karen Pine and Avril Nash of the University of Hertfordshire found that watching alone made children more susceptible to advertisers' messages, as their viewing was not tempered by the scepticism of their parents.

In the UK, advertisers are not allowed directly to tell children to buy something, nor are they allowed overtly to tell them to ask their parents for it. So advertisers have to work around the issue. They have to reach children on an emotional level and manipulate their feelings to create a need or want for the product they are selling. The way they do this is very simple. One advertising executive, cited by the Child Poverty Action Group, puts it like this:

'Advertising at its best is making people feel that without their product, you're a loser. Kids are very sensitive to that. If you tell them to buy something, they are resistant, but if you tell them that they'll be a dork if they don't, you've got their attention. You open up emotional vulnerability, and it's very easy to do with kids because they're the most emotionally vulnerable.'

Such boastful candour is not employed by Martin Lindstrom, bestselling author of *Brand Child* and America's most sought-after 'brand-marketing guru'. He applies a more positive spin: 'Dreams are the hard currency in the life of a tween. Every brand and every product has to appeal to the imagination of tweens. It

'Marketers are after our children.'

National Family and Parenting Institute

has to give them something to dream about.' It is interesting, psychologically, that Mr Lindstrom does not use the emotive word 'child' but prefers 'tween', an abstract concept invented by advertisers to describe the pre-teen age-group. It is not *children's* dreams that businesses are manipulating and exploiting but those of 'tweens'. Whatever they are.

The psychologist Dr Aric Sigman responded to an enquiry into the ethics of advertising to children by explaining how adverts directed at children were designed to 'address and exploit' basic needs. He identified four specific vulnerabilities: the need for nurture and protection, the need for stimulation, the need for role models and the need for peer-group acceptance. Certainly the last three come into play in the creation of crazes, especially where celebrity endorsement can be used.

While there is recent evidence to show that 'tweens' will respond to billboard advertising, television is the jewel in the child-advertising crown. According to Pine and Nash, in a typical Saturday morning's viewing, children can be exposed to up to 174 different advertising messages, while pre-school children see more than 18,000 advertisements per year. Once the message is lodged in the child's consciousness, the pestering may begin. Pine and Nash have concluded that the more television children watch, the more they 'yearn' for material things and so by extension may feel disappointed or inadequate if they don't have them.

The syndrome intensifies in the run-up to Christmas. The BBC's parenting guide advises parents to 'be absolutely firm about a date when listing can start'. Listing? They mean 'making lists'. The BBC might well give out advice to parents, but the UK Campaign for LogofreeTV alleges that our licence-funded public service broadcaster is a wolf in sheep's clothing. Parents who carefully monitor their children's access to commercial television may be missing something when they tune into the BBC, some parents claim. While commercial stations have clear boundaries between programmes and advertisements, LogofreeTV claims the BBC's line is not so clearly demarcated. *The Teletubbies, The Tweenies, Bob the Builder**: three of the biggest merchandising crazes of recent years were all introduced to children via BBC 'learning' programmes. While the BBC cannot show advertisements, it can and does imprint the content of its trusted shows on to commercial items, an activity carried out by BBC Worldwide, the Corporation's commercial arm, which acts 'at arm's length' from the production teams. Between 2000 and 2002, the *Tweenies* franchise alone earned the BBC £32 million. The corporation was not fussy, it seems. The Food Commission forced the BBC to remove *Tweenies* branding from fast-food packaging. Is the name 'Tweenies' in fact a message to prospective licensing franchisees about the 'tweens' market?

LogofreeTV claims the corporation apes a commercial enterprise while simultaneously collecting a licence fee to ensure it stays just the opposite. As such the broadcaster occupies a position of trust. It's the sort of 'Aunty' we're happy to leave our kids with. When an individual uses a position of power to

* 'Bob the Builder' is owned by Hit Entertainment Ltd. and not the BBC.

take advantage of a child's trust in order to further their own agenda, we call it abuse. When a corporation does it, we call it marketing.

'Our BBC has been caught at questionable practices recently,' LogofreeTV claims. 'We are calling for proper "Parental Control" systems and greater corporate accountability and honesty.'

The BBC is dismissive of the claims and denies its practices are questionable. A spokeswoman for CBeebies, the BBC children's programming arm, said that the Corporation was only responding to demand. 'Nowadays there's often an expectation by parents that there will be certain products available which will complement the child's experience of a TV programme. In some cases where BBC Worldwide and other commercial rights-owners have *not* produced any merchandise… they have been contacted by viewers and parents asking where they can find merchandise relating to the show.' This said, the spokeswoman acknowledges that 'the absence of advertising on CBeebies is one of the key reasons cited by parents as to why they choose CBeebies as their first choice in pre-school programming.'

BBC Worldwide said that learning through play was one of CBeebies' 'key themes' and the toys and publishing range were designed to 'create a dialogue between the character and the viewer'.

Jeff Taylor, director of global marketing and brand development at BBC Worldwide, expects such 'properties' as *The Tweenies* to reach children via a range of media channels. 'While today's children still tune in to television, they take for granted a far wider choice of media and products, including the internet, books, videos, magazines, toys and other associated products. Our vision for the future is to engage children around the world and across all media in a way that makes a real difference to their lives.'

But what sort of difference? While children may 'yearn' for the products they see decorated with familiar cartoon characters, film tie-in products or items

> 'Children, through their pester-power and their influence over parents, have a significant say in how household income is spent. Kids can also be good indicators of future consumer trends.'
>
> Fox TV, owners of *The Simpsons*

with familiar logos, parents responding to surveys carried out by the National Family and Parenting Institute repeatedly said that their kids 'lost interest' in the product once it had been bought. 'It's all about having it,' one parent said. 'And then once they've got it, I don't know about anyone else, but they don't want it. He's much happier with a ball in the garden.'

The NFPI found that, rather than asking broadcasters for more, parents consistently complained about the rise of tie-in products and collectibles. Tie-in products work because the child sees the familiar picture on the packet and wants the product, whatever it is. Barbie® spaghetti, for example, exists. Collectibles work on a child's feelings of dissatisfaction. A single Care Bear or Pokémon is not enough. The instruction is to collect the set. Therefore the child risks feelings of inadequacy if he or she fails to do so. When his or her friends have a bigger collection, then peer-group pressure will intensify this feeling. 'What's really being marketed,' the NFPI says, 'is a picture, a dream, a construction of identity. And alongside that is being created a brand-aware consumer, looking to find belonging and acceptance through the marketplace.'

As parents, we understandably kick against such manipulation of our children's feelings and try to resist the advertisers' use of emotional blackmail to make us spend on their behalf. But businesses such as TheManageMentor.com, quoted above, claim parents react 'hysterically' to marketing aimed at 'their little ones'. There is no doubt that the efforts of advertisers to create crazes for their products are extremely irritating to parents. But are they actually harmful to our children? The jury is not so much out as ill-informed. The fact is that most of the research into the effects of marketing on children has been carried out by advertisers and not by parent groups, the NSPCC or independent psychologists. Even the groundbreaking research by Pine and Nash was commissioned by the commercial broadcaster Channel Four.

Is legislation an option? Yes, but equally unlikely. While Tony Blair's government seized upon concerns over child obesity, perhaps for its own reasons, during the crisis in Iraq, it felt that less rather than more regulation was needed of television advertising and had no general stance on marketing to children.

In their research paper, *Dear Santa*, in which children's letters to Father Christmas are set against their television viewing figures, Pine and Nash suggest that parents can lessen the impact of television advertising by insisting on watching with their children. But other psychologists believe parents have a role to play beyond monitoring or censoring television viewing. 'You have to look at it in the context of our culture,' child psychologist Stephanie Pratola told *Time* magazine back in 1999. 'We are all obsessed with acquiring things, and we can't expect our children to rise above our culture. Children will always grab on to fads, but parents are helping to feed this artificial economy.'

The Pet Rock

The Emperor's-New-Clothes syndrome that takes hold of intelligent people in the grip of a craze was never demonstrated better than with US snake-oil merchant Greg Dahl's Pet Rock empire. This genius, this king of crazes, this demi-god of fiddlefaddle made masses and masses of people buy rocks off him in the mid seventies, just because he told them to.

'Look,' he said. 'They're your pets. Love them and care for them. Don't pick rocks up off the street for free. They're not your pets. Only my ones, which I've picked up off the street for free, are your pets who love you. Buy them from me.' So we did. Greg Dahl, this book salutes you. The craze was sadly short-lived, but there's no reason why other entrepreneurs shouldn't take the pet-rock baton and run with it.

FAD RATING ✪✪✪ *'See the dirt from my shoe and the lint from my pocket? They are your pets.'*

The Pog

The game of Pogs was born on Maui in the 1920s (*see* **Surfing**) as a simple pastime played with milk-bottle tops. It later acquired the Pog tag from the popular fruit-drink made from passion-fruit, oranges and guava. In this respect it mimics the genesis of the **Frisbee**®. The craze migrated to America, where licensers and marketers saw the potential to fatten their wallets. Pog mania hit Britain in the mid nineties, with collectible tie-in Pogs adorned with images from movies. What you do: you stack them up face down, then your opponent smacks them viciously with a Pog of his own (*see* **Marbles**). Any of the stack that land face up are then claimed by the aggressor. The denouncing and banning spree that followed the rise of Pogs in the UK was swiftly eclipsed, like the craze itself, by the arrival of the **Pokémon**. Crap toys would never be the same again.

FAD **RATING ✪✪✪** *'Miss, he's nicked my Pog.' 'Your what?' 'My Pog.'*

The Pogo-Stick

In March 1962 the *Times* parliamentary correspondent noted a curious exchange between the Labour spokesman on health matters, Kenneth Robinson, and Enoch Powell, at that time the Conservative Minister for Health.

Mr Robinson wryly commented to the House that Mr Powell had contrived to be photographed 'bouncing around Eaton Square on a pogo-stick... in order to give the impression that beneath his arid exterior, a human heart beat on'.

It's always possible, though, that the Minister for Health was trying to lead by example. The pogo-stick, patented in 1919 by George Hansburg, is a fine tool both for developing balance and for burning calories. Had it been the Minister for Transport, an altogether more stark message may have been communicated.

While the fad for pogo-ing lived and died during the 'roaring' twenties, when such a thing must have seemed unspeakably modern, Mr Powell would have benefited from numerous improvements in the basic design of the beloved jump-stick. The original 1919 model was made from wood, but warping due to humidity caused Hansburg to recast his creation in metal. By 1947, he had achieved a far superior steel construction and better, more durable suspension. A further patent in 1957 enhanced the device to such an extent that the design now remains almost unchanged.

The pogo-stick, declining in the seventies, fell out of fashion completely during the eighties and wasn't to reappear until the late nineties, when it made a brief but impressive comeback, along with the scooter, in shiny chrome.

While the image of post-war race-hate pioneer Enoch Powell demeaning himself on a spring is an amusing one, Mr Robinson's comment was intended to goad his right-wing rival on the subject of the then current nurses' pay claim. Mr Powell's response is not recorded, though we are told that he 'limited himself in reply'.

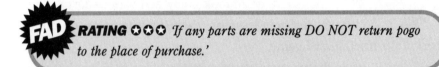

FAD *RATING* ✪✪✪ *'If any parts are missing DO NOT return pogo to the place of purchase.'*

HOW TO START A CRAZE

License your property

One of the quickest ways to reach saturation point is to let others do the work for you (*see* **How to Start a Craze no. 4: Make it a sport**). Why bust your chops overseeing the manufacture, sales and distribution of your product when others can take the chores away from you? License others to make it, use it, emblazon it over their tins of spaghetti. The first licensed character was Walt Disney's Mickey Mouse. Nowadays we are bombarded with licensed goods such as the BBC's *Tweenies*, Beanie Babies in McDonald's or film tie-ins such as *Finding Nemo*. Successful licensing works like pyramid selling. Everyone else does the work, and yet it all comes back to you. Pokémon and Hello Kitty are two good examples: if you want to make a mint in today's world, all you really need to do is a doodle.

Innovators with brilliant ideas who failed to license their properties include the groundbreaking Apple Computer, which now takes a back seat in the PC market, and Sony, with its long-extinct Betamax video format.

The Pokémon

'Gotta catch 'em all.' The Pokémon, or 'pocket monsters' craze took many and various forms, but its sinister pointlessness reached a stunning apex in the form of the trading-card game.

When 150 badly drawn cartoons of monsters were secreted into the US and European markets in 1998 from a raft of orifices, even an untrained eye could tell they were a bit rubbish. There are many talented cartoonists around the world, producing great work in animation or in comic books. But these pictures seemed to have been done by an animal with a lazy eye. Adding to this foolhardy proposition was the fact the Pokémon had really quite startlingly silly names. Jigglypuff was one. Wigglytuff was another. Diglett, Blastoise, Squirtle and Gloom. Butterfree, Lickitung, Gastly and – unusually – Mr Mime. Then there was the expectorant range: Koffing, Weezing and Drowzee. But the very best was the name that surely contained its creator's own cynical comment on the fad: Farfetch'd.

Far-fetched indeed. Early market research revealed that kids found the trading cards, er, a bit rubbish. How could they rival the **Tamagotchi**? But it didn't matter. That could be changed. Children's opinions, their hopes, desires and feelings: these are easy to manipulate if you have the means and the right sort of conscience. Children were carefully and deliberately manipulated into caring very much indeed about a piece of cardboard on to which something – possibly a Rhesus monkey – had done a doodle. Someone was laughing all the way to the bank.

And that person was Minoru Arakawa, chief executive of Nintendo of America and son-in-law of the Japanese parent company's chief executive

Hiroshi Yamauchi. After he had observed Japanese children travel hundreds of miles by train and queue in the rain simply to glimpse new squirrel/tortoise combinations done with felt pen, Arakawa imported the 150 cartoons from his pops-in-law in the form of a trading-card game. The card game itself had been created under licence from Nintendo by the Japanese firm Media Factory, as a spin-off to the popular Nintendo Game Boy version of *Pokémon*, already then making waves in Japan. Arakawa saw the opportunity for global dollars and licensed the card game's translation into English and European languages.

But that is not all. You can't just put trading cards on to the market and hope kids will go out and buy them. Hope doesn't come into it. You need certainty, and that's where the feature films, the comic books, the toy figures, the Burger tie-ins and the TV animation series come into it. What better than a TV show that not only can be sold all over the world but is also an advert for your other products? Perfect. That way it doesn't even have to be good. Just cheap and clearly branded. And you can't get cheaper labour than a Rhesus monkey (possibly not true). Your next task is to leave absolutely no ambiguity about what you expect from the child: 'Gotta catch 'em all!' Then you license other companies to use the brand to make whatever they like, as long as they cut you in. As the Pokémon brand spreads across the world like smallpox, you sit back and watch the money flood in from a million sources. The Pokémon brand began to pervade every area of children's consciousness and that of their parents. Arakawa made it so and he reaped the rewards. The first film alone grossed $51.2 million in its first week. 'I still don't even understand the game,' Arakawa says.

To be fair, nor did anyone else. 'Attack [ppp] Confuse Ray (30) Flip coin, if heads, the defending Pokémon is now confused.' Beg pardon? 'Attack [2] Lure () If your opponent has any benched Pokémon, choose 1 and switch it with his or her active Pokémon.' Great. Oh – wait. 'This power cannot be used if Venosaur is asleep.' Damn. Mind you, 'This attack does 30 times number of heads.' Or, even better, how about this chilling, if cryptic, punishment: 'Leek slap.'

No, it was no good. Learning the rules was for wimps. You might know it was something about training basic Pokémons to evolve into better ones: hence Diglett becomes Dugtrio, a drawing of three Digletts that have partially burrowed into the earth. Dug + Trio – do you see what they've done there? Or perhaps it was something about fighting them. Or swapping them. In any case, all that was irrelevant. What you really wanted to do was simply own more cards than your peers, and you didn't mind what you had to do to achieve this. Steal, rob, slash, cut, smash, grab, victimize, bully. Pushers could sell rare cards to addicts for vastly inflated prices. Nintendo claimed the game encouraged 'nurturing' behaviour, and the corporation may well have been genuine in its belief. But the news reports told a different story.

'The fourteen-year-old produced a knife and told the victim that if he didn't give up the cards, he was going to cut him,' Sergeant John Jeter of the Bossier City Police Department told news agency reporters. 'He took the slogan "Gotta catch 'em all" to a new level.' The boy, aided by two ten-year-old accomplices, had hatched his Pokémon plan earlier that day when he saw an eleven-year-old showing off a large collection.

FAD Fact Psychologists have found that children aged two and three believe the sparkly objects they see on television are real things inside the set. Therefore, they believe that if they get these objects they will look the same and do the same things as they do on television. (Pine & Nash)

This was only the beginning. In South Carolina, a fourteen-year-old boy was arrested after smashing a window to steal $250-worth of Pokémon cards, ignoring several thousand dollars worth of rare coins that were displayed next to them. A grown man slapped a Burger King bus boy in the face when he failed to supply a Pokémon toy with his meal. In

Quebec, a boy was stabbed in the belly with a four-inch knife when he tried to recover the Pokémon cards that thieves had stolen from his ten-year-old brother the day before. The litany of violent Pokémon crime goes on. Children were pulling knives on friends, stabbing, slapping, bullying and beating, all to get hold of 'rare' Pokémon cards, worth hundreds of dollars on the black market. Hooked on the adrenalin, the spending and gambling, and driven by the status afforded by holding rare Pokémon, children were edging into ever more dangerous behaviour. In Sarasota, Florida, an eleven-year-old boy agreed to be burned on the arm with a cigarette by a thirty-three-year-old man when promised a rare Pokémon card if he did so.

The UK craze was considerably less violent than its transatlantic counterpart, but no less fevered. Soon Pokémon were everywhere. Every petrol station, every newsagent had a Pikachu in the window. Waterstone's was full of Pokémon books. The papers carried Pokémon cartoon strips. Teachers went on a banning spree. Parents wrote to the newspapers. Everyone had a view on Pokémon. The nation's pundits churned out Pokémon opinion for the press. Politicians were let off the hook as *Private Eye* editor Ian Hislop used his platform on TV's *Have I Got News For You* to rail against the monster drawings. Muslim leaders called for a ban on the products because they believed the badly drawn cartoons were part of a Jewish conspiracy to overthrow Islam. Sunderland police attempted to cash in on the craze by releasing their own set of collectible stickers. 'We hope the stickers will become as popular as Pokémon,' said a spokesman. The stickers featured Sunderland police officers dispensing anti-crime advice.

The Pokémon could work other magic too. Nigel James, an IT clerk from London, recalls an unfortunate experience at the Japanese gift shop. 'There were all these Pokémons you could get, like little figures on a key ring, but the only one I wanted was Lickitung.' Ah, yes, poor old Lickitung. A sort of squat, mauve squirrel with a big red rolled tongue.

As an 'uncommon' Pokémon, Lickitung was often overlooked. 'So I went into this Japanese shop in Chinatown, that sold all this Pokémon stuff, and I went up to the girl and said, "Hello, I'm looking for a little Lickitung."' It seems she ran from the shop floor and a man came to remove him. 'Unfair, I thought,' says Nigel, who never did acquire his plastic collectible. 'I went back there recently. There was a new girl. She shook her head sadly and told me the truth. "Pokémon all gone now."'

And it was true. Like your pocket money, no sooner had the beastly cretins arrived than they were gone. 'You don't hear so much about Pokémon anymore,' the Knoxville News Sentinel lamented recently, in its lonesome Tennessee way. This was good news for the state of the world's psyche, but bad news for box offices, as the fifth Pokémon feature film had just hit American big screens. The response from the US media was this: 'Yawn.'

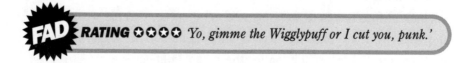

FAD ‹ *RATING* ✪✪✪✪ *'Yo, gimme the Wigglypuff or I cut you, punk.'*

Pong

See TV Games.

Punk

Erstwhile Sex Pistols manager Malcolm McLaren would have us believe he invented the aggressive, saliva-happy punk-rock movement of 1976–8. But English bands like the Canvey Island-based Doctor Feelgood had been tapping into the disaffection of the young working classes for some time. This new, aggressive rhythm with attitude in drainpipe trousers and short hair spoke to a section of society that felt economically marginalized, excluded from the disco party and unimpressed by the intellectual navel-gazing offered up by the prog-rock and folksy outfits that had developed from hippy psychedelia. What they didn't have was a name.

Punk, in the UK, was about short, angry songs with shouted lyrics and simple chords badly played by yobs who rejected the muso cognoscenti. It was about sticking up two fingers, or preferably one, at respectability, the government, the privileged classes and the royals. For the fan, it meant pogo-ing up and down (*see* **The Pogo-Stick**), spitting at the band, moshing, fighting and generally rioting. Punk rejected everything the hippy movement had embraced, such as love and peace. In their place punk promoted disorder, hate, vandalism and violence. Hoorah.

Socioeconomic forces were the real drivers in this trend, but what McLaren undoubtedly did influence was our adoption of the name and the New York-influenced sartorial fashion that came to represent punk in the eyes of the media and outraged parents. Here, the trend was for ripped clothes, leather jackets, DIY safety-pin piercings, spiked hair, mohican cuts, zip-heavy 'bondage' jeans, T-shirts printed with offensive slogans and, best of all, tartan. McLaren marketed the fashions himself, along with designer Vivienne Westwood, from their Kings Road shop, 'SEX'. Cheaper boutiques soon caught on, and before long the anti-establishment rebels were buying into a marketing plan (*see* **The Skateboard**). Among the SEX clientele were Glen Matlock and John Lydon, who were recruited into the fledgling Pistols as gobbing, shouting, shrieking, squawking living dolls.

McLaren may also have influenced the Pistols' music, drawing heavily as it did on his former wards the New York Dolls, on the Ramones and on other denizens of the New York 'punk' scene centred on the CBGB club, such as Television and Richard Hell. In keeping with this name idea, Lydon was redubbed Johnny Rotten and the band later acquired a Sid Vicious.

But the British punk movement, given McLaren-free musical voice via bands like The Clash, The Damned and Stiff Little Fingers, was so much more than a few bands and a clothing idea. While McLaren successfully imported a fashion, the British take on it differed from the New York music scene in that its aggressive nihilism struck a chord with a generation that felt ignored, saw little hope of employment or recognition and would make themselves felt at all costs by attacking the establishment and combusting into wilful self-destruction.

But where American music fans had a scene, the British really only had a craze. When the Sex Pistols gobbed their last, the former Mr Rotten rose phoenix-like from its ashes in 1978 as frontman of Public Image Ltd, an altogether more articulate and cynical outfit, while punk splintered, Hydra-like, into a thousand heads, veering off into the New Wave of punk-influenced bands such as The Stranglers, The Jam, Elvis

Costello, Siouxsie and the Banshees and the Undertones in the UK, while New York New Wave segued into nerdy latecomers Talking Heads, Blondie and plastic-hair apologists Devo. This 'new wave' was ultimately to disappear up its own frilly sleeves in the New Romantic 'movement' of the early eighties amid the likes of Adam Ant, Spandau Ballet and Duran Duran.

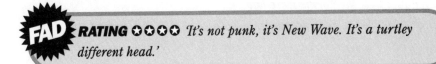

FAD ❯ **RATING** ✪✪✪✪ *It's not punk, it's New Wave. It's a turtley different head.'*

Purple Ronnie

Was there ever a better-made fad
For adults who still were infants?
It's not just that the poems were bad
But also the blokes wore no pants.

Giles Andreae's range of stick-man greeting cards, sold through the Hallmark empire, peddled the reluctant grown-up poetry on subjects such as 'bottom burps' and 'doing it'. In the early nineties, no birthday, baptism, Valentine's day, stag night or wedding was safe from Andreae's doggerel and the ubiquitous outline-people he used to illustrate his world. For God's sake, man, put some trousers on them. The Licensing Company – which controls the rights, along with **Star Wars** and the insipid 'Love Is…' series – has dubbed 'Mr Ronnie' the UK's most successful poet. The grisly truth is that if success is measured in revenue this is undoubtedly true.

 **FAD RATING** ✪✪ *'Unsanitary.'*

The Raleigh Chopper

Raleigh's bestselling Chopper bike has come to signify the seventies like no other piece of hardware. Heavily influenced by 'dragster'-style race motorbikes, the Chopper, like its motorized namesake, featured a small front wheel and a large back wheel, a laid-back saddle and high handlebars. It also had a gearstick mounted on the central beam. This meant you had to take your hands off the 'wheel' to shift gear. This meant you had to fall off. Perfect: in a world where **Evel Knievel** was king, bike-stunt injury was a badge of honour. Odd that such an unstable vehicle should become an icon of design. Perhaps because no one had tried anything like it before.

Our Knievel-scented Chopper fantasies were helped by a popular cartoon strip in *Whizzer and Chips*, in which the bike-bound hero was always escaping danger on his trusty Raleigh (a selection of horns and other accessories [*see* **The Pea-Shooter**] were generally available for purchase through adverts in the back pages of the comic, no doubt eased in by the appearance of such a strip), his **flared trousers** almost always getting caught on barbed wire. If only we could get that bike, we could be like him.

As a cult bike, the Chopper was only toppled by the appearance of the ridiculous, gearless **BMX** and Raleigh's proto-mountain bike, the Grifter. If you had any of these, you really were king of the road. Until you slid under the wheels of a car.

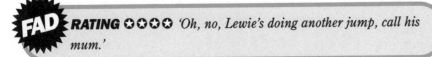

FAD **RATING ✪✪✪✪** *'Oh, no, Lewie's doing another jump, call his mum.'*

The Ringtone

There was once a time when the Post Office Trim Phone's electronic bleep was the height of modern glamour. It is now impossible to own a telephone that does not play a tune instead. There was also a time when fashion accessories were less sophisticated (*see* **The Deely Bopper**). These days, though, the ringtone of a young person's portable telephone (*see* **The CB Radio**) makes a statement about who they are, where they're at and indeed where they're coming from. There is hardly a pop hit that is not available to download in ringtone format, while many records are released straight to ringtone, the modern equivalent of the direct-to-video phenomenon in film-making (*see* **The Betamax Video**). But if you really want to make a statement with your ringtone, you could simply live there. The sleepy Somerset village of Wrington has seen an unexpected rise in property prices in recent years.

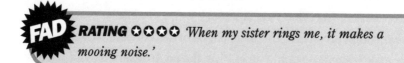

FAD **RATING** ✪✪✪✪ *'When my sister rings me, it makes a mooing noise.'*

The Roller Skate

The author's first tentative steps into the world of foot-held transport were taken on a pair of adjustable metal clamps, fitted with four wheels in 'quad' formation and leather straps. The wheels appeared to have been made out of solid Tarmac and when set in motion they sent forceful, juddering vibrations up the author's legs and torso and into his brain.

Basic perambulation was achieved after two days' practice along the seafront at Portishead. Experiments were made into the viability of the skates as a mode of transport. These experiments produced disappointing results. The wheels, while they did in fact roll, did not roll very much, owing to their inability to negotiate major obstacles such as tiny specks of gravel and imperceptible cavities in the road and pavement. Thereafter, the author relied upon his trusty Grifter, a giant, lumbering geared version of the popular **BMX** bicycle.

Some years later, the author discovered the roller boot. These skates came with footwear attached and boasted light, flexible plastic wheels, suspension and, most importantly, a brake. Low-cost transport was thus obtainable, and the author successfully achieved extended perambulation around the Aldgate East area of London. Sadly they were not his own roller boots and had to be given back. There followed a period of some years during which the skate fell away from view only to reappear during the nineties as the Rollerblade® and the Bauer®. During this era only branded wheelwear would do and so the generic tool of human-powered transport became a must-have label and fashion accessory.

Like so many things, the roller skate was most probably invented by many people all at once. The first name to be associated with the innovation, however, is generally given as that of the Belgian inventor

Joseph Merlin. His in-line skate (wheels all in a row) appeared in 1760. This we gather from a report of his entrance to a London masked ball playing the violin on said skates. He glided well but realized moments too late that he had not designed a brake. Having sustained rather more than minor injuries, Merlin decided not to develop his invention. According to the American National Museum of Roller-Skating, the first patent belonged to a Parisian named Petitbled, who laid claim in 1819 to another version of the in-line skate. The fact that the early skates were all in-line models lends credence to the theory that they evolved from the ice skate. In 1849 the French actor Louis Legrange wore a pair of ice skates with added wheels to simulate ice-skating on stage.

But Petitbled's skate had recessed wheels, which meant they could only go in a straight line. Like the ice skate, they also required strong ankles. But as interest grew, so the technicians went to work. The roller skate acquired much-needed stability in 1863 when James Plimpton made the first 'quad' model, which also included a rubber pad that allowed the skater to steer by leaning. However, it wasn't until the advent of the toe-stop and the ball-bearing in the last years of the nineteenth century that roller skates became more than just a fad gadget. The ball-bearings were added by Robert Henley, whose uncle Micajah began mass production from Richmond, Indiana, in 1881 under the name of the Chicago Skate Company.

These developments ignited the first wave of the roller-skate craze. During the first half of the twentieth century the activity grew in popularity, but it was not until the seventies that the real worldwide mania took off. In the seventies, roller skates finally gained shock-absorbent plastic wheels. This made skating easier, more comfortable and much more fun. Roller rinks had been around for decades, but once disco fever had caught the world, there was no stopping us. The roller disco was born. The age of the first Sony **Walkman** also saw roller-skating finally permeate mass culture. The combination of sneakers and wheels in the form of the roller boot made skates hip. From 1979 on, the skating loon with the Walkman's iconic orange headphones strapped to his or her ears was a common sight.

But 1979 also brought one last major development in skating technology. Although the quad skate had dominated the roller-skate industry for decades, the machine lacked the elegant simplicity and fluidity of the ice skate. The push for a good in-line skate had been driven in the US and Canada by the hockey world. Sports players seeking a way to practise during the spring and summer were limited to places where they could find a good ice-rink. But when Minneapolis hockey player Scott Olsen found an old pair of the popular but flawed Chicago Company in-line skates in a second-hand shop, he grabbed them and added his own modifications. The toe-stop became the heel brake,

his wheels gave more fluidity, and Olsen began to market his skates to the hockey world. In 1984 he sold his business to Bob Naegele, who took the skates to market under the name Rollerblade Inc. Through Naegele's marketing muscle the roller skate and the ice skate finally fused into a worldwide craze for inline skating. The blades gave unprecedented freedom of movement, speed and agility. Finally roller-skating could compete as a sport, with unlikely sounding offshoot styles, such as 'Naked', and 'Aggressive', which, according to one of its leading exponents, is 'all about fun'. The author gathers figure-skating on wheels is now considered respectable practice by grown adults.

Such has been the success of the new breed of in-line skate that it is now hard to find a good pair of old-fashioned quad roller-boots. Such

THAT WAS THE YEAR...
Eighties Toy Crazes

1980 Rubik's Cube, *Pac-Man*.

1982 BMX Bikes, ZX Spectrum.

1983 My Little Pony, He Man & The Masters Of The Universe.

1984 Care Bears, Christmas Cabbage Patch Kids®, Trivial Pursuit.

1985 Transformers. They were robots in disguise.

1986 Panini Football stickers. Half paper, half toasted ciabatta.

1987 Sylvanian Families. Mouse and stoat fun.

1988 *Ghostbusters.* Well, who else were you 'gonna' call?

1989 *Batman.* Holy licensing and marketing!

moments, then, belong here in this paean to the nostalgic and ephemeral, along with other obsolete vehicles, such as the **Space Hopper**. In this writer's opinion, transport really didn't get any better than that. As for the author's own forays into portable wheel-based motion, he appears to have missed the zeitgeist at every opportunity. Roller boots, much like the **SodaStream**, were not thought in his household to be a solid investment. A child with growing feet could make do with the bone-breaking skates with solid wheels that he got for Christmas years before. And by the time the branded inline skates came into fashion he was an impecunious student whose money went on Tesco value beans (*see* **The Teasmaid**) and Nutella. None the less, he looks fondly back on the days when he wheeled around the deserted **skateboard** parks of East London armed with a **spud gun**, looking for mischief.

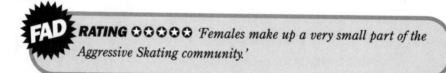

FAD RATING ✪✪✪✪✪ *Females make up a very small part of the Aggressive Skating community.'*

Rubik's Cube

Spring had sprung in Budapest. A crisp light played on the Danube as the crocuses poked though the soil, but Ernö's mother was worried about her son. He never seemed to go out and play like the other boys. And for nearly a month he had been shut up in his room with his wooden building blocks. Suddenly one night, the door opened and a triumphant Ernö burst forth, clutching his latest model.

'I remember how proudly I demonstrated it to her when I found the solution,' Rubik later wrote in his memoirs. 'And how happy she was in the hope that from then on I would not work so hard on it.' It was 1974. The boy was in fact twenty-nine years old, and the crude prototype cube he had first constructed with wooden blocks and elastic bands would go on to become the world's fastest-selling toy.

And how. Rubik's Cube burst on to the western market in 1981, captivating the minds of infants and adults alike. Absurd in its simplicity, almost infinite in its complexity, it was a masterpiece of design and the puzzle to end all puzzles. Six bold colours marked the faces of the cube, itself constructed of individual mini-cubes in a 3x3x3 formation. Each row and column could be twisted, shifting the locations of the fifty-four coloured squares from order into chaos. And, if you were very clever, or very lucky, from chaos back into order. But therein lay the maddening appeal of Rubik's Cube. There was only one winning combination and – count them – 43 quintillion ways to lose.

Speaking on his own account, the author struggled for a day with a knock-off model from Brick Lane market before pulling the thing apart and going swimming. He thought this a superior method to the preferred playground cheat of simply peeling off the coloured stickers and putting them back in the right place. But solving the cube was not nearly so compelling as the urge to own and display it as a badge of social conformity.

The key to understanding the craze lies in recognizing that the cube was at once a playground fad and an **executive toy**. Everyone wanted to solve the puzzle, and even those who harboured no hope of twisting it back into harmony simply had to own one. As aesthetically pleasing as it was mathematically troubling, Rubik's Cube was a must-have object, a fashion item, talked about endlessly in the bus queue, the schoolyard, the office, the factory. Even on radio and television, it became a focus for hired punditry. Intelligent people were driven to distraction by its difficulty. Less intelligent people twisted it at random and ended up solving it by accident, parading it proudly while blinking excitedly with their lazy eyes (*see also* **Magic Eye**™, **Pokémon**).

'The only people who can do the Rubik Cube are children and morons,' the comedian Jasper Carrot observed, voicing, it seemed, the frustrations of everyman. None the less, over a hundred books were published claiming to provide the solution. Many dedicated twisters did indeed find methods. The world record for solving the cube is held by American 'cubist' Minh Thai, who in 1982 took a mere 22.95 seconds to reach the finish, depriving the Dutch seed Razoux Schultz and Hungary's own Zoltán Lábas of the coveted title. Such racing cubes were often 'lubed up' for speed-twisting.

Though its shelf-life was relatively short – the craze proper had dwindled by 1983 – Rubik's Cube became so much more than the sum of its parts. At once a toy, a puzzle, a sport, a teaching aid and an iconic piece of design, it also asked us to consider much deeper questions of man's relation to nature. Or at least it did according to Rubik's thinking.

'Space always intrigued me,' he later wrote. 'Movement in space and in time, [its] correlation [and] repercussion on mankind, the relation between man and space, the object and time. I think the Cube arose from this interest.' That and his fascination for games. 'I particularly like games where the partner, the real opponent, is nature itself, with its really particular but decipherable mysteries.' These were the preoccupations that led Rubik to create the cube that troubled the world. But the puzzle's worldwide success had little to do with its designer, who would rather have been at home with his wife and daughter than giving it eyes and teeth with corporate moguls in the West.

Ernö Rubik was born in 1944, in an air-raid shelter in Budapest, Hungary. His father was an aircraft engineer and an innovative designer of gliders. His mother was an artist and a published poet. A solitary boy, Ernö veered towards the visual arts and passed his unhappy school days learning sculpture. At a school dedicated to the fine arts, the young Rubik's dislocation stemmed from his inability to bond and blend in with his bohemian classmates. A serious thinker, Rubik was never happier than when he was canoeing alone down the Danube, walking his dog, alone, or working on chess problems. Alone. None the less, the sculpture awoke in him an interest in technical applications, and he went on to gain a diploma in architecture at the University of Technical Education in Budapest, drawn by the discipline's blend of science and art, fascinated by the technical, aesthetic and philosophical problems architecture posed.

He liked the way a space would change depending on what was put into it and, conversely, the way an object would change according to the space around it. Architecture, coupled with a second diploma in interior design, appealed to both the artist and the engineer in him – two elements completely evident in his cube.

On graduating as a designer in 1970, Rubik began to lecture at the Academy of Applied Arts and Crafts in Budapest. A man of modest ambition, he was rewarded with an even more modest salary. Not enough to afford a place of his own. Since his parents had divorced, the former Mrs Rubik had taken a small flat in Budapest. It was here that Ernö lodged. In the evenings he spurned the company of his colleagues, preferring to ruminate alone on man, space and nature and to tinker with the multitudes of wooden or cardboard structures he built in his bedroom to demonstrate such things to his students.

It has often been suggested that Rubik first designed the cube for this purpose, but this story glosses over Rubik's fascination with games and puzzles and with the exactitudes of geometry. He was impressed by the Ancient Chinese tangram, and the way a few very basic elements would yield a multitude of figures. He enjoyed Golomb's Pentomino, Hein's Soma Cube and the classic nineteenth-century '15 puzzle' designed by Sam Lloyd. This is the well-known flat puzzle in which locked tiles may be moved independently to create an alphabetic or numeric sequence. Rubik deliberately set out to design a classic puzzle, one that would reflect nature as he saw it: at once infinitely complex and elementally simple, with a beauty that reflected the geometry in all things, from a leaf to a drop of water.

He experimented with various combinations of blocks before he hit on the perfect three-by-three. He held them together with elastic bands at first, enjoying the structure as it twisted this way and that. When the rubber bands snapped he persevered. Rubik claims the inspiration came from the Danube. Watching pebbles that had been smoothed and rounded by the water, he hit on the cylindrical internal structure that holds his cube together.

Once unleashed, the cube took on a life of its own. The compulsive enthusiasm of his students and colleagues prompted Rubik to apply for a patent in Hungary and hunt for a manufacturer. This proved more difficult, but eventually the small toy-making cooperative Politechnika took it on. The puzzle was more complex than anything it had tried to make before and raising finance in communist Hungary was a laborious, centralized process. Three long years later, in 1977, the first cubes drifted into the shops.

There was no promotion, but the cube's popularity spread by word of mouth. It absorbed people. It held them. It pissed them off. It pissed off one Budapest waiter so much in 1978 that he sold his cube to a fascinated customer for a dollar. The coffee drinker was one Dr Tibor Laczi, a Hungarian-born computer manufacturer based in Vienna. He had never seen the cube before, but wasn't about to let it go. When the dollar signs lit up in his eyes he sought an audience with Rubik. He told the lecturer he could sell millions in the West. If only he could get permission to cross the Iron Curtain with it.

The Hungarian state trading company mocked Laczi. They said cube sales had fallen off and their efforts to show it at international toy fairs had met with no outside interest. Laczi, who understood the workings of capitalism, suspected their state-funded hearts had not been in it. He took it himself to the Nuremburg Toy Exhibition, where he met a British-Hungarian called Tom Kremer.

Kremer was an established toy inventor and ran his own licensing and marketing company in London. He was similarly excited by the cube's international potential. But his efforts fell on deaf ears. None of the big manufacturers was interested. They considered it too cerebral and too expensive to make. Only after Kremer dragged the vice president of Ideal Toys to Budapest to witness the craze in motion did he secure an order. For one million cubes.

That posed a problem for Konsumex, the Hungarian state trading company. Persuading the Eastern Bloc country to trade with a capitalist fat cat in the West took a great deal of diplomacy on the part of Laczi and Kremer. But, in a glowing testament to the zeal of the greedy, eventually both the free market and the people's republic were convinced of the international appeal of the 'Magic Cube', as Rubik had called it.

The UK toy market is worth £1.9 billion.
(British Association of Toy Retailers, 2003)

The pre-school 'market' for toys, food, clothes and other consumer goods is worth £4.3 billion.
(*Guardian*, 2002)

That posed a problem too. Rubik had not thought to patent his geometric abomination beyond Hungary. It was too late for Ideal to secure an international patent, but they could copyright a name. So 'Rubik's Cube' was birthed unto an unsuspecting world. And that posed a problem for Politechnika, the tiny Hungarian co-op tasked with making them. They just couldn't do it in time. Demand outstripped supply, allowing 43 quintillion (approx.) pirate 'Magic Cubes' to flood in from the Far East. These ended up accounting for about half of all sales. Ideal tried to sue, certainly in the UK. The court ruled in 1982 that the Taiwanese cubes breached the Hungarian copyright but found against Ideal's claim that the pirates were 'passing off' their imports as the real thing. This might have influenced the creation of 'Rubik's Revenge' – a 96-squared big-brother to his cube. Nevertheless, thanks to Ideal's insistence on a trademark, Rubik will for ever be the name attached to the cube. The name also added an appealing dose of eastern mystery. Who was this enigmatic Mr Rubik – whose name rhymed with 'cubic'?

Well, now you know.

The cube became an icon of eighties pop culture, but is now enjoying a second wind as nostalgia hits the thirty-something generation. In October 2004, the children's charity Barnardo's told Scotland's *Buchanan Observer* that it had seen a boom in sales of authentic eighties Rubik's Cubes. The report said Barnardo's was 'really pleased that so many people are using the charity to source collectible toys' cheaply, and then sell them on eBay for personal profit.

On the subject of profit, one of the happiest facts in this story of capitalist exploitation – at least in capitalist terms – is that Rubik never lost his rights to the various companies and individuals who helped bring his toy to market. Though he only took a reported 5 per cent of the profits, he certainly became a multi-millionaire and is still benefiting from sales of his puzzle, still innovating and marketing new toys and puzzles.

But did success change the loyal worker? Laczi noted that the chief difference in Rubik's habits was that he started smoking a better class of cigarette, post-cube. But did it make him happy? The journalist John Tierney visited the inventor at his lavish Budapest villa in 1986 and discovered a withdrawn, laconic man. Tierney wondered why Rubik had no dining room. 'Do you plan to have many people over to dinner?' he asked the designer. 'Rubik puffed on a Marlboro 100, gazed out at the walled yard in back, and frowned. "I hope not."'

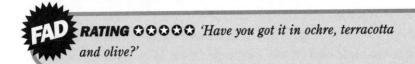

FAD RATING ✪✪✪✪✪ *'Have you got it in ochre, terracotta and olive?'*

SEE THE JOIN

The Traffic Warden, NASA and the Cabbage Patch Kid®

Yo-Yo® promoter Donald Duncan found his company's finances went up and down like its product. When bankruptcy loomed, Duncan's other money-spinner – the parking meter – bailed him out and in turn gave meaning to the lives of thousands of traffic wardens.

In a giant leap for marketing-kind, Duncan was also the first to launch the breakfast-cereal-packet offer we now regard as commonplace. Homing in on children at their most receptive – while eating sugar-coated food – Duncan's first deal offered a toy space rocket in return for tokens collected from the special boxes.

Later, one of his Yo-Yos® actually went up in a space rocket, ensuring worldwide coverage for his product. This trick was later copied by Xavier Roberts, the creator of the Cabbage Patch Kids® range of ugly dolls. But since the Yo-Yo® had already made its name as first toy to blast off, and since 'second toy in space' isn't much of an accolade, 'Christopher Xavier', the doll chosen for this NASA mission, had to make do with the honour of 'First Cabbage Patch Kid® in Space'.

Rubik's Snake

All the rage for a short while in the aftermath of Ernö Rubik's seminal cube, the Snake was a long, straight sequence of pleasingly constructed triangular segments that could be twisted to produce a finite number of shapes, including the cobra and, er, hm. At it's most satisfying, this two-coloured, candy-striped puzzle folded into a compact, fist-sized ball, which could be launched at smaller siblings. At its least satisfying, it was nearly a doggy with pointy ears, sort of. All the same, the Snake was the most commercially successful of Rubik's post-cube toys.

 **RATING ✪** *'That's nice, dear.'*

The Sandwich Toaster

The sandwich toaster looked nice enough in your kitchen, until it became covered with a permanent Asda decal transfer after you accidentally left the carrier bag leaning against the hot appliance (*see also* **The Shrinky Dink**®). The ritual of greasing up the ribbed hot plates with butter was matched only by the ritual of scrubbing it off afterwards, along with the little nuggets of fried cheese that clung to it like dairy limpets (*see* **Milk**). Once you'd gone through that a few times you generally left the thing alone, occasionally bringing it out of the cupboard to **crimp** your hair. The sandwich toaster, once standard issue to all students, has now been superseded by the flat-plated panini-maker, which could possibly double up as a trouser press. Tip: do the trousers *before* the mozzarella panini.

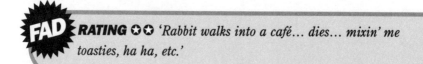

FAD **RATING ✪✪** '*Rabbit walks into a café... dies... mixin' me toasties, ha ha, etc.*'

Scalextric

FEATURING SLOT-CAR RACING

Scalextric. How were you supposed to say that? It's unpronounceable by the human tongue. You refused even to try. What you said was 'Scay-letrics', like everyone else, but at least you knew it was wrong. This iconic but oddly named slot-car racing system captured our hearts like no toy before. This was **Hornby** train sets on speed, modelling in the fast lane. Competitive **Dinky**. You had to have it.

There were one or two drawbacks of course. The cars would tend to fly off at bends, teaching you valuable lessons about selective deceleration. Then they would need to be slotted back into place by the gimbal. The car on the inside slot had an unfair advantage, as it had less ground to cover, though it was subject to tighter bends. Also, because of the slots, Scalextric differed in one important respect from the Formula One races it aimed to emulate: cars could overtake and lap, but they could not cut each other up and block their opponents, a cornerstone of real-life motor racing. But, just like train sets, the system was expandable, so your own track designs could be accommodated, along with chicanes, bridges and a wide range of cars and motorbikes. You dreamed of giant race-tracks that covered the whole floor. However, because it cost a small fortune, you invariably made do with what was in the box.

Ideal solved the lane-changing conundrum with its rival TCR, or Total Control Racing. This slotless system allowed cars to swap lanes at the flick of a hand-held switch. The system also featured a rogue car or truck

> **FAD Fact**
>
> Almost all children in the UK write a begging letter to Father Christmas each year, asking for specific products. (Pine & Nash)
>
> Father Christmas was invented by Coca-Cola®. (Coca-Cola®)

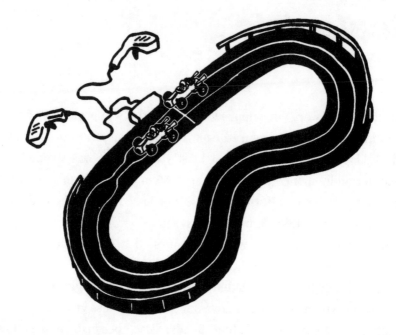

whose sole function was to block you to hell. It was collisions ahoy with TCR.

But the pick of the bunch, for this writer at least, was Race and Chase from **Matchbox**. Drawing, perhaps, on the popularity of TV's *The Dukes of Hazzard*, Race and Chase dispensed with the worthy sportiness of Scalextric in favour of lawless anarchy, as an American cop car was unleashed in hot pursuit of a souped-up saloon. This set featured a swing bridge. If you were clever you could trap your opponent underneath it, forcing the use of the reverse function unique to Race and Chase.

But however good they might have been, such competitors ultimately fell by the wayside. Scalex was first launched in 1952 by a company called Minimodels, the brainchild of Havant-based designer Fred Francis. The original product was a free-running metal car with a clockwork motor. In fact Francis's motor design lives on in numerous generic low-end toys. The motor was wound up by pulling the car backwards on a gear wheel underneath the chassis. When you released the car, off it shot. Francis added the slotted rubber track, the hanging gimbal and electric motor later that decade, when sales of Scalex began to thin out. Plugging into the mains also sparked off the unspeakable trade name of Scalextric. A sale to Tri-Ang in 1958 brought both a switch from rubber track to cheaper plastic and the marketing resources to make it sell. Championships were launched (*see* **Meccano** *and* **The Yo-Yo®**), bringing Scalextric into the public eye, and the sixties saw steady growth. But the phenomenon had its heyday during the seventies, when the quality of the product, the range of accessories and the level of marketing all hit critical mass.

The author, it should be pointed out, had none of the above racing sets, but that did not stop the longing. Scalextric skill was acquired over time, at a succession of other people's houses, necessitating frequent visits to places known to harbour a track. 'You don't know me but I was passing your window and couldn't help but notice you have a chicane. Do you think I could possibly…' The explosion of home computers (*see* **The Sinclair ZX Spectrum**) and video games in the early eighties did the same for the slot-car fad as it had for **Action Man**. While rivals bowed out of the match, the brand is now owned by Hornby, ensuring the continued presence of the slot-car sets we know and love, if not the craze.

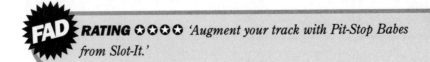

FAD **RATING** ✪✪✪✪ *'Augment your track with Pit-Stop Babes from Slot-It.'*

The Scented Eraser

The author's own first perfumed eraser, a vanilla-scented ice-cream-cone shape, was finally eaten one morning during a long double-maths session, with lunchtime near and yet so, so far. The intrinsic appeal of the scented rubber was – much like the flavoured condom – also its downfall. None the less, its very pointlessness earns it a place in the fad hall of fame. Sadly, perfumed erasers are less commonly found now. But readers wishing to correct pencil mistakes (*see* **The Etch A Sketch®**) fragrantly on a budget can make their own olfactory-enhanced apparatus at home by the medium of osmosis. For this experiment (*see* **The Chemistry Set**), you will need one clove of crushed garlic, one W. H. Smith porous rubber (smooth, coated Staedtlers are not suitable) and some cling-film. Leave overnight to maximize infusion, remove from the cling-film and impress your friends. The same technique will also work with condoms, although your friends will be less impressed. (*See also* **The Pencil Top**.)

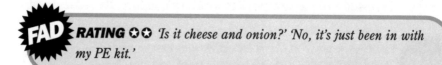

FAD **RATING ✪✪** *'Is it cheese and onion?' 'No, it's just been in with my PE kit.'*

The Sea Monkey

Sea Monkeys is the brand name for the brine-shrimp toy developed and first marketed in 1960 by Harold von Braunhut. The particular strain of brine shrimp von Braunhut discovered was called *Artema nyos*. What von Braunhut exploited was the shrimp's peculiar evolutionary gift: the creature is able to preserve itself out of water in a state of suspended animation, via the medium of protective cyst (*see* **The Metal-Detector**). Using this trick, the *Artema nyos* is able to cheat death when stranded above the tideline, flipping back into a kind of eerie life the instant water is added (*see also* **Cup-a-Soup**). The canny marketer saw in these rather unpleasant-looking, ghostlike creatures an opportunity to sell instant pets via mail order. And so he did, initially under the brand Instant Life, via the back pages of comics (*see* **The Pea-Shooter**). A change in favour of the rather misleading term 'Sea Monkey' brought rather more success, and a brine-shrimp craze developed. Mr von Braunhut made all sorts of startling claims: they could do tricks, they could be trained to race each other. No. Whatever these three-eyed foot-breathing monsters do, they do of their own accord. Tests have shown (the author bought a pack) that what they do in fact is eat each other. What you then have left over, you can feed to your Siamese fighting fish.

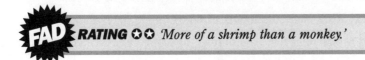

FAD **RATING ✪✪** *'More of a shrimp than a monkey.'*

BEHIND THE SCENES
Customer for life

One of the best ways to prise open the wallet of an adult is to take control of him or her when he or she is still a child. By entering and influencing the imagination of a child at their most impressionable, a company's champion brand can actually become a kind of folklore, an early subconscious root inextricably linked with those first moments of play. A good example of this subtle but alarming intrusion is Coca-Cola's® famous repackaging of Christmas and its creation of Santa Claus, in carefully branded red and white.

Other examples, more pertinent to the creation of crazes, include American Greetings' Care Bears and Strawberry Shortcake brands. AG was not content to sell teddy bears in toyshops. The company launched a range of branded products to take control of the whole learning process. Care Bear colouring books and nursery songs on audio tape effectively meant the Care Bears brand 'owned' key moments in the learning process. Who forgets their first visit to the cinema? In releasing four branded Care Bears feature films, the company ensured that for a significant proportion of the target market, that powerful memory will have a special Care Bear glow.

Creating folklore is powerful. In its branded children's stories AG cleverly made a sweet fudge of the popular legend of King Arthur and the round table. Camelot became Care-a-lot. The round table was a heart-shaped table. And so on. When legend and folklore are rebranded, a very powerful association is made in the mind. How many thousands of times during his lifetime will an English-speaking person hear, half-hear or read the word 'Camelot'? When that word becomes 'Care-a-lot' in his imagination, strange things can happen. We are no longer talking about parents picking up a product from a display, weighing up its pros and cons – its aesthetic appeal versus educational merit, its safety values versus desirability – and making a reasoned value judgement on behalf of their child. We are talking about instinctual urges. Camelot, Care-a-lot. It's the oldest story on earth. This way, you'll get a customer for life. First Pester Power, then Pocket-Money Power; give it a few years and then Nostalgia Power kicks in. Add a new generation of children, and the whole delicious cycle starts again. Doesn't that make you feel warm inside? This strategy was taken up by Xavier Roberts for his famous Cabbage Patch Kids® range of dolls: Roberts

> '**Children have lost the ability to please themselves, to be creative, resourceful, self-reliant…**'
>
> National Family and Parenting Institute

even goes so far as to label his rather trite fantasy story about the discovery of the 'orphans' as 'folklore'. Albeit a 'folklore' dashed off one afternoon around the marketing table. We see the same technique countless times, where early learning books, for example, are published with the sole purpose of raising awareness of a brand of toy consumables. The trick is getting into the child's imagination when he or she is learning, say, to read. On seeing the familiar characters in a shop, the child will make a subconscious connection and reach out for them.

Another way to slip into a child's unconscious is to brand their learning resources, as our friend American Greetings did when it sponsored – and heavily branded – a learning programme for 'kindergarten' students about how to take care of pets. 'The Strawberry Shortcake In-School Program', launched in association with the highly reputable American Society for the Prevention of Cruelty to Animals (ASPCA), declared its objectives thus: 'To familiarize children with pets' needs and how people can provide for them. To encourage empathy and humane treatment of animals. To introduce children to the differences between wild and domesticated animals and how to be safe around all kinds of animals. To reinforce literacy, observation, science, and recording skills.' Of course, the aims of American Greetings were entirely altruistic – indeed, decorating each of its activity sheets almost exclusively with pictures and the names of its Strawberry Shortcake range of collectible products was clearly a key part of this learning and caring strategy. That the materials were free – AG had no problem with them being endlessly photocopied, downloaded, redistributed and shared to 'meet the needs of your students' – can only have been a plus point to budget-conscious schools and nurseries.

It's not just restricted to toys. Fast-food companies, soft-drink and sweets manufacturers are all sneaking into your child's school through the back door. The much publicized Cadbury 'Get Active' campaign famously offered to invest £9 million in school sports equipment using collectible tokens on chocolate wrappers. This, at a time when one in five children is overweight. The NFPI calculated that children would have to eat 5,440 bars of chocolate to collect enough tokens for a single volleyball kit. Tesco and Walkers also used token schemes offering school equipment in order to market to children.

Other examples, though certainly far less troublesome, include the sponsoring of literacy events by bookshop chains. Large companies such as Borders have teamed up in the past with literacy charities to sponsor reading events. To their credit, the companies are open about the reasons for this work.

'Securing youth appeal not only establishes brand loyalty at an early age, but has a dramatic influence on parents' purchasing patterns.'
Martin Lindstrom in *Brandchild* (Kogan Page, 2003)

They want customers for life. This is a lesson they have learned from the likes of Martin Lindstrom and other brand-marketing gurus who peddle strategies for manipulating the 'dreams' of our children. Getting access to children when they are young and helping them to have a positive, fun learning experience in a heavily branded environment is a great way to persuade them to associate books with a certain store, to trust a brand to deliver, rather than, say, their school or a library.

Even the NFPI admits that 'there was no golden age when children were not exposed to marketing.' Big business argues that to protect children from these messages is to deny their development into choice-making, media-savvy individuals, to deny children the analytical skills they will undoubtedly need later in life. To this end, the advertising industry has funded the creation of Media Smart, an organization that provides worksheets and materials to schools with the aim of teaching children from primary age up about advertising and the media. The NFPI asks: 'Should valuable lesson time be spent teaching our children to become sophisticated consumers?' It answers its own question: 'There is no easy or straightforward answer because as yet there is no agreement on the problem.'

The Shrinky Dink®

Open your cereal packet, pull out the large, flat sheet of plastic printed with a goofy design and colour it with felts. Then pre-heat your oven to 325°F (163°C) and bake for two to three minutes. When it's done, your colouring will have reduced to the size of a postage stamp and can then be thrown away or simply lost.

The cereal-packet giveaways (*see* **The Yo-Yo**®) were as close as many of us got to the 'magical world of Shrinky Dinks®'. But the oven-fun pastime had been on the market since 1973, when two cub-scout leaders from Wisconsin went into business together. Akela Betty J. Morris and her Baloo, Katie Bloomberg, discovered the technique during a cookery demonstration for their youthful wards. From there it was but a short hop from Wisconsin to inside your Shreddies packet, clocking up retail sales of more than £40 million. In fact, Shrinky Dinks® are still innovating in the US, although the British market, er, diminished in size.

Similar fun can be had by baking your empty Quavers, Skips or Wotsits packet to create a shrivelled but perfectly formed mini-packet. Ideal as a key ring, which will be stolen from you within minutes of revealing it in the playground. **Yoghurt** pots are good baking, too. Place your pot upside-down on a heatproof tray, and minutes later you have a passable **Frisbee**® emblazoned with the words 'Asda Zinc & Banana yoghurt'.

Shrinky Dink® use is alleged to be a gateway activity and can lead to experiments with glue. For example, white PVA glue can be spilled in a massive slick behind the classroom

FAD Fact In 1952, four hours of television a week were dedicated to children. In 2002, the figure was 620 hours.
(Cowling & Lee)

radiator and allowed to solidify overnight into a clear patty. This can be recovered in the morning during break, adorned with felt-tip-penned insults (such as 'I have shag yor sister and she smellt') and launched at the class fleabag.

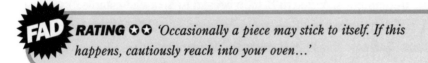

RATING ✪✪ *'Occasionally a piece may stick to itself. If this happens, cautiously reach into your oven...'*

Silly Coffee

In the mid nineties, coffee in Britain ceased to be a daily staple, provided in jars of dehydrated granules by global food-giants Nestlé and Kraft (*see* **Instant Coffee**). Instead it became a fashion accessory, a lifestyle indicator that marked discerning drinkers out as Young Urban Professionals (*see* **The Yuppie**). Along with *Frasier*, slacker culture, Nirvana and Amazon.com, the North American city of Seattle sold us silly coffee.

As the internet was just beginning to peep into mass consciousness and something called 'Britpop' ushered in such characters as the New Lad, hip style-magazines such as *The Face* published guides to adopting the all-new coffee craze: what to say, what not to say, what to ask for, what the words meant. Here are some of the phrases the switched-on and wired urbanistas were expected to use in daily life: 'Excuse me, Barista, I'd like one tall, no-fun, skinny latte with cinnamon, please, one vanilla frappuccino, two macchiatos, a double tall amaretto latte, a ristretto, a doppo, a freddo and a lungo, six punés and a why bother breve, one cake in a cup, four quads and a dry, but make it wet and harmless, one whipless with legs and a zebra on a leash – oh, and an ambulance please. Quickly.'

Of course, you couldn't ask for this sort of produce at your local greasy spoon, where you'd be lucky to get a bit of Maxwell House. No, you'd need to attend one of the many specialized chain cafés opening up all around you. The Seattle Coffee Company was first on the scene, swiftly followed by Starbucks, Costa, Café Nero and Coffee Republic. No longer would a steaming mug of watery Mellow Birds cost you 50 pence. Now you paid £3 for a cappuccino and nearly £2 for a single espresso, while simple filter coffee, once rather Ferrero Rocher, became the Pomagne of hot beverages (*see* **Babycham**). The new coffee was good, we understand this. But it was also expensive. Having updated our tastes, the new chains then fought each other bitterly for control of the multi-million-pound market, with the ubiquitous Starbucks gradually emerging as the dominant force.

Along with more sophisticated tastes came three important realizations. As we tried to emulate the new coffee-bar fare at home we realized that proper coffee was quite cheap and easy to make, which put the lid on Instant for a generation of drinkers. We also realized that the stuff we bought for home was in fact rather better than the mass-produced, portion-controlled guff being served up in Starbucks et al. So, sadly, in our bid for a European-style café culture, we had bowed down and succumbed to the McDonald's of bean-drink providers. This caused a backlash of protest-boycotting in favour of 'fair trade' coffee produce. Some chains currently provide this option at an extra cost. 'Would you like to pay more to drink fair-trade coffee, or would you rather oppress the developing world for 30 pence less? You choose and we'll do it.' Symbiosis in motion.

The third realization was that there is no way on earth ordinary British people, however upwardly mobile, could possibly give vent to such silly words in the pursuit of a simple cuppa. While the craze for talking Seattle coffee like Frasier and Niles has, metaphorically, left a note and blown its brains out, its sonorous legacy has become part of our lives. When you walk into a noisy café and ask for 'a cup of tea, please' you *will* be served a cappuccino. And that's a fact.

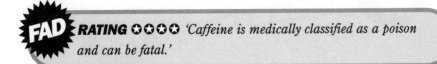

FAD **RATING** ✪✪✪✪ *'Caffeine is medically classified as a poison and can be fatal.'*

The Sinclair C5

British inventor Clive Sinclair's heart was in the right place, with no question. But ours was not. Having long pondered the feasibility of a silent, pollution-free electric personal vehicle, Sinclair finally launched the result of years of research in 1985. It was a low-lying, battery-powered invalid-carriage that looked like a **Dinky** toy, which we dutifully mocked, attacked and ultimately ran out of town.

On 14 January of that year, *The Times* published a large display advertisement from the Electricity Council congratulating Sinclair on his achievement and offering the glorious new green-powered vehicle for sale at its showrooms.

The following month *The Times* was already describing the vehicle as a 'formula-one bath-chair' and devoted the bulk of one article to quoting dissatisfied customers. The technology was considered either 'not very innovative' or 'disappointing', and unhappy owners were 'thinking of selling' or had already 'sent it back'. According to the Journal of Record, customer comments ran the gamut of gripes from lack of power to uncomfortable design.

By August 1985 the writing was already on the wall. Retail prices were slashed by up to 50 per cent in a bid to boost sales. This coincided with Hoover, which manufactured the C5, issuing Sinclair with a writ for £1.5 million in alleged arrears and halting production. The media were having a field day, while Sinclair, understandably, blamed poor sales on 'bad publicity'. By October it was all over. Sinclair was forced to call in the receivers to his C5 company when debts to 110 individual creditors reached £700,000.

Clive Sinclair had hoped to revolutionize motor transport, creating a quieter, safer, greener way to travel. It was a vision he believed in to the tune of £7 million of his fairly earned **Spectrum** money, but one that was doomed to die. The C5, of course, was never a craze. But mocking it and willing it to fail it was. We slated his half-baked jacuzzi on wheels at every opportunity, while burning fossil fuels at a rate of miles-per-hour, and never gave peace a chance. Forgive us all, Sir Clive, for we knew not what we did.

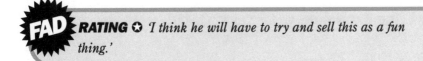

FAD *RATING* ✪ *'I think he will have to try and sell this as a fun thing.'*

ELEVEN TRANSPORT FADS

1. **Stilts.** More economical to fall off than a pogo-stick. Handy for swamp-living.

2. **The Yuppie-Scooter.** Your boss rode it to work. He looked very silly. No one told him.

3. **The Bond Bug.** Orange cheese triangle on three wheels.

4. **The Bubble Car.** Only ever seen on *Blue Peter*.

5. **The Reliant Robin.** When invalid carriages go bad.

6. **The Invalid Carriage.** Obsolete now that we have banned invalids.

7. **The Budget Airline.** 'They're cheap because they don't give you any food.' Yes, what a shame to say goodbye to that luxury £100 meal in a plastic tray.

8. **The Microlite Aircraft.** Hang-glider with motor, and sitting duck for air rifles.

9. **The Go-Kart.** Your old pram wheels, two bits of wood and a free trip to Casualty.

10. **The Raft.** Some empty petrol cans, some old tyres, three bits of wood and a visit from the river police.

11. **The Batmobile.** Well – wouldn't *you*?

The Sinclair ZX Spectrum

Clive Sinclair made a number of mistakes, but the Spectrum was not one of them. Following from early successes with the programmable microcomputers ZX80 and ZX81, Sinclair imbued his most popular release with not only more processing power and more memory but colour graphics too, hence the name. For its market and its time, the Spectrum could not be beaten. The size of a celebrity memoir but with so much more inside, this fun-sized console dispensed with the touch-sensitive flat keyboard in favour of individual rubberized keys, giving its users a tactile thrill that was compounded by the unit's versatility as a working computer. Yes, it had everything. For the boffins, there was the programming, which allowed boys with lank hair to use words such as 'gosub' in ordinary conversation. For the rest, there were games. Whether you laboriously typed them in from the comics and magazines which had sprung up to service the expanding craze or uploaded the data in audio format from gaudily packaged cassette tapes, Spectrum games opened up a world of screen-based entertainment that was both a satisfying development from the standalone **TV Game** (bip-bop tennis anyone?) and a tantalizing forerunner to the Game Boy and Sega Megadrive. It was a toy adults felt they could play with too, and progressive parents could indulge their offspring while pretending they were helping with learning. Spectrum habits developed. You might put your hand in the fridge hoping to pull out a *Munch Bunch* **yoghurt**, only to find 'your' 24k-RAM booster pack chilling quietly under a lettuce. Dads believed putting microchips in the cooler would improve their performance.

The Spectrum burst on to the scene at a time when most computers were the size of a fridge and best given a room of their own. Not only was the Spectrum affordable, but – unlike the giant IBM PCs that now clog up our offices – it worked. Having designed and built the bestselling micro-computer of all time, Sinclair should have been poised to take a seat at the top table of the information age, in which names like Bill Gates and Steve Jobs still dominate. Sadly he stood still and let Amstrad buy his business. 'I don't like running a company,' he told the *Financial Times* recently. 'I'm not averse to making money but I just don't like managing people. It's a distraction.'

 RATING ✪✪✪ *'My dad says only I'm allowed to use it.'*

HOW TO START A CRAZE
Publicize

In the early eighties, *Harpers & Queen* editor Peter York made full use of his media contacts and influence in spreading the word about the Sloane Ranger. Newspapers loved talking about these social archetypes, and cartoonists loved mocking them in pen and ink. York followed all the rules of craze-making: he kept his ear to the ground by knowing the market for his magazine; he picked up on a trend that existed anyway, but repackaged it as something all his own; then he sold, sold, sold. Remember, folks, he had a book out. It became one of the bestselling books of the whole decade. The same thing happened with the Chav. Getting editorial media coverage is even better than advertising. It goes deeper and lasts longer.

The Sindy Doll

Poor old Sindy. British Mattel-rival Pedigree tried enviably well to topple the reign of **Barbie**®, queen of the bimbos, with the homegrown Sindy, an altogether more wholesome girl. Despite being petite, svelte, better looking and owning her own whole house, Sindy simply could not compete with that brash all-American glamour. Now that Barbie® has finally dumped Ken for her ski instructor, Dave, and is swanning around the pistes with her preternatural tan, where is our Sindy? Behind the till at Lidl, that's where. She really was the **Betamax** of toy dolls.

 RATING ✪✪✪ *'Sindy says will Action Man go out with her?'*

THAT WAS THE YEAR...
Nineties Toy Crazes

1990 The Teenage Mutant 'Hero' Turtles. Censored ninja fun.

1991 Nintendo Game Boy. Thumb-ache ahoy.

1992 *Thunderbirds* are go. Again.

1993 Power Rangers. Not to be mistaken for Sloane Rangers.

1994 Magic Eye™. Migraine antics from the USA.

1995 Pogs. Cardboard was never so expensive.

1996 Buzz Lightyear lands. Aisle-rage soars.

1997 *Teletubbies*, Tamagotchi and Beanie Babies. Four-syllabic mania.

1998 The Yo-Yo®. Keeps on coming back up...

1999 Pokémon. Doodles were never so expensive, etc.

The Skateboard

Surf's up (*see* **Surfing**). Hooray! But what if it isn't up? What if surf's not only down but taking Prozac for Seasonal Affective Disorder (*see* **Fimo®**)? What then? Well, fear not. You can always attach a pair of **roller skates** to your board and surf the sidewalk or pavement. This, some skate historians will have us believe, is how the skateboard developed. What lunacy. It might be true, but the beloved wheely board was already about in the form of the **scooter**. All you had to do was break off the central pole and handlebar. That's when foot-propelled transport started to feel as free as the sea. Well, almost.

Early skateboards appeared in the fifties, their design influenced gradually, rather than initially, by surfboards. But as with so many crazes (*see* **The Yo-Yo®**, for example), it wasn't until companies began to brand their boards that serious purchasing commenced. Hobie Alter's board, launched as early as 1962, was an early mass-produced must-have, taking its lifestyle cues from the surfing world. The first 'wave' of the craze swiftly followed, ridden by the hip but broken early on by a sea-wall of health-and-safety enthusiasts. This blip would soon pass; in fact, the skateboard tide would turn many times as the trend gathered momentum. As with the roller skate, the fashion really didn't hit critical mass until the technology caught up with our aspirations.

The early seventies brought skateboard wheels out of the solid-clay era and into polyurethane. A smoother, more comfortable ride was thus offered, as well as the 'kicktail', allowing for greater control over lift and the tricks that would afford. Precision bearings were introduced in 1975, giving less friction and so greater speed. As the skateboard became less like a gimmick and more like a sport, with its own professionals, so our interest grew.

More interesting than the boards themselves was the image of the skater. Getting the right sneakers was as important as getting the right board. As skateboarding took off in the UK, local authorities went on a banning spree (*see* **Marbles**). Just as storm drains had proven popular in the US, concrete-heavy shopping precincts were Brit-skater heaven and, predictably, the issue of health and safety was raised again. The answer to such liberating, freelance skateboarding was clearly to contain the phenomenon. So began the era of council-funded skateboard parks. As far as the author can discern, this is when interest began to decline again.

Skateboarding never disappeared, it retained a grass-roots, perhaps even cultish, appeal. Always an urban thing, it was almost certainly the approbation of the authorities that helped to lend the sport an underground, streetwise feel. Many pro-skaters, such as Steve Rocco, went into business for themselves, shifting power away from toy

---

ELEVEN SKATEBOARD TRICKS

1. **Nose Grab**
2. **Melon Grab**
3. **Sex-Change**
4. **Willy Grind**
5. **Barely Grind**
6. **Salad Grind**
7. **Roast Beef**
8. **Laser Flip**
9. **Nose Slide**
10. **Lip Slide**
11. **Ollie**

manufacturers and into the hands of the dedicated. As the eighties and nineties rolled on, skateboard chic grew to encompass not only a sport and a board but a taste for grungey, punk-style music, low-slung jeans and baggy casual clothes. Skater types became icons of youthful rebellion, and kids identified with this, a bona fide sport for city drop-outs, summed up in so many ways by teen songstrel Avril Lavigne's 2002 hit paean to baggy clothes, 'Skater Boy'.

Lavigne's carefully targeted song of love across the class divide (ballet girl rejects skater boy, Lavigne gets him and gloats to the West Coast beat) was probably more an indication that big business had begun to recognize the boy-centred skater culture as a legitimate target. As skateboarding, inline roller-skating and extreme sports such as snowboarding began to cross over, large companies saw a way to reach the youth spending-power they so dearly craved. By associating their clothes, shoes, crisps or whatever with skater chic, they found a way to make young males want the guff they made. That's when the activity stopped being an underground, cultish movement and the boundaries of ownership began to blur. While skateboarding has enjoyed a new spike of popularity among American and British kids in recent years, it is not certain whether corporate dollars are driving the trend or simply trying to follow it.

But while fashions change, skateboarding remains rather more than the sum of its lifestyle accessories. Though subject to craze-like activity, it seems unlikely that the sport/mode of transport will ever go away. Like the surfboard, it found its own technological apogee, established its own range of sports, its own clothing fashion, its own music and its own lifestyle long before the big bucks got involved. You can't ignore that. That's culture. Go, 'dude'.

FAD *RATING* ✪✪✪✪✪ *'Bogus.'*

Skipping

Her Majesty's purveyor of punk, Malcolm McLaren, did his level best to convince us that this classic rope-based playground activity for girls could make it as a hip new 'street' craze, with his hit single 'Double Dutch'. He was wrong. That did not stop the tune from flying up the charts, but he was looking the other way when Breakdancing took hold. Never mind, Malcolm.

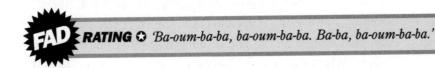

FAD RATING ✪ *'Ba-oum-ba-ba, ba-oum-ba-ba. Ba-ba, ba-oum-ba-ba.'*

The Slinky®

There is something special that distinguishes the entrepreneur or inventor from the rest of us. Most of us will experience at least once or twice in our lives something odd and new that excites or intrigues us: a chance action or series of events might reveal a strange phenomenon or unexpected result. What we tend to do is wonder, marvel, perhaps exclaim. And then we have a nice cup of tea and a good sit-down, perhaps switch on the television, and let our brains quietly atrophy before bed-time. The inventor, however can't let it go. And the entrepreneur makes a leap of faith, puts money on the line or energizes others into funding his or her vision. When the two are combined you get something that either a) changes the course of history, technology, communication or thinking for ever or b) becomes the Slinky®.

Ours is not to judge the merits or demerits of such items. What has the author of this book invented today? He'll tell you: the condensed milk and Ritz biscuit taste sensation. Unmarketable. His chief leap of faith on this rather bitter December afternoon has been to risk a wind-lashed trip across the road to the Village Post Office Store on the off chance that there might be a warm pasty in there with his name on it. This hazard, in fact, paid off, but otherwise it's been a quiet Sunday.

For Richard James, in 1943, things worked out differently. He was in Philadelphia, where he worked as a naval engineer. His task was to find a way to prevent recoil on a large scale from damaging instruments and navigational equipment when the ship's guns were fired. With this in mind, he was looking into tension springs, when one of his prototypes fell off the bench. Except it didn't. It walked off.

The first time you see a Slinky® in action, this is precisely the sensation it evokes. The thing appears to be alive, and this proves to be thoroughly engrossing. It's metal, it's industrial. And yet it moves in an organic, fluid way. How can this be? You watch it walk down the stairs, you coax it into behaving more and more like an animal, doing tricks and amusing your friends and family. Before you know it, hours have passed.

In truth, James's spring did not really walk at first. But he saw in its movements the potential, and simply couldn't let it go. It was a question of getting the right steel and the right tension. The key is getting a low tension and a big mass. All springs can move in waves, but these are generally too small and fast to see, as springs usually have high tension in order to 'bounce'. The lower the tension and bigger the mass, the easier it is to see these longitudinal waves. This is what happens with the Slinky®: it is the slow wave that allows it to walk. James worked at it, eventually perfecting the tension-to-mass ratio in 1945.

When he took his coil home to the kids, he saw that, before long, the neighbours' kids were playing with it too. And here's where James took his leap of faith. He spent his own money at a local machine shop and turned out several hundred springs. Thus stocked, James convinced a local retailer to give him a concession stand, where he offered his half-inch coils at a dollar each. He had absolutely no trouble in shifting them. James's wife, Betty, recalls: 'We had 400 "Slinkys"® and sold them all in ninety minutes.' From that point on the Slinky® boinged its way into the hearts of 250 million fans.

Most entrepreneurs would be happy with that result. But wealth did not make Richard James happy. Seeking answers to the human conundrum that coiled steel simply could not provide, James became involved with a marginal religious group, to which he donated large amounts of his company's money. In 1960 he left Betty and his six children to join the cult in Bolivia, where he died in 1974. It was left to Betty James to protect the company from the jaws of the receivers. During her time at the reins she instigated massive marketing campaigns and innovated new designs, including plastic Slinkys® which were safer for children. They are also rather more reliable walkers. It is down to Betty's acumen that the walking steel sparked off further Slinky® crazes in the sixties, the seventies and now again in the twenty-first century.

If you're having trouble getting your Slinky® to walk, you may have misjudged the angle. According to data collected by leading Slinky® expert Erica Byrne, of Slinky.org, the critical angle for Slinky® walking is 24 degrees. Anywhere between 24 and 41 degrees should guarantee success. Above 41 degrees and you're asking for trouble. Just bear that in mind.

Over the years, the toy has had many other uses. Just the other night on television the author witnessed the walking metal spring being used as a model to represent the male rectal passage. A man poked the spring round about the prostate and a woman winced. That's show business. Others use it for physics demonstrations: it's adept at showing compression waves, centripetal force and harmonic waves. Betty James claims it can be used as a pecan-picker. These days she can afford to put it on to more domestic chores: she sold the brand in 1998 to a company called Poof Toys, who wisely market it under the Ideal Toy brand. But the author's favourite part of the Slinky® story is that the address of James Industries Inc. is Slinky Avenue, Hollidaysburg. If that ain't success, what is?

FAD RATING ✪✪✪✪ *'Look, it walks downstairs. Hold on, I'll try again.'*

The Sloane Ranger

'Sloane Ranger' is a term coined by the British writer Peter York in his bestselling 1981 book *The Official Sloane Ranger Handbook*, co-written with Ann Barr. Named after a cross between Sloane Square in London and The Lone Ranger, the 'Sloane' character typified a specific genre of the British upper-middle-class. Typically, this Chelsea-dwelling, Range Rover-driving socialite would hang around in London's expensive West End clubs speaking, or whinnying, a horsey dialect of abbreviated public-school *patois*.

They wouldn't really have chosen to be at the club, but they felt *motg*, or morally obliged to go since the *wrinklies*, 'Ma and Pa' to the *hoi-polloi*, were throwing it for some charity do, and would probably have a *sohf*, or sense of humour failure, if they failed to get their privileged behind off the *sofa* and put on a ball gown. In any case it was better than minding the *ankle-biters* or entertaining Priscilla's 'husband,' that *bolter* who suddenly returned from Malaysia to find his wife had set up her own cosmetics range and didn't need him *tyvm* (thank you very much). Stiff upper lips all round, but *wrm*, or what really mattered, was braying to each other about such pressing issues as 'what's the best Glyndebourne you've ever been to?'

These were the well-heeled but feckless offspring of wealthy, preferably royal parents who lazed around with nothing much to do except wear navy blue, denounce the fish-knife as 'non-u', flaunt ill-

---

THAT WAS THE YEAR
Twenty-First-Century Toy Crazes

2000 Robotic Pets and Aluminium Folding Scooters.

2001 Bob the Builder, Pogo Sticks bounce back.

2002 Beyblades, Micropets.

2003 Yucky Yo Balls. Banned.

gotten finance (Pa's chargecard) and speak too loudly in affected stretched vowels. This successful rebranding of the Hooray Henry was lapped up in the eighties by newspapers such as the *Daily Mail*, especially by class-obsessed columnist the late Lynda Lee-Potter, whose readers aspired to but could never reach this level of privilege and breeding. The Sloane is not to be confused with the **Yuppie**, who had to work for every wad. Mr York, meanwhile, was uniquely qualified to comment as he was then editor of *Harpers & Queen*, the glossy Sloane style-bible and a self-confessed Sloane.

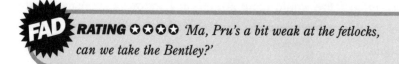

FAD **RATING** ✪✪✪✪ *'Ma, Pru's a bit weak at the fetlocks, can we take the Bentley?'*

GREAT BETTYS IN HISTORY

Betty J. Morris

The 'B' in K & B Innovations was a Wisconsin Cub-Scout leader who in the course of doing her 'duty to God and to the Queen' discovered, along with her Baloo and subsequent business partner Katie Bloomberg, that certain plastic pots and packets could be shrunk in a domestic oven. What fun. But this Akela, like all great inventors, could not let it go. She developed her own sheets of shrinkable plastic which could be manipulated, cut, coloured and assembled into fun arts and crafts. These were marketed under the name 'Shrinky Dink'®. Betty's singular cookery demonstration led to total retail sales estimated at $76million (£40million). She told *The Bumper Book of Fads and Crazes*: 'Thirty years and counting. Some fad, hey?' Hooray for Betty.

The Slogan T-Shirt

Frankie said 'RELAX' originally, the Liverpool-based one-hit wonderband Frankie Goes To Hollywood having ripped off the idea from Katherine Hamnett's popular political T-Shirt range. This soon led to all sorts of things appearing in bold black type on white T-Shirts. Before long everyone was in on the act, including **designer stubble** hero George Michael and his Wham! partner Andrew Ridgeley. Within what seemed like days, the slogan T-Shirt had taken over where the badge had left off. We were wearing our hearts on our sleeves, literally. The only drawback was that no one except Hamnett, whose designs were eclipsed, had anything much to say.

 RATING ✪✪✪ *'Frankie says open your wallet.'*

Slot-Car Racing

See Scalextric.

The Smurf

Rivalled for pointlessness only by the **pet rock**, the Smurf was the creation of Belgian cartoonist Pierre 'Peyo' Culliford. A package from the outset, the Smurfs were a cartoon strip, a series of animated television shows, a string of bad novelty pop songs by Pierre 'Father Abraham' Kartner and, worst of all, an endless range of affordable toy figurines. Basically blue trolls with silly hats, the Smurf empire managed to outsell the deluge of **Star Wars** merchandise from about 1979 to 1982. Then, as swiftly as they appeared, they were gone. Wherever they were coming from, they all went back to Smurf land where they belonged. No one had a major problem with that.

FAD ★ *RATING* ✪✪✪✪ *'Why did they all talk this way?'*

HOW TO START A CRAZE

Release a pop song

Would anyone really have thought American line dancing was cool if Steps had not released their carefully packaged song and dance set? Even better was the Smurf song: a three-minute advert for useless blue toy collectibles that went out on prime time BBC television and radio. You have to be sneaky if you want to advertise on the Beeb. Malcolm McLaren made a sterling effort with his Double Dutch song in a bid to send the country into a skipping frenzy. Sadly the song was better than the craze. The slew of Mike Batt-penned Womble tie-in songs were an easier proposition. *The Wombles* was already a BBC show, and how we bought those PVA toothbrush holders! The author's was Tomsk. After a bit he smelled bad. Best if we don't dwell too long on 'The Birdy Song'.

The Snake Belt

It was elasticated. It was striped. It was adjustable. It fastened with two interlocking S-shaped snakes. It was the snake-belt. Once, it was everywhere. Now it is gone. But the snake belt was not mere ephemera. This brilliantly designed waist appliance has an admirable pedigree and deserves a place in the fad hall of fame.

Appearing first in England in the late nineteenth century, the snake belt was a favourite among cricketers. It was less restrictive than braces and indeed would expand with the movements of the players. That it was finely adjustable by means of a loop and slide made it a first choice for school wear too. With three stripes in a two-colour combination, the belt was perfect for displaying school-uniform or sports-team colours. Its use was often compulsory in schools, and the item could usually be bought at uniform outfitters. The elastic, coupled with the metal snake, also meant the belt was perfect for whipping siblings or troublesome classmates.

The snake belt enjoyed widespread patronage from the turn of the last century until the sixties. During the seventies, however, it dwindled in popularity until it hissed its last and disappeared from view, perhaps under a rock. In the eighties, the decade the **Yuppie** made his own, braces made an unwelcome comeback, while belts became more rudimentary.

The snake belt simply fell out of fashion but should be remembered for its faddish design. Modern belts use the primitive pin and pim-hole system. When the wearer expands due to

FAD Fact According to the Advertising Standard Authority, the adverts most likely to cause complaint are those aimed at children.

laziness and gluttony, a new belt must be bought. Should the wearer contract due to stress or the fad diet, additional pim-holes must be drilled into the leather, leaving a dangling long end, or *fribulum*. But the snake belt overcame this, first by elastic and second by the ingenious loop and clasp system. The reader might think that the snake belt was nothing more than a single brace, and that girdling oneself into what is essentially a rucksack strap with lumpy serpentine appendages is somewhat complex and uncomfortable, allowing for all kinds of unseemly belt-side snarl-ups. But that's where the reader would be wrong. The beloved snake belt will always be the **Betamax video** of waistline apparel.

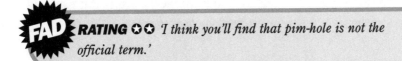

FAD RATING ✪✪ *'I think you'll find that pim-hole is not the official term.'*

The Snood

The authentic snood of hair history is a kind of crocheted net or 'bun-warmer'. A wartime favourite, the snood enjoyed an early flush of success from around 1939, as women found it practical for keeping their hair out of the machinery in the bullet- or parachute-factories. Snood-wearing did not last, but the word itself enjoyed a much vaunted renaissance in the eighties at the hands of pop stars such as Nik Kershaw, Paul King and Duran Duran. This version was little more than a baggy woollen tube worn loosely about the neck, preferably coupled with a pair of the infinitely more ridiculous **leg-warmers**.

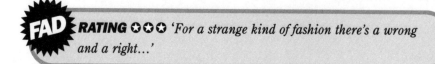

FAD **RATING** ✪✪✪ *'For a strange kind of fashion there's a wrong and a right...'*

The SodaStream

Home from school at last. Pausing only to take off your **snake belt**, you head for the kitchen and begin the ritual. Fill up the swirly glass bottle from the tap, ram it up the chute, pull on the lever to lock, then jam down the button on the top to carbonate. Hoorah. Then pour in the syrup. Since you filled the water up to the top, the addition of syrup means the whole glutinous mixture overflows, your fingers are sticky and so you must lick them. It is 1979. You are, of course, the height of fashion and that is why you must 'get busy with the fizzy.'

But in fact you are *so* seventy-six years ago. The SodaStream – a machine for laboriously creating carbonated water in the comfort of your own home – was first marketed in 1903 by Gilbey's Gin. It was an upmarket product in which only the wealthier households – such as Buckingham Palace, which was an early implementer – could afford to invest. No sickly syrups for His Majesty, though. Pure carbonated H_2O was ambrosia enough and, luckily, that was all that was available. It took twenty or so years before concentrated flavourings such as Sarsaparilla and Cherry Ciderette were introduced. It is not known whether the current queen invested. Sources close to Buckingham Palace suggest she put her money into **Tupperware**.

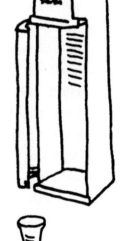

In the thirties, the machine, then known as the Penny Monster, was sold mainly to retailers, who fizzed on demand for their customers. And the SodaStream's rise to domestic power was hardly meteoric. It wasn't until the seventies that the company began to

FAD Fact

A third of under-sevens fail to reach minimum recommended activity levels. Two-thirds of fifteen-year-old girls are classified 'inactive'.
(British Heart Foundation)

In 2002, 95 per cent of children's television advertising was for fatty, salty or sugary foods.
(Sustain)

advertise the home carbonation centre as a consumer product. Popular fez-wearing entertainer, Tommy Cooper, was enlisted to endorse the home-brew pop. According to Mr Cooper, with the SodaStream you could make your favourite fizzy drinks at home, 'just like that'. The result of this drive was a full-scale craze, peaking in the eighties.

Everyone who was anyone had one. Your best mate had one. Your cousin had one. The author did not. The author's mother, already lumbered with a hyperactive child, was suspicious of any combination of sugar and money, and the SodaStream became a forbidden fruit, only adding to its appeal. In almost all households, SodaStream use was rationed in one form or another. Some mothers simply banned it. Others allowed one drink per day. Some parents believed bubbles were the problem and limited the carbonation to frankly unworkable levels.

But bubbles were not the problem. The problem was this. They simply weren't your favourite fizzy drinks. No amount of advertising could mask the fact that Sodastream Cola did not taste like Coke. Nor did any of it taste like what it ought. In fact, a surfeit of bubbliness was the least of the problems. There is a reason why brand-marketing works. SodaStream, in effect, offered kids the beverage equivalent of Tesco's trainers. Plus, there was all that ritual. Why should we get busy with the fizzy when someone has already done it for us, and better? Serious child-obesity is impossible with all that work to do. Far better to steal the money your mam left out for the milkman and gorge yourself on Cresta.

But the milkmen were in on it too (*see* **Milk**). Gilbey's weren't letting go without a fight, and during the nineties it was possible to get your

SodaStream requisites delivered with your daily pinta. TV's Lenny Henry was employed to encourage consumption, but by now consumers were on a health kick. Perhaps the milk-run idea was a step too far for protective parents. In 1998 Gilbey's sold the brand to the Soda Club Group. SodaStream is now available worldwide, but somehow the craze is dead. You can get the current incarnation at Argos, complete with new-style plastic bottles. Or, if nostalgia prompts you to seek out those swirly glass bottles, you're sure to find an unwanted vintage model at Kessingland car-boot sale. It's fair to say they haven't held their price.

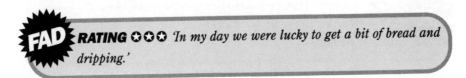

FAD **RATING** ✪✪✪ *'In my day we were lucky to get a bit of bread and dripping.'*

Space Dust

Powdered candy that popped and crackled in your mouth giving momentary excitement and mild pain. Banned in every school, mistrusted by all parents, leading to covert use in all playgrounds. The thing to do was to snort it or give it to the cat.

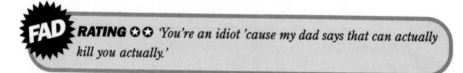

FAD RATING ✪✪ *'You're an idiot 'cause my dad says that can actually kill you actually.'*

ELEVEN SWEET FADS

1. **'Sweet' Cigarettes.** Cheap rice paper and chocolate snack offered by beneficent tobacco company… Or starch stick with pink end. Your choice, until they were banned.

2. **Fizz Bombs.** Dry on the outside, dry on the inside.

3. **Gold Rush.** Tiny pink bubblegum off-cuts coated in 'gold' and sold in a Wild West pouch with a drawstring.

4. **Splicer.** That mythical tricolour chew bar. But where did it go?

5. **Bazooka Joe.** Cult bubble gum and cult comic strip all in one.

6. **Jaw-Breakers.** Alternately sweet and sour, the challenge was to keep the mammoth gob-stopper in your face for the three hours it took your saliva to break it down into a tiny ball of chewing gum. Mmm.

7. **Fisherman's Friend.** No friend of yours though.

8. **Victory V.** Ether-based entertainment without prescription.

9. **Spangles.** Was a boiled sweet ever so sorely missed?

10. **Sherbet Fountain.** Last desperate attempt to sell licorice.

11. **Black Jack and Fruit Salad chews.** At least one is still sewn into the lining of your parka.

The Space Hopper

This iconic inflatable was a giant orange blob with a grinning printed face and two ribbed antennae. You straddled its girth, gripped its feelers and space-hopped down the street, round the corner and right into your neighbour's paddling pool, causing widespread hilarity. Either that or you fell straight off and hurt your tailbone.

This quintessential seventies character was manufactured and marketed in the UK by Mettoy and bounced its way into our affections over the summer of 1971. Mettoy told the story that one of their bosses spotted kids bouncing on inflatable buoys in Italy and got the idea from there. But might they not, in fact, have been Pon Pons?

The original inflatable hopper was indeed called the 'Pon Pon' and was invented in 1963 by an Italian called Aquilino Cosani. Cosani patented his creation in Italy in 1968 and in America three years later, for 'recreative and sporting use'. His ball had a hard handle grafted on to the vinyl. If the soft moulded antennae of the Space Hopper were a welcome innovation to safety-conscious parents, and the cheeky face a turn-on for kids, the truth is, they were most probably patent-busting necessities for the myriad imitators. Although the Space Hopper we know and love came to us via Mettoy, various

FAD Fact Kiss goodbye to the pogo-stick and the space-hopper. Research by the Children's Society and the Children's Play Council found youngsters were afraid of being told off and threatened by adults for playing outside. The research found that adults were becoming increasingly intolerant of activities such as bike-riding. A MORI survey in 2003 found that 75 per cent of adults supported an evening curfew for teenagers.

other companies turned out their own Hoppity Hops and the Kangaroo Hops. Cosani's company, Ledraplastic, is still in business, marketing inflatable balls as aids to good posture and gymnastic exercise.

Numerous outfits now market 'space hoppers', offering the full seventies nostalgia experience and urging punters to relive their childhoods. But the author warns you now that, though the new crop are good, if it ain't got the curly horns and the grinning face, it ain't a real Space Hopper. Original seventies Mettoy models are now collector's items fetching ridiculous prices on eBay: up to £200 in original boxes.

As with any collectible, there are communities devoted to the propagation of hopper love and the sharing of hopper information. And as with any collectible, there are those who understand the affection and those who cannot or will not let rubber love bounce into their life. Dave is a man who knows such pain and has allowed the author to reproduce his anguish: 'My wife decided she would burst my original hoppers if they were not sold – well, I did not let her sell them, so we got a divorce, and the night she came to pick up her stuff, she popped the original hoppers. I am now on anti-depressants and see a psychiatrist. I also need a new wife. Are there any women who would want a man with only three original hoppers (used to have six)? They are the main thing in my life.' Readers wishing to avoid such heartache might find it prudent to go down the **pogo-stick** route.

FAD **RATING** ✪✪✪✪ *Does anyone have any pictures of women on Space Hoppers? I would be most grateful to have some emailed to me!'*

Space Invaders

Taito's *Space Invaders* was launched in 1978, a year after **Star Wars** shook our worlds. **Star Wars** may not in truth have influenced Taito's decision to replace the original human soldiers with evil, mandible-waving carnivores from outer space, but surely space mania did nothing to inhibit the growth of this groundbreaking video game.

Is it conceivable that any reader might not be intimate with the game plan? *Space Invaders* pitched a moveable gun (you) against an armada of forty-eight invading alien space ships. You had three chunky shields to hide behind, which were destroyed piecemeal by fire from the marauding fleet, which in turn shifted annoyingly from side to side to fox your attempts at hitting home. In general they advanced on you quicker than you could blast them to kingdom come. The game required almost relentless attacking of the fire button, an annoying and energy-consuming trait overcome by 1980s **Pac-Man** from rival Japanese game company Namco. All this to a soundtrack of menacing bop-bop electronica, a technique later employed by TV's *Who Wants To Be A Millionaire?*

This original shoot 'em up, generally credited to programmer Toshihiro Nishikado, offered an escape from the sporty domain of **Pong** and its competitors, into a sidereal fantasy world attainable simply by putting money in the slot. And how we needed to put money in that slot. *Space Invaders* crime never matched that of the **Pokémon** craze, but even so, kids were still looting Granny's mattress and holding up the corner shop to fund their gaming habits. In Japan, where the game was first released, the craze famously caused a coin shortage. Happy days for Taito. *Space Invaders* also gave a massive boost to the fledgling arcade industry, although younger children could often access it via their local swimming pool, the game being the first such to cross over from arcades. So they could flex their budding muscles for an hour and sustain a decent repetitive strain injury afterwards. Both the yin and the yang there.

FAD Fact During the summer holidays, seven out of ten children spend more time playing with computers or watching TV than in any other hobby. A quarter of parents said their children spent seven hours a day or more in this way. (Powergen)

Space Invaders was not the first electronic arcade game, but it was certainly the one that made the world sit up and take notice. It was swiftly licensed for the **Atari** home console. Never more would we be content with an **Action Man** or a **slot-car** set. Taito's game ushered in a brave new world of inactive gaming, where running in the woods was replaced by staring at a screen. Obesity beckoned. It also confirmed the concept of 'space' as an ongoing concern. A year later, clearly in response to this **Star Wars**- and **Space Invaders**-induced enthusiasm, **Lego** produced its wild new range of Space Lego.

Following the early successes of the **Atari** and the **Sinclair ZX Spectrum**, the world of electronic games has come to be dominated by home-based consoles, while the games themselves offer ever more realistic graphics and sound effects, ever more challenging terrains and missions. So does this clunky, monochrome retro gun-fiesta hold up against the hi-tech millennial fare? Frankly, yes.

FAD RATING ✪✪✪✪✪ *'Classic killing fun.'*

Speak & Spell™

'Now? Spell? Abscess! A... B... S... C... E... S... S, Correct?'

In 1978, in the days before personal computers, chunky gadgets such as Texas Instruments' Speak & Spell™ gave us a hopeful promise of a bright future (*see* **The Teasmaid**), where technology would seamlessly take over dull, menial jobs, such as teaching your first-born to read and write. Speak & Spell™ looked like a giant red and yellow calculator with a built-in carrying handle. Once switched on, to the sound of the familiar bee-boo-bee-boo melody, it launched a spelling-bee contest, limited only by the user's ability to understand American pronunciation coupled with ropey early voice-simulation software. 'Now? Spell? IGANOBANIM!' What *was* that word?

Its limitations aside, the gadget did actually perform its task. Spelling *was* more fun because of Speak & Spell™, a trick that Texas Instruments' follow-up, the arithmetic wizard Little Professor™, failed to master. While Speak & Spell™ fell to the home-computer revolution begun at the turn of the decade with Clive **Sinclair's** ZX80, the machine, like the **Stylophone**™, found a home as a musical instrument on Kraftwerk's 1981 *Computer Love* album.

FAD **RATING ✪✪** *'Now? Spell? Windows 2000!'*

Spirograph®

Things to do with ballpoint pens: (1) Your homework. (2) Make a **pea-shooter**. (3) Eat the end off and replace with a **pencil top**. (4) If all else fails there is Spirograph®. These plastic cogs, impaled by your humble Biro on to a blank sheet of paper, the wallpaper or perhaps a tablecloth, allowed you to make intricate geometric designs for no reason. Hours filled. Things to do with completed Spirograph® designs: (1) leave them taped to the fridge door for weeks until they are curled and stained with spots of fat and coffee. (2) Throw them immediately away. (3) Tidy them into a drawer and throw them away a year later.

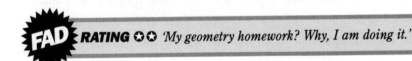

FAD **RATING** ✪✪ *'My geometry homework? Why, I am doing it.'*

The Spokey-Dokey

AND OTHER MOTORBIKE SOUND-EFFECTS

In fact a brand-name bicycle spoke-key, 'spokey-dokey' is also one of a few names given to any device placed on the spokes of your **Raleigh Chopper** or similar fad-bike wheels to make it sound like **Evel Knievel's** motorbike. The author's preferred method was to attach a low-rent **Star Wars** card, such as R2D2, to the forks of his Grifter with a clothes peg in such a manner that it brushed against the spokes as the wheel rotated. This should provide the user with a solid half-hour of motorbike-engine fun. The sound can be augmented with the use of multiple cards placed at strategic intervals, but all are guaranteed to fall off if the rider wheelies off a kerb. This technique came as a replacement for the more widespread Grifter sound effect, created by flipping the mudguard back on itself. The fun lasts as long as your mudguard, i.e., not very.

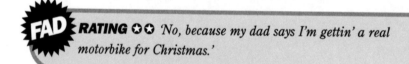

FAD **RATING** ✪✪ *'No, because my dad says I'm gettin' a real motorbike for Christmas.'*

The Spud Gun

There are no two ways about it – the Lone Star Spudmatic pistol was a masterpiece of design. It was genuinely satisfying to hold this weighty firearm in your soiled hands and seek out your prey, be it a Ringos packet flapping in a shrub, or be it a sibling. As the author's older brother recalls: 'When you were six, I fired it at your head every day until you were seven.' The author replies: 'It's funny, I don't recall that at all. In fact, that whole year is a blank.'

The appeal of the Spudmatic was partly tactile. All-metal and solid, it felt like a proper weapon. That's because it was. The pump-action barrel, if thrust with appropriate force into the hard but yielding flesh of a potato tuber, made roughly the same noise – one imagined – as a genuine shot-gun loading up. What's more, using the supplied attachment, the same mechanism could be converted into a water pistol.

It was partly sensual. The potato would weep milky juice from its lesion, the tuber itself would throb in your hand, hot with potential energy. Once loaded into the gun, the vegetable projectile was capable of covering serious distance at high speed, thus ensuring the sought-after mild sting on the face or leg of your victim. It was also possible to load caps, giving a dual thrill.

It was partly practical. The 'piece' was, despite all its power, small enough to fit into the pocket of your Mothercare shorts, to be whipped out and deployed at a moment's notice, wherever you were.

FAD Fact Parents feel under increasing pressure to supply according to their children's demands. They are particularly worried about 'tantrums and tears' when they refuse or fail to provide the right toys. (NFPI)

Sunday School, round your cousin's, at the school fête. In the playground. This is all the information we need to explain both its high popularity and its sudden demise.

Or perhaps it fell foul of new EU regulations on vegetable firearms. Or perhaps it was more insidious still, a victim of the decline of the independent toyshop. But whatever the reason, its wilderness years could not last. This book can report that, after a prolonged absence, the Spudmatic is back. Available from www.gointernational2.co.uk and other outlets, the pocket firearm has returned in all its former glory. Home trials have confirmed its ability to sting a grumpy, tree-felling neighbour from ten feet. This is a good thing. Time for a rebirth of the craze.

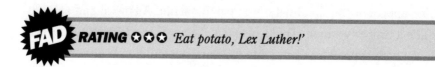

FAD **RATING ✪✪✪** *'Eat potato, Lex Luther!'*

Star Wars

SUPERFAD 'My only concern with Lucas,' admitted Sir Alec Guinness on the UK launch in 1977, 'is that the cinema system will force him into a series of follow-ups to *Star Wars*. He should resist that.' The author is tempted to leave it there, with the unheeded words of Obi-Wan ringing on across the galaxies. But there is a craze to document, so let's just close our eyes, feel the Force and push on.

Of course, by the time the film was finally released in the UK, just after Christmas, we already knew almost everything there was to know about *Star Wars*. In a publicity campaign of unprecedented size and breadth, we, the punters of the future, had been teased almost to the point of death. The radio had been playing a disco version of the theme tune for what seemed like years, building a sense of giddy anticipation even before details of the film were released. Closer to the event, the British papers had been running stories about the movie's success in the States, while in the final run-up to Christmas, reviews, previews, interviews and an inundation of factual trivia about the making of the film thickened into a kind of creamy hype-soup. The beauty of *Star Wars*, though, was that the product did not disappoint.

The story was a familiar one, especially at this time of year. Jack is sent to market to purchase a droid, he comes away with the runtish R2D2 who, in a spasm of malfunction, projects for him a 'vision' of a beautiful princess (Carrie Fisher) captured by the giant Darth Vader (Green Cross Code Man David Prowse). No, let's start again. The unknown actor Mark Hamill played the callow, impetuous Knight Errant (Luke Skywalker) to Sir Alec's venerable Merlin. The wise old druid passes

Excalibur, or the light-sabre, to the younger man. Luke's quest is to rescue the Princess from the evil clutches of Imperial warlord Darth Vader and restore health and prosperity to a sick kingdom. Thus charged, the budding Jedi 'knight' sets off on his steed, the rusty shitbucket known as the Millennium Falcon, along with the tin man (C-3PO), the softy lion (Chewbacca) and the scarecrow without a heart (Harrison Ford's Han Solo). Though few involved in its making and promotion actually believed in its commercial viability, there was really no way this cartoonish fairy tale, liberally sprinkled with 'cutting-edge effects', could fail. It was the oldest story on Earth – *in space*.

But George Lucas's classic film, written and directed by a true artist on a creative mission and labour of love, was itself only a small cog in the machine. Lucas insisted on keeping merchandising rights, and 20th Century Fox, seeing little use for them, since the film was surely destined to flop, let him have his way for free. This was an error. The *Star Wars* craze fed the merchandising game like no craze had done before, with no stone left unturned in pursuit of trinket-based profit. Such mass consumption helped nourish the film-tie-in business into the multibillion-dollar licensing and marketing industry we've come to know and hate. While, in 1977, everyone was taking a major gamble, nowadays merchandising rights are a cornerstone of any film contract.

Entry-level participation was secured with the *Star Wars* trading cards by Topps. Combine these proto-**Pokémon** with the collectible Kenner action-figure toys and you've got the beginnings of mania. Open the branded lunchbox and drink from the Burger King tie-in Coca-Cola glass (due to the non-existence of Burger King in the UK, the author popped into the Toronto branch to get his) at lunchtime, and the drone-like purchase of another pack of trading cards on the way home from school would be quietly suggested to you. Get a pack, get a pack.

Once home, you could don your Darth Vader costume and mask, fire up the official branded battery-powered light-sabre, or the cheaper, not-so-long one from the supermarket, and challenge school friends and siblings to a duel. Actually this 'game' – a robotic re-enactment of a scene from a film – could only have one outcome. 'You be Ben Kenobi and I'll be Darth Vader,' you would bark, offering your hapless opponent a potato sack as a costume. Once you had smote him to death with your over-long red torch, you could get out your figures and do it all again, working them from behind.

Star Wars action-figure play took two basic forms: lining up all the ones you had and boasting about the ones you were 'getting', or acting out selected scenes from the film. Trading could sometimes occur, with the strict proviso that you shout the phrase, 'No swap-backs' before they twigged that Princess Leia was not really and truly equal in value to Darth Vader (*see* **Marbles**). With careful use of these retail products, it was actually possible to live and breathe *Star Wars* all day and all night. *Star Wars* could and would dominate your every thought and influence your every action.

This was the mania side of your disorder. The depression came when you simply could not get a Grand Moff Tarkin card for love nor money. Mainly money. Or you could not find a retail outlet willing to sell you the plastic Millennium Falcon or Tie Fighter you so coveted. That's when the Dark Side got its grip on you. The only treatment was to 'Own *Star Wars* Now on **Betamax Video**'. Then at least you could slide into your fantasy world, do up your **parka** hood and pretend to be a jawa.

The first knock-on effects of *Star Wars* mania could be seen the following year, when Universal released a film remarkably similar in theme yet notably poor by comparison: *Battlestar Galactica*. The same year, the electronic arcade- game industry sparked into life with Taito's **Space Invaders**, Taito having changed human soldiers to marauding aliens at the last minute.

Star Wars fever was kept simmering by our love of space-related merchandise until the second instalment – *The Empire Strikes Back* –

was released in 1980. While tie-in toys have now become the rule, back in 1977, Kenner, who made the original action-figures, took a considerable risk. It paid off, and by the time *Return of the Jedi* burst forth in 1983, *Star Wars* had become a fully fledged brand, a household name that even lent its name to America's controversial plan for a space-based anti-ballistic missile system.

But crazes cannot live on merchandising alone, the driving product has to contain that x-factor. The original *Star Wars* film was the right fantasy at the right time, a vision of an anticipated, perhaps feared, technocracy at a time when home computers were some way off, along a with a 'Force'-shaped reassurance that some values and powers could never be replaced by a microchip. But the gulf between *Return of the Jedi* and 1999's *Phantom Menace* was not just one of time. Overestimating the size of the renewed craze brought ruin to the venerable book-publisher Dorling Kindersley, whose gamble on tie-in books caused a £3 million operating loss and a £14 million write-off against unsold stock. By the time those fateful sums were done, the noble but weakened independent had been captured by the Pearson empire and imprisoned at its Penguin-shaped Death Star on the Strand. The trouble was that times and tastes had moved on. We were, in fact, ready for an altogether different kind of fantasy.

If Lucas's original film owed a lot to Tolkien's *Lord of the Rings* – in its epic opposition of absolute good to absolute evil, in the characterization of Guinness's Gandalf figure to Hamill's unlikely hobbit Skywalker – the makers of the *Lord of the Rings* film trilogy, and the totalitarian merchandising empire that flourished on its back, owed it all to *Star Wars*.

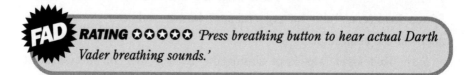

FAD **RATING** ✪✪✪✪✪ *'Press breathing button to hear actual Darth Vader breathing sounds.'*

THOSE CRAZY STAR WARS SPECIAL EFFECTS

Exclusive to all newspapers and magazines c. 1977–8

1. The sound of the laser blasters was made from banging a pylon coil with a spanner.

2. The sound of a 'light-sabre' is made from a movie projector and feedback from live microphone wire in front of a TV.

3. The sound of Han Solo's footsteps in the Death Star were made by dropping uncooked polenta on to cork tiles.

4. The sound of the landspeeder was made from a Flymo engine and a faulty hairdryer, the audio converted to binary, the number sequence perforated on to paper strips, which were then rolled backwards through a restored 1876 Dutch carousel organ by Van den Hooger (now in the Smithsonian).

5. Princess Leia's hair was made from two Chelsea buns on a wire.

Strawberry Shortcake

Strawberry Shortcake, the branded toy doll who is half child, half carbohydrate coma, was marketed to children in America via their teachers. American Greetings, who made the doll and its accompanying range of accessories, offered teachers 'learning materials' for kindergarten children. Through an association with the respectable American Society for the Prevention of Cruelty to Animals, AG was able to target children at the very first stages of learning. Or, as AG put it, 'With these materials, we're pleased to introduce Strawberry Shortcake to a whole new generation.'

The educational kits, which were offered free, aimed to teach children all about pets and how to care for animals, but in fact there were few illustrations of animals on the worksheets. Rather, each one was very clearly branded with Strawberry Shortcake and her 'berry special' friends, including her cat, Custard, and her dog, Pupcake.

'The ASPCA is a non-profit organization whose mission is to prevent cruelty to animals,' the accompanying letter boasted. Yes, but American Greetings is not. That's the company that brought us the **Care Bears**.

FAD Fact Research by the University of Hertfordshire shows that the more television children watch, the more material things they want to own. (Pine & Nash)

So what's the link? Why should teachers use these materials? AG executives Roberta Nusim and Joel Ehrlich, both former teachers, explained: 'Embodying both warmth and charm, this sweet-natured character demonstrates caring, generous, thoughtful behavior as well as shares the meaning of friendship.' That's nice of them. And what's even nicer is they're offering the materials free of charge. 'Feel free to share these materials with fellow educators, including preschool teachers and second grade teachers,' they instructed.

FAD *RATING* ✪✪ *'When Teachers Go Bad.'*

ELEVEN CRAZE-MAKERS

1. **George Hansburg:** The Pogo-Stick (1919).

2. **Donald Duncan:** The Yo-Yo® (1929).

3. **Richard Knerr, Spud Melin:** The Frisbee® (1958); The Hula-Hoop® (1958).

4. **Brian Jarvis, Bert Coleman, Rolf Harris:** The Stylophone™ (1970).

5. **Greg Dahl:** The Pet Rock (1976).

6. **Malcolm McLaren:** Punk fashion (1976).

7. **George Lucas:** *Star Wars* (1977).

8. **Toru Iwatani:** *Pac-Man* (1980).

9. **Tibor Laczi and Tom Kremer:** Rubik's Cube (1980).

10. **Peter York, Ann Barr:** The Sloane Ranger (1981).

11. **Minoru Arakawa:** Pokémon (1999).

The Stylophone™

'I'm a celebrity, buy a small and irritating electronic musical toy.' While these may not have been the actual words uttered by leading marsupial bondage apologist, Rolf Harris, the phrase neatly sums up the Dübreq Stylophone™ story.

Once the initial shock of opening your Christmas package only to come face to face with Rolf's gurning visage was contained and medicated, there was the insertion of the battery to contend with. Proper parents had done this already, of course, but if not, you had the treat of competing against the laws of physics to fit a squat PP3 in the hole without damaging any of the circuitry which this cavity exposed with gay abandon. This *Krypton Factor* task completed, some hours and tantrums later, you were ready to give Mum, Dad and Granny a collective aneurism. Pick up the stylus, prod the 'keyboard' and beeeeeeeeeep beeeeeeeeeep all day long.

This whining parent-irritator, roughly the size of a **Betamax video** tape, was devised in England in 1967 by Brian Jarvis, who ran the broadcast post-production company Dübreq along with Ted and Bert Coleman. Jarvis allegedly hit on the idea while 'fixing' his niece's toy piano. Imagine handing over your pleasantly tinkling percussion instrument and receiving this miniaturized Dalek in return. Poor girl. It was left to Bert Coleman to spot the marketing potential, though, and it wasn't long before he fixed on Rolf Harris, the variety act and painter, as his conduit.

Harris was an obvious target. All the rage on television with his *Rolf On Saturday* show, and backed by The Young Generation, Harris was already an accomplished musician. He was, for example, a virtuoso on the atonal wobble-board, the monotonous didgeridoo and the puffing-your-cheeks-out-and-going-'a-choof-a-hoofa'. The Stylophone™ would clearly be in great company. Coleman stalked the bearded entertainer, finally cornering him at a rehearsal and pressing a Stylophone™ into his paint-spotted antipodean hand. From here on in, the Dübreq Stylophone™ *would* be known as the Rolf Harris Stylophone™.

Once the celebrity endorsement was in place, there was no stopping the thing. Harris promoted it mercilessly on television, even supplying a rather frightening recording of him using it to 'play' the 'William Tell Overture' on a free flexi-disc and releasing books of songs, all with his cult-lobotomized grin plastered over the covers. The result of all this mass brainwashing was a rather daunting demand for the fledgling Dübreq, prompting the tiny company's expansion from basement to factory.

Exposure and celebrity endorsement will get you so far. But after that it's down to the product. And here's where the Stylophone™ fell down. It was rubbish. Oh, it looked great, an iconic and futuristic piece of late sixties design, possibly the most beautifully crafted electronic instrument ever created, especially the woodgrain model. And in an age when electronic music was still in its foetal stage, the Stylophone™ really did look as though it was from space, an image hardly hampered by David Bowie's use of the 'instrument' on his hit album *Space Oddity*.

But there the comparisons to music must end. In the hands of talented multi-instrumentalists, the Stylophone™ could be persuaded to play music, but that did not mean it was an instrument. Firstly, it was monophonic, meaning that only one note could be played – or, more accurately, switched on – at a time. Secondly, the attached stylus, which closed a circuit to make the note, was a very unmusical device: as any pianist will tell you, ten fingers beats a pointed stick hands down. Lastly, the machine, though it could be coaxed into vibrato, was not velocity-sensitive, so there was no scope for expression. In fact it was less a musical instrument and more a deluxe siren.

All this meant that the novelty soon wore off. German techno-music pioneers Kraftwerk may have pictured themselves Stylophoning it up a treat on the sleeve of their 1981 album *Computer World*, and indeed used the instrument to provide melodic sounds throughout their record. But it was a kind of ironic, Teutonic joke on a record carried by a hit single called 'Pocket Calculator': other non-instruments for the album included the **Speak & Spell**™ and a Texas Instruments electronic translator.

Sadly, Dübreq itself had shut up shop only a year before the release of this record, when the three directors suddenly decided to pursue 'new career paths' (*see* **The Team-Building Weekend**). Those were the wilderness years, but today, the Stylophone™ is making a comeback as a 'vintage' collectible. Nostalgia-happy wallet-holders are clamouring for the little monsters, and just as well – it's one less plastic gremlin tweeting in the land-fills. Oddly, it has kept its 'value'. The original price was £8 18s 6d – around £95 in today's coinage – and the second-hand price is roughly the same. This new interest has prompted Dübreq to re-form and ask for money to make more instruments. Good luck with that. Meanwhile, the original pieces can be bought from various websites and the occasional music shop, so if you feel that urge to point and squeak, go right ahead. They can mock all they like, but they can't touch you for it.

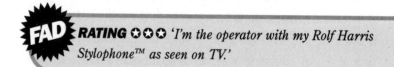

FAD **RATING** ✪✪✪ *'I'm the operator with my Rolf Harris Stylophone*™ *as seen on TV.'*

Subbuteo

This cult flick-based football game was designed in England by Peter Adolph and launched in 1947. You had a mat with a football pitch marked on it. You laid that on your table. Then you positioned your players. Subbuteo players were tiny models of men on a **Weeble**-style half-globe base. The idea was to flick the players with your fingers and make them hit a ball into a net: all the skill and excitement of a football match. Subbuteo players wobbled. Unlike **Weebles**, however, Subbuteo players did fall down. Despite this, or perhaps because of it, Subbuteo has, along with **Dungeons and Dragons**, become one of the most avidly collected and severely 'hobbied' games of the twentieth century.

The original players were flat cardboard drawings stuck into half a Malteser (fact!), but celluloid followed swiftly after. The first heavy, three-dimensional players appeared in 1961, followed by a more detailed design in 1967, including ripples and folds in the players' jerseys. Collectors have distinct categories for all of these players. Do you have a 'walker,' a 'scarecrow,' a 'zombie' or a 'dwarf'? If so, it could be worth money to you.

There are two schools of thought about Subutteo. Some say it is a fiddly, silly game that is nothing like football. Others contest that it is, in fact, a complex game of extreme skill. These people have set up clubs and associations to give credence to this philosophy. There is undoubtedly one near you. One thing is certain, the players are rather satisfying to behold and eminently collectible. And that is enough to push this odd, finger-flicking pursuit into the Fad Book of Records.

And if you're wondering about the name, well – Adolph originally thought he would score by naming his game after his favourite bird, the

Hobby Falcon. The British Patent Office, however, declared 'The Hobby' offside. Not to be cornered, Adolph deftly passed the name into Latin translation to give Falco Subbuteo. And that's the Beautiful Name.

FAD **RATING** ✪✪✪✪ *'Flick it, flick it, flick it, flick it!'*

HOW TO START A CRAZE
Make a film

If *Wayne's World* had never existed, the whole of the Anglophone world would never have insisted on putting the word 'not' after every sentence. Catchphrases are useless tools for marketing – *not*. Once you've got the world talking your language, you can sell them anything. The success of products relating to *Toy Story*, *Shrek*, *Pocahontas* et al might seem like a recent phenomenon, but would the CB radio ever have caught the imagination of the masses if it hadn't been for *Smokey and the Bandit* or *Convoy*? That's not to mention *Star Wars*, the outsider film that broke the merchandising mould.

Surfing

Dennis Wilson was in fact the only so-called 'Beach Boy' who did any surfing, in the USA or otherwise. The others were along for the ride. But the famous 1963 song and its all-singing group were as much a product of the craze for surfing as, say, Avril Lavigne and her 'Skater Boy' tune were a function of twenty-first-century **skateboard** power. Where there are crazes there are markets, and where there are markets there are opportunities.

The sport of riding waves on a board developed among the seafaring Polynesian peoples of the eastern Pacific and was first recorded in Kealakekua Bay, Hawaii, by James King, Captain Cook's lieutenant, in 1779. Enmeshed in the culture since the dawn of time, Polynesian wave-riding had ritual and religious significance as well as its place as a sport. There were chants, taboos and worshipful practices in which surfing played an important role. Standing up on belly-boards was a development of a deep-held custom as widespread as the Polynesian people themselves, a refinement that Hawaiians claim as their own.

Within years of Cook's discovery of the Hawaiian islands and the subsequent publication of his and King's diaries, Christian missionaries arrived to convert the age-old culture and polytheistic religion of the Polynesians to their way of thinking. These Calvinists, the historians say, effectively suppressed surfing by discouraging its support system. Hawaiians were urged to work more, wear more clothes and exercise a stricter division between men and women socializing. Like many strict religious organizations, the Calvinists saw sport and recreation as a corrupting influence. By the time the US Marines arrived in 1898 to

occupy and annexe the islands (*see* **Action Man, Barbie**®), surfing in
Hawaii had dwindled to a minority pastime.

The migration of the sport to California, however, may have started
long before this, possibly brought across by Hawaiian boat crews. The
writer Jack London discovered the joys of surfing on a visit to Hawaii in
the first years of the twentieth century, when he fell in with the journalist
Alexander Hume Ford and Irish Hawaiian George Freeth. Inspired by
the 'manly' sport, London wrote articles on the subject. The oxygen of
his publicity prompted a Californian captain of industry to invite Freeth
across to give a demonstration. Meanwhile, Hume Ford had been
lobbying the Hawaiian authorities for an area dedicated to the
preservation of the ancient culture at Waikiki, stressing the
opportunities for tourism. This was effective and, simultaneously, native
Hawaiians formed surf clubs and began competitions. In 1912, Hawaiian
beach boy Duke Paoa Kahanamoku, already a sporting celebrity on
Hawaii, visited California and caught the fancy of the masses with his
athletic demonstrations of swimming and surfing. An Olympic gold-
medal winner, the master swimmer was courted by Hollywood. He
appeared in numerous films and introduced his influential new friends to
his favourite sport of surfing. He also visited Australia in 1915, kick-
starting interest in the sport there.

Surfing in California grew steadily in the following years, with clubs
and competitions springing up along the coast. Alluring images in books
ensured widespread dissemination of the surfing lifestyle. By the early
fifties, the scene was beginning to boom, and then in 1959, the first surf
movie, *Gidget*, was released. Its future fate was sealed. It needed only the
efforts of pop stars Dick Dale and the Beach Boys to send America into
full-blown mania.

And full-blown industry.

The British surfing boom in the late twentieth century and across the
millennium – while driven by the international success of the

professional sport and a slew of cool films – was as much about wearing the right Rip Curl fashions and painting your nose with fluorescent sun cream as it was about actually getting into the water. A sport in which the ancients hewed their boards directly from the hardwood trees and wore a loincloth had developed into a multimillion-pound industry and a beach lifestyle to which many aspired. While the sun and surf of Bondi did not readily translate to the freezing coasts of Cornwall, there was no end to the accessories with which a dedicated surfer could console himself. Hard pressed to assimilate the skills of the pros, the majority opted simply to wear the fashions down the pub and enjoy the credibility afforded by a label paid for with money.

This, as the budding beach bums from Bristol to Manchester had discovered, was because surfing is actually really hard. You have to be a skilled, strong swimmer to be in with a chance, standing up is a challenge, catching a wave an art and riding it a lifetime's pursuit. You also need a bit of sea. Whereas, with a **skateboard**, you're in the clique pretty much straight away. These days surf- and skate-wear are often described by boutiques as 'urban' fashion, helping to fuel the notion that the miniature wheelie-board we know and love evolved from the sea. Perhaps it did.

FAD **RATING** ✪✪✪✪✪ *'Surf wear. All the brands. Buy now online.'*

The Sweat Band

Tennis stars such as John McEnroe made the sweat band an attractive choice of fashion accessory for boys. Essentially a flexible towelling Alice-Band, with wrist-sized companions, the idea was that it would absorb your bodily fluids to stop them running into your eyes, or on to your fingers, ruining your grip on the racquet that could win you the championship. The truth was that, away from Centre Court, it became simply a place to store bad odours and wetness, the better to insinuate them into the front porthole of your enemy's **parka** hood.

 **RATING** ✪✪ *'Eeww. Touch that.'*

The Tamagotchi

You know the routine. You pay your 50 pence and win a goldfish at the fair. Just like that – way too easy. Now you are the proud owner of a tiny, living, swimming creature, in all its orange frailty. Whoops. Now you need to keep it alive. You can't keep it in that plastic bag. Luckily, the stallholder has a tiny plastic bowl for sale for a mere twenty quid. Phew! Where else are you going to get a tank at this time in the evening? You hand over your mother's money and take home your new pet. You love it. It's so beautiful and shiny. Two days later it is dead. You cry, you wail, you sob, you bury your head. How can something you loved so much be taken from you, in the prime of its life? It's so unfair. A hard lesson, cruelly won.

There's no training for this sort of thing. Or at least there wasn't until 1996, when Bandai, the Japanese conglomerate that brought you **Hello Kitty**, released its series of virtual pets. These electronic key-ring playmates were said to have crash-landed on earth, *en route* from the planet *Tamagotchi*, the Japanese word for 'loveable egg'. Once fallen, the midget aliens were taken in by 'The Professor' and his assistant Mikachu (not to be confused with Pikachu, *see* **Pokémon**). The altruistic scientist built his microscopic wards egg-shaped protection-cases so they could survive the Earth's atmosphere. 'Then Mikachu painted the eggs, took them into school and started a craze.' That's the official spiel from Bandai, in any case. Note how the story contains the frankly blunt instruction to take them into school and start a craze. That's marketing.

In truth, the egg contained a tiny LCD screen and three buttons. The idea was to hatch a baby creature, feed it when it cried, play with it to make it happy, clean up its mess and try to keep it alive for as long as possible. Up to five Tamagotchi 'years' was amateurish. Six to ten years left room for improvement. Over ten was getting to expert level, but once you broke the twenty-three-year barrier, strange things began to happen. Secret characters could evolve.

To hatch the egg, you set the timer. It ticked away, prompting pre-set belly-aches and transmutations. Once unleashed, the cyber creature 'lived' in real time and could be quite demanding. It was supposed to be 'on' twenty-four hours a day, sleeping at night. Luckily, by use of a clever 'cheat' you could put the unit on pause if you weren't going to be able to look after your little one for a while – a bit like, say, employing a nanny. If you thought the sorry bleeder was just whingeing, you could press the discipline button, but at your peril, as this course of action could cause your mini-pet to grow up bad.

As with goldfish, so it was with Tamagotchi. Chances are, your first ever electro-pet died the death within ten days. But here was the healing genius of Bandai: when the grim reaper culled your beloved, you simply reset the timer and hatched another. No wonder the Tamagotchi caught on. Children could, as Bandai boasted, 'experience the fun and responsibility of feeding and caring for their digital pet' – without having to bury it down the toilet. At its zenith the Tamagotchi craze saw fifteen eggs sold every minute in the USA and Canada alone, while 40 million 'units' were sold worldwide. The toy spawned a generation of similar evolving cyber-pets, of which **Pokémon** is the best-known. In truth, the Tamagotchi itself looked like a chicken.

Beyond the world of playground status-symbols, Tamagotchi was a genuine success with Japanese adults. Media commentators claimed that the Japanese lacked space but longed for emotional connections. The Tamagotchi was deemed ideal. Indeed. Why share your square metres with a live-in partner when you can just stick one in your pocket. Not just a toy, then, but a real relationship that transcended 'projections of desire' and replaced them with 'acceptance of otherness'. And so cheap too! If you believe what you read in the press, this emotional attachment to what was basically a plastic clock was of utmost cultural significance. In 1997, *Neo-Tokyo* magazine claimed Japanese youth was suffering a deep-seated personality dilemma: 'The crisis consists of young people dealing with their own cultural hybridity, in which their identity is put into question. In this respect, caring for tamagocchi [sic] is fundamentally an identity-affirming action.'

FAD Fact In September 2002 in New York City, Kidscreen's fifth annual conference on Advertising and Promoting to Kids taught delegates how to 'own fun' and 'own kids'. (*The Lancet*)

That's as may be, but goldfish had the last laugh. Where are the Tamagotchi now? Car-boot sales, that's where, while goldfish live to die another day.

Oh. Hang on, what's this?

'Over the past five years, we have heard Tamagotchi fans ask for the return of this brand,' Bill Beebe, senior vice-president of sales and marketing at Bandai America, told his own press office in 2004. 'We couldn't be more excited to bring back America's favorite digital pet with more interactive features and options. We believe Tamagotchi Connection is just the product to boost toy-industry sales and top holiday wish-lists this fall.' Uh-oh... According to reports, the new generation of Tamagotchi will be able to fall in and out of love. By the time you read this, we may be forming still deeper clock-based relationships.

FAD RATING ✪✪✪✪ *'Never mind, we'll get you a hamster.'*

The Team-Building Weekend

This corporate abomination is the bastard child of two awful, undiscriminating parents. The daddy is the American tendency to talk about tawdry companies as though they are basketball teams. The business philosophy that gave rise to such expressions as 'I want you to take the ball and run with it' naturally required all employees to be 'team players'. This is when the daddy had bad, possibly illegal sex with the whorish 'consultant', who then gave birth to the team-building weekend.

'Consultant' is another word for 'recently-fired manager'. Other titles were considered, such as 'contributing executive', 'manager-at-large' and 'job-seeker', but 'consultant' was found to command a higher rate of pay while simultaneously satisfying the status anxiety of the recently-fired manager.

The consultant's job is to make the remaining managers feel insecure about their ability to direct their business without him or her. He or she must then find ways to make them give away money for no actual work. The trick is to find out what the managers want to do, then tell them to do it. This, 'in real terms', takes little more than an hour, as the only thing managers want to do is 'grow revenue, enhance customer relations and minimize cost-base'. So, to extract top dollar, the per-hour consultant must construct time-consuming activities based on what he has told the managers they want. One way to cut costs, he will say, is to avoid hiring and training new staff. To build 'staff loyalty' and avoid losing staff to the competition, the company must normally pay its drones more money. This clearly does not fit the required strategy, so the consultant must find a way to 'boost staff morale' while failing to raise pay. A cheap way to do this is take them away from the office for a day – or preferably a weekend, as then it's on their own miserable time – and give them biscuits.

Once subdued with Jammy Dodgers and trapped in a conference centre far from home, the workforce will then be subjected to any number of 'fun' games. Anything will do, as long as it fills the hours. 'Trust-building' exercises such as falling backwards into the arms of your line-manager can work. Role-play is good too. 'You pretend to be on the end of the phone and I'll pretend to be an unhappy customer.' Games that encourage workers to reveal more about themselves than they want to are good for building 'rapport' among colleagues, the consultant will say. For example, each staff member could write a secret about their life on a piece of paper, while everyone tries to match the secret to the colleague. This sort of crap can go on all day, especially if Paintball is involved. If time is short, tea-breaks can be taken 'on the hoof'. This means there is no break, only tea.

Such away-days should always be rounded off with a thorough 'brainstorm'. This is where staff members are encouraged to feel 'empowered' by suggesting ideas for the business which will be ignored by managers but will allow them to identify creative, forward-looking people who can then be made redundant. When all the games are over there might be time for enforced socializing with a room full of all the people you would never choose to know were you not trapped in a conference centre far from home. If the 'team-building' gets to this stage, drunkenness is encouraged, as that's when people really 'bond'.

Once safely back at their desks, the newly built team-players will put their lost weekend behind them and continue to stab one another in the back as before. Only now they will know each other's secrets, the consultant will be several grand richer, and the business will have increased its cost-base by the same amount with no 'positive impact on the bottom line'. Hooray for consultancy.

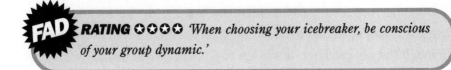

FAD RATING ✪✪✪✪ *'When choosing your icebreaker, be conscious of your group dynamic.'*

The Teasmaid

When the author was ten he enjoyed watching science-fiction films such as *Soylent Green*, in which the starving futuristic millions are forced by a giant corporation to eat plankton and eventually themselves. The author also enjoyed reading in the school library highly illustrated books with titles such as 'The Future'. Such utopian fantasies made a number of consistent promises that were attractive to the average ten-year-old.

The first was that in THE FUTURE, more work would be done by machines, giving humans 'much more leisure time'. The pages showed images of calm, fulfilled citizens drifting around angular leisure complexes that looked suspiciously like Milton Keynes with limitless supplies of New Monetary Units.

What the creators of these books clearly meant was that more work would be done by machines, giving humans a much higher incidence of redundancy and unemployment and that, through a lack of New Monetary Units, hordes of such dislocated, unfairly defeated individuals would drift around brick estates eating economy 'baked beans' made by large corporations.

The other promise was that in THE FUTURE, our luxurious houses, or leisure-spaces, would be filled with robotic domestic servants who would satisfy our every whim at the flick of a switch or the assured, privileged cadence of a voice-command. This could still happen of course – in THE FUTURE – but until then, there is the Teasmaid.

The first person to have a shot at it was a gunsmith called Frank Smith. In 1902 he produced a rudimentary tea-making device by attaching a kettle and meths burner to an alarm clock to create a sort of tea-shaped bomb. It did not catch on. It was left to Goblin, now better known for its

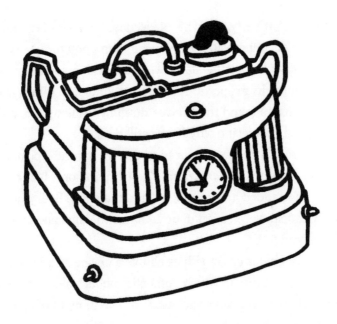

vacuum cleaners, to market in 1937 a user-serviceable tea-making device, which the company called 'the Teasmaid'. The beauty of this idea, apart from the amusing pun, was that the machine could be programmed to make tea in the morning and wake you up with a full cup. First an electric timer activated the element that heated the water. The boiling water was then decanted through a pipe and on to the tea, which sat on a pressure pad. When the pot became heavy the machine activated an alarm. And that's science.

Despite regular appearances alongside the **hostess trolley** and cuddly toy on the glittering conveyor-belt of gifts that formed the end-piece to TV's *The Generation Game*, it took some time for the Teasmaid to really make it as a generic household appliance. During the eighties, the device enjoyed enough success to register on the author's patented Craze-o-Meter™, as various companies provided cheap Teasmaid clones.

But there was a problem. In order fully to discharge its duties, the Teasmaid required ideally to be placed in the bedroom. When the machine worked properly, the whir of circuits, the roar of the kettle and the rumble of decanting water were more than enough to wake even a heavy sleeper long before the alarm went off, which somehow took the shine off the miracle magic of Teasmaid technology. When it did not work properly, users found themselves dutifully drinking tea at three in the morning and wondering why it was still dark.

This latter scenario was captured perfectly in one episode of the eighties BBC sitcom *Terry and June.* The Corporation's blanket ban on trade-name plugs added a delightful twist to the show. Every time actors Scott and Whitfield were called upon to name the appliance they had to call it a 'Teasready'.

Given the margin for error with as simple a device as a Teasready, the author now fears a future in which domestic robots walk stiffly about the house doing chores we'd rather not take on. The thought of being woken during the small hours by the sound of R2D2 sanding down the floorboards and regrouting the bathroom, swearing in bleep-talk as he nails his robot foot to the radiator and floods the house fills the author with a dread surpassed only by the thought of receiving a Teasready for Christmas.

Sadly for Goblin, no one much outside England drinks tea in the morning, which limited the scope for global domination. Now Goblin don't make the Teasmaid at all, but their former rival Swan bangs out a reported 30,000 Teasreadys a year for the UK market. Swan calls its Teasready the 'Teasmade'. Cunning. But who buys them?

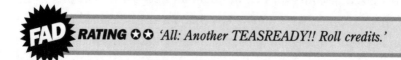

FAD **RATING ○○** *'All: Another TEASREADY!! Roll credits.'*

Top Trumps

Long before the **TV Game** and the **Digital Watch**, there was Top Trumps. A simple card-game series, it appealed to boys, as the only tactic was competitive one-upmanship. That, and you got to collect the set.

Each pack had a theme, such as Football Stars, Military Aircraft or Motorbikes. To the author's knowledge, Wild Flowers of Great Britain and Ireland and Broadway Musicals were never made. Each card featured a different member of the set. Under its picture was a list of statistics. Cylinders: V-12, for example, beat Cylinders: 6. Top speed 200 kph beat 100 kph. Essentially, whatever was more, bigger, faster or quicker to kill won the day.

To play you divided the pack equally between players and held your hand face up, so you could only see the top card. Without revealing the identity of his card, each player chose a statistic he thought would beat the others in that category. The winner of each round collected the losing cards from the other players, and the first to gain possession of the entire pack won the game. That's it.

Given its collectibility and portability, Top Trumps found favour in the playground, or under the desk. And while in many ways it was a game of chance, the scope for bluff, tactics and cheating should still not be underestimated. The author's brother had Aircraft Carriers in his Christmas stocking, while the author was given Formula One Racing Cars. Apparently, an aircraft carrier 'beat' a Formula One racing car, so the latter pack was never played.

The game may have temporarily fallen from grace as Sega Megadrives ruled the day, but never underestimate the power of nostalgia. Top Trumps is back. Now marketed by Winning Moves, the old classics such as Predators remain (Polar Bear: killer rating 2; Tawny Owl: killer rating 5; hand it over), but the new company has succumbed to the Faustian lure of tie-in licensing and marketing. The new range includes *Buffy The Vampire Slayer*™, *The Simpsons*™, and *Lord of the Rings*™. The author has invested in a *Simpsons* pack for research purposes and can reveal that Millhouse trounces Maggie in the 'Biggest Nerd' category. But in the 'Fattest' contest, Patty and Selma's 86 per cent walks all over Itchy and Scratchy's mere 60 per cent. Come on, you blimps. And to think those are real statistics.

But you don't have to buy into the marketers' dream. You could collect vintage Top Trumps. They're not worth much, and you can pick them up for less than a new set on eBay. Or, better still, you could make your own sets. Be careful to call them 'Excellent Trumps' to avoid an infringement of the Winning Moves trademark and subsequent legal action. Then simply make a card for each of your work colleagues (*see* **The Team-Building Weekend**), and rate them accordingly. Most Transparent Sycophant, Biggest Unethical Trader, Worst Shag. Hours of fun. You saw it here first, kids.

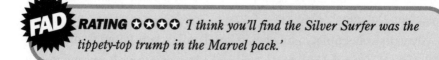

FAD **RATING** ✪✪✪✪ *'I think you'll find the Silver Surfer was the tippety-top trump in the Marvel pack.'*

HOW TO START A CRAZE

Make your intentions clear

Collect the set. 'Gotta catch 'em all.' The first issue comes with a free presentation ring-binder worth £19.99. What's the point in selling one thing when you can release an endless stream of subtly different variations? Never underestimate the willingness of the consumer to fulfil your demands, especially if the consumer is a child. Marketers adept at manipulating the emotions of children are aware that the instructions above work on children's need for acceptance and on their feelings of dissatisfaction. One *Star Wars* figure will never be enough. This worked for the Kewpie Doll, for the Cabbage Patch Kid®, for the Care Bear, for My Little Pony, for Pokémon and countless others. The Tamagotchi electronic pet included a blunt instruction in its 'folklore story'. Once those crazy space-eggs had landed, the kind professor 'took them into school and started a craze', according to manufacturers Bandai. The Furby® only really came into its own when communicating with other Furbies®. Afro Ken, we are told, is a cute dog that 'likes to get near things that look like Afro Ken'. And happily, lots of other products look like Afro Ken, so pleasing him is easy. With collectibles, you need to work on the consumer's feelings of disappointment, the marketers say. Be sure to make a number of your football stickers, trading cards or Pogs extremely 'rare'. They'll buy again and again, hoping against hope. Sorry, you have not won this time, please try again. Keep looking for acceptance, you're so close.

Trivial Pursuit

Cheese segments or pieces of pie? Trivial Pursuit was marketed as a 'party in a box'. But what sort of party? Where was the bottle of Bailey's and the sexually aggressive divorcée, where was the coked-up gatecrasher? Hardly a proper party. No, Trivial Pursuit was in truth the ultimate tool for competitive dads whose seven-year-olds were beginning to beat them at chess.

'What element of the periodic table, Timmy, is signified by the symbol Pb?'

'Plobium?'

'No, boy, it's LEAD, from the Latin *plumbium*, whence we derive the humble plumber, which is what you'll end up as if you don't pay attention. Next. The riparian nations of *which* European river include Germany, Austria, Slovakia, Hungary, Serbia, Croatia, Montenegro, Bulgaria, Romania, Moldova, Russia and Ukraine? Quickly!' *(For a clue, see* **Rubik's Cube**.*)*

The genesis of 'Triv', or 'Pedant's Joy', as it is sometimes known, can be traced back to Montreal in 1979, when two 'good buddies' (*see* **The CB Radio**) called Scott Abbott and Chris Haney argued over which one of them was better. Judge for yourself: Abbott was sports editor of the Canadian Press and Haney was photo editor for the *Montreal Gazette*. This bantering competition between journalists resulted in the pair devising their very own board game. They thought they were pretty smart, but of the first 1,100 copies of the game, which they launched at the 1982 American International Toy Fair in New York, only a very few were sold. The buddies faced crippling debts. Other buddies baled them out. However, later that year they swung a Canadian distribution deal with Chieftain Products and followed it the next year with a US deal. As a result, sales went from a few hundred to around 20 million in 1984.

The game took off, and fast. Why? Well, they were pretty smart after all. Firstly, the board game promised an educational slant, boosting its appeal to parents. This was something new. It was also well packaged, in the manner of a box of After Eights, and the board was tastefully decked with Victorian-style line-drawings. A rather stylish thing to own. A game for discerning adults. It oozed class and sophistication, the antithesis of, say, Buckaroo. On the marketing side, it was pushed as an antidote to television, while the high price and weighty box found favour with its target market, the well-to-do. One got it to keep up with the Joneses, and playing it only helped to confirm one's status as a highly intelligent and successful person. The subliminal marketing meant hosts thought it quite the thing to whip out after dinner, the better to impress their guests. In short, it appealed to the vanity of the middle classes. It was a great success.

The object was to collect a coloured plastic segment for each subject category and place it in a circular receptacle. You gained segments by answering questions correctly. As long as you stuck to History (Yellow), Geography (Blue), Science and Nature (Green) or Art and Literature (Brown), it was a matter of general knowledge, or lack thereof. When it came to Entertainment (Pink) or Sport and Leisure (Orange), you were lost to the world of hobbyist arcana or cruel generational differences. What team was disqualified during round two of the 1963 FA Cup? In the 1970 sit-com *Keep Your Clogs On*, what was the profession of Hattie Jacques's character? What is Midori? These two categories led to over 6 million child tantrums and divorces in Surrey and Buckinghamshire alone (legal note: this is not true). Disillusioned youngsters, mocked for not knowing who played Frank Spencer in TV's *Some Mothers Do 'Ave 'Em*, ran in tears to the comfort of the **SodaStream** and mince pies, while wives mentally called their lawyers as husbands chirruped, 'Oh this one's *easy*, surely you know *this* one. *I* do.'

FAD Fact In Sweden, television advertising aimed at children under twelve is banned.

Given the obscurity of many questions, the key to winning at Trivial Pursuit lay not in knowledge but creativity. You simply made up your own questions and answers. 'Who starred opposite Doris Day in the 1959 film *Diamonds and Rust*? No? Alec Guinness, believe it or not. No, I didn't know that either. Never mind, my go.'

The creators endeavoured to balance things by issuing alternative sets of questions, such as the Baby Boomers Edition (Who played bass in Jefferson Airplane?) or the Junior Game (I saw a mouse. Where?), while a 1988 sale to Tonka, followed by Hasbro's 1992 acquisition, brought film tie-in and pop-culture versions galore. But this hardly addressed the issue. Just give us the answers with a four-pack of Strongbow and leave us be.

Trivial Pursuit is still selling and innovating, although it's safe to say that the craze is long gone. Successive corporate takeovers took the product arguably downmarket, to the extent that, under Hasbro, the 2002 celebration of twenty years of Triv did not feature, for example, TV boffins Stephen Fry, Bamber Gascoigne and Jeremy Paxman, as one might hope, but Village People and the Sock Puppet.

'I'm here today to remind people that it's OK to laugh, enjoy life and celebrate the good times,' said former New York City mayor Rudolph Giuliani, opening the festivities. 'I'm for anything that brings people together to have fun.'

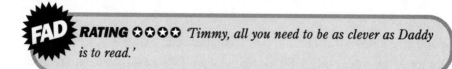

FAD RATING ✪✪✪✪ *Timmy, all you need to be as clever as Daddy is to read.'*

The Troll

An ugly, flesh-toned folklore miniature with a shock of brightly coloured 'hair' made from raw sheep's wool, the ubiquitous troll toy was first marketed in 1959 by Danish woodcutter Thomas Dam. Beginning as a homespun craft, the troll was drafted into a Danish toy shop and from there took over the world. Why? It seems hard to believe that these menacing little Rumpelstiltskins became as popular in sixties America as the **Cabbage Patch Kid®** would years later. In Britain, wherever small pocket-money toys are sold you will find the troll. While the collectible doll-size range seems to have secreted itself under a rock in Moominvalley, the creepy Scandinavian ne'erdowell (*see* **Chintz, chucking out one's**) is still available as **pencil top**, keychain or gonk. And he still hasn't put his top on.

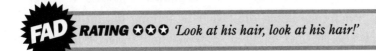

FAD **RATING** ✪✪✪ *'Look at his hair, look at his hair!'*

Tupperware

No one ever went broke underestimating the appeal of putting things in other things. First, get some things. Any things will do, but you could begin with dry lentils, sugar lumps, homemade cakes, tea-bags, crayons, **Lego**, biscuits – or indeed any other small item, such as thimbles, **marbles**, bouncy balls, cheese crackers, **French toast** or Oxo cubes. Then take the item or items out of their original packaging and put them inside a plastic Tupperware container. Make sure to compress the lid as you clip it shut for that damp-proof hermetic seal. Congratulations, for you have just successfully put one thing into another thing. Now take the Tupperware container and in turn put that into a cupboard. Now you're stuffed. You can't put the cupboard anywhere.

The best thing about the Tupperware container is its aid in rattler identification. Strictly speaking, the rattler is nothing but an innocent-looking margarine container found in any household fridge. It goes like this. The toaster pops up and you scramble for the fridge to reach for that margarine, get it spread before the melt-factor decreases. But when you open the fridge you see not one margarine tub but four. Four? What diabolical test is this? Which one, which one? Quickly! Make a choice, the toast is getting colder and each precious second counts towards decreased liquefaction. You lunge, you lift.

It rattles.

Margarine shouldn't rattle and – you know you shouldn't look but you can't fight it – when you open up the lid, there, inside the tub, away from everything else inside the tub, is a lone floret of last week's broccoli, shrinking in on itself, hardening, compacting, rattling.

Why do we keep these things? When exactly do we think we might like to suck on a bit of withered cauliflower, half a detumescing potato and a solitary stiff green bean?

If you think your cohabitee might be harbouring rattlers you could do worse than invest in some Tupperware. It's see-through, you see. It's not disguised as margarine. Imagine your joy when you reach triumphantly for your spreadable butter substitute. 'I can't believe it's not a rattler!' Limitless glee awaits you at your every toast moment.

The place to get your Tupperware is not in a shop. What you need is the Tupperware Party. It's much like an Ann Summers party, or a swingers night, only more exciting. Here's how it all happened.

It's 1946. In Orlando, Florida, Earl Tupper is besieged by things. He longs to put them into other things. During the war, his work in plastics had given him a few ideas for the sort of thing he might put his things into. A glass bowl? Why, no. It's breakable. A ceramic bowl? So heavy! A lightweight and fashionable plastic bowl? Say, there's an idea. Tupper's 'miracle' Wonderlier bowl was born. But would it catch on? Tupper's press department puts it like this: 'With the onset of the post-war "baby boom", (*see* **Trivial Pursuit**) women dedicated themselves to caring for their growing families. The "Tupperized" kitchen was born – a kitchen that was well organized and neat.'

If this description has you reaching for the gin, fags and valium, take heart. Tupperware didn't really sell. Shoppers, sorry – women – didn't really understand how to use the revolutionary patented seal. So Tupper decided the in-home demonstration would be the best way to sell. Accordingly, in 1948, the Tupperware Party phenomenon began. It worked. So well, in fact, that a short three years later Tupper removed his products entirely from retail shelves, freeing up a lot of space for other things no doubt, and sold direct. The Tupperware Party, the company claims, 'was a welcome diversion for women, whose involvement in the community mostly revolved around their family'.

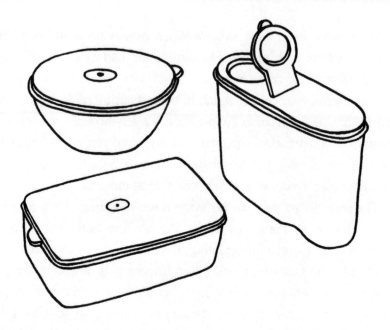

Given these commitments, what a wonderful opportunity for such women to earn! They could do it from home, without leaving their children, without having to go out to work and embarrass their husbands. It wasn't even working, it was a social event. These women were not cogs in a large corporate selling-machine, they were suburban hostesses. 'Come round, eat light snacks and buy storage products for your own kitchens, that they might look as neat and fashionable as mine. And when we are done eating the light snacks, we may put the remainder in a Tupperware container, keeping them fresh as the day they were opened.'

Tupper innovated. He made toys, travel desks and special Tupperware for 'ethnic dishes'. Tupperware wouldn't melt in the microwave. Tupperware wouldn't crack in the freezer. Tupperware operates across borders. In Japan, consumers can choose from the Kimchi Keeper, the Kimono Keeper and the Japanese Bento Box.

As a fad, Tupperware is a distinct success, innovative, modern and once fashionable. As a craze, it worked well, and Tupperware parties were *de rigueur* in many countries worldwide. But then the whole Tupperware scene fell into decline. Had housewives bought all the storage they could store? Had housewives ceased to be housewives? Had plastic ceased to be modish? Had environmentally conscious consumers reacted against the deluge of plastic in favour of traditional, recyclable fare? Had prices risen? Well, yes, all of these things are likely causes for the fall-off in Tupperware activity.

The nineties were tough times for Tupperware's image, if not for sales. The children of the Tupperware generation marry and cohabit later than their parents. They have more money, more information, more freedom and more choices. When kids can record a hit song in their bedroom, who has time for Tupperware?

But as this encyclopaedia goes to press, a report has flooded in of increased Tupperware awareness on 'the continent'. In France, young professionals are coming back to Tupperware, drawn by the fun and convenience of home-selling and by thirty-something nostalgia. The rub, of course, is that Tupperware has moved on. Oh, you can look, but you'll never find those utilitarian translucent tubs of yore.

Still, as revealed via covert photographs taken inside the Royal family's private quarters at Buckingham Palace by *Mirror* reporter Ryan Parry, our own Queen is fully Tupperwared up. With this Royal endorsement, it is entirely possible that a whole new generation could discover the simple pleasure of putting things into other things and perhaps even consider 'a career in Tupperware'.

FAD **RATING** ✪✪✪✪✪ *'Discover the new interactive Tupperware party experience, "A Taste of Tupperware." Experience the taste. Taste the experience.'*

TV Games

FEATURING PONG

Bip bop. I'll have to be careful how I word this. Once upon 1966, an American called Ralph Baer, an engineer at a company called Sanders Associates, hit on a system for moving dots around a standard television screen. He believed the innovation could be made into what he termed a 'home TV game' – an alternative use for the television. Indeed it could.

Called the *Odyssey*, Baer's eventual box came pre-programmed with ping-pong, volleyball, handball and hockey, along with various shooting games involving a special 'light gun' which players 'fired' at the television. The game was patented by Baer (Sanders rejected it) and commercially released by Magnavox in 1972. It was the first time such a game had been designed for use on a home television.

The author's own home TV game entered the household during the Christmas of 1980, to the soundtrack of Jona Lewie's yuletide hit, 'Stop The Cavalry'. Made by Binatone, this device was essentially a continuation of Baer's original idea, with the difference that tennis, squash and 'football' could be played. The playing fields and courts shone bright green, and two vertical bars formed the racquets or virtual players. Actual players sat in their **bean bags** and each held a handset, which consisted of a single potentiometer (or rotating knob), which moved the bar. Clockwise for 'up'. The other way for 'down'. Bip bop. Hours of fun. Really.

It's easy to see why such a thing caught on. An action game played in real time with sound and vision, simple and pure, far from the greed of the Monopoly board and safe from the rigours of actual movement. Why wouldn't such a thing appeal? Crucially, it also allowed people to continue to stare at the television long after the national anthem had been played and transmissions put to bed for the night.

Years later, while Baer was successfully defending his patent against the electronic-games giant Nintendo, a story emerged about an engineer called William Higginbotham. It transpired that Higginbotham had devised a game called 'Tennis for Two' in 1958, long before Baer's patent. The difference was that Higginbotham, who created his game for a one-off physics demonstration at his company, had connected a laboratory oscilloscope to a large analogue computer, which he programmed himself. Nintendo used the story and Higginbotham, who testified, to attempt to discredit Baer's claim to have invented the video game. Nintendo lost that case.

Let us, though, note that in 1971, a year before Baer's *Odyssey*, Nolan Bushnell and Ted Dabney created the first electronic arcade-game, which they called *Computer Space*. In 1972, Bushnell released *Pong*, a simple ping-pong arcade game. Bip bop. The same year Bushnell and Dabney founded **Atari** computers and soon brought their *Pong* into our homes.

We now live in an age of video games. Computer games. Electronic games. Call them what you will and hang the lawyers' expenses. Walk into any media megastore or video-rental shop and you will be assailed with choices for various games consoles or home computers. The chunky, rudimentary graphics may have long gone, the irritating sounds may have been replaced by real audio, the ping-pong and light-gun target practice may have been replaced by a million shoot-'em up or platform jumping games, but bip-bop tennis will for ever hold a special place in our hearts. Thank you, bip-bop tennis.

FAD **RATING** ✪✪✪✪ *'Can you turn the sound off?'*

The Virtual Pet

If the **Tamagotchi** introduced a generation of children and emotionally challenged adults to the joys of loving and caring for plastic, then the urge to nurture an automaton found expression at the turn of the millennium. The robot-dog craze of 2000 saw a number of battery-operated friends enter the lives of children everywhere. One such was Tekno, from Manley Toy Quest. He was apparently programmed to act just like an eight-week-old puppy, except that he would not shit on the carpet or savage your **Care Bears**. Except that he sang songs. Except that he spoke useful English words, including 'Tekno'. Except that 'behaviours' had to be 'launched' by pressing buttons on his head. Unlike a puppy, Tekno would not lick or love you, would not fetch a stick or play with a rubber ring, would not go for a walk with you, roll in fox dung or curl up on your lap. You would not find Tekno asleep next to you on your pillow, and Tekno would not play with dog biscuits, jump into your arms at the sound of the door bell or indeed act like a dog in any way shape or form. Apart from that, he was a fantastic canine companion and soul-mate who you could deactivate instantly by removing the electrical power to his circuits. A boon for those who like controlling relationships (*see* **The Friendship Bracelet**). On the minus side, he snored.

I-Cybie was a better proposition, as he could recognize your voice, get up when he fell over and communicate with other virtual pets Poo-Chi and Super Poo-Chi. Despite its name, this latter 'unit' did not shit either. Fisher Price's 'Rocket' had some impressive dog-like features, but his scope was limited by the fact that his master needed to wear a headset at all times. And still no poo. That came later with Hasbro's 'My Real Baby' (not included).

Virtual pets were everywhere for a short time. The **Furby**®, designed by Dave Hampton at Sounds Amazing and launched in 1997, was intended as an evolution of the **Tamagotchi**, which he saw as tyrannical and inorganic. He wanted a pet that had a physical shape and was intelligent enough to learn new tricks, socialize and 'dance with other **Furbies**® when the grown-ups were trying to watch TV'. In the wake of his success, other companies looked for virtual pets of their own. Most were, in fact, inferior to the **Furby**®, if more pleasing to the eye. The Nano Puppy and the Giga Frog both made a dent in the market, but while the technology of the new wave was advanced for toys, it was primitive when compared to, say, a dog brain. So limited was the scope of virtual pets that the novelty soon wore off.

But the craze for virtual-pet toys gave social commentators pause for thought. While owning and caring for a real pet teaches children how to nurture and respect a living thing (*see* **Strawberry Shortcake**) and helps wean them off the idea that they alone are the centre of the universe, a digital pet cannot do these things. If it 'dies', you reset it. If you're bored, you switch it off. Further, the digital pet risks drawing children into a dislocated world of simulated activity where the links between cause and effect are not so readily made, where responsibility has no real meaning and, compared to the comforting predictability of which, actual reality, with its infinite capacity for change, surprise and upheaval, might seem too daunting a prospect. What will this do to our children? Will they grow up unable to form lasting attachments? Will digital-dog love lead to controlling behaviour in their own relationships with other people? Will they see digital company as a viable alternative to actual friends? When your first live-in girlfriend dumps you because you won't stop playing video games, will your **Furby**® offer you a sofa to sleep on? I don't think so. Luckily these questions need not trouble us too deeply. Because, unlike a real doggy, these mechanized counterfeits really were just for Christmas.

FAD ✦ *RATING* ✪✪✪ *'Real digitized puppy sounds and songs.'*

The Wacky WallWalker®

In Japan, in 1982, Mrs Hakuta sent her son Ken a plastic octopus. The idea was to throw it at a wall, whereupon the tacky, sticky creature would proceed to crawl downwards without falling off. Ken loved the octopus so much that he bought the rights, renamed it the Wacky WallWalker®, registered it as a trademark, renamed himself Dr Fad and proceeded to sell 240 million of the things. By 1983 the craze was everywhere and 'Dr' Ken Hakuta was advising companies on how to start crazes.

No doubt he told them how he got the *Washington Post* to write a full-length feature on his new toy, how he persuaded CBS evening news to cover it as a news story and how he did a deal with Kellogg's, who distributed shiploads of the cheaply made beasts via their cereal packets. He might have mentioned that keeping overheads low meant you could hit critical mass by flogging the brutes for twenty-five cents in vending machines. Ken did all of these things and more to make his gravity-fun octopus a success.

The downside, of course, was that in order to 'stick' to the wall or window, the critter needed to shed particles of itself. This unstable plastic, part solid, part fluid generally left a slug trail of chemical detritus which home-owners appreciated. But why did we, the consumers, love our Wacky WallWalkers® so much? In 1983 there was not the range of entertainment options that today's youngster takes for granted. The octopus represented one last chance to lob stuff at other stuff before computers took all the physical fun out of it.

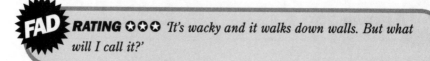

FAD **RATING ✪✪✪** *'It's wacky and it walks down walls. But what will I call it?'*

The Walkman

Sony's groundbreaking personal stereo cassette player changed the way we listened to music for ever and introduced a whole generation to the joys of tinnitus. No longer did you need to be Ozzy Osborne to gain access to that delicious, high-pitched ringing in the ears that will be your constant companion and friend. Oh, they warned us in the user manual, but did we heed their words? It was entirely our own fault. To develop a really good tinnitus it is necessary to listen to your headphones at full volume for prolonged periods of time. This can be achieved by spending your entire adolescence strapped into your Walkman as a statement about your sense of societal dislocation and ennui (*see* **Punk**). A good choice of soundtrack to this would be The Smiths, The Cure and Echo And The Bunnymen, all of whom were musically active at key Walkman moments.

Developed in 1979 and unleashed in the early eighties, the Walkman forever dispensed with the need to carry around the fridge-sized 'ghetto blaster' that terrorized neighbours and passers-by. Music became a private, personal thing and collateral irritation was reduced to stifled winces from fellow public-transport users. The Walkman was adopted early on by joggers and **roller-skaters** – and how we coveted those funky orange headphones. You have to understand that until the Walkman burst on to the scene, stereo headphones could double up as plant pots. Later models used black foam pads and eventually the dreaded 'in-ear headphone', lessening the appeal.

Other manufacturers soon jumped on the personal-stereo bandwagon, to such an extent that now, in the age of the iPod, we forget how remarkable these gadgets were. The author's first Walkman was in fact not a Walkman but a Sanyo Personal Stereo Cassette Hi-Fi which he won in an essay-writing contest and which hooked unobtrusively on to his belt, much like a brick, allowing him to listen to Kraftwerk (*see* **The Stylophone**™) while mowing his granny's lawn.

The Walkman heralded the age of the personal stereo but soon faded. The trouble was not with the player, but with the cassette (*see* **The Eight-Track Cartridge**). The compact disc put paid not only to vinyl but also to the tower of clattering plastic monsters we fed into our Walkmen. The CD Walkman was duly ushered in, but much-needed miniaturization was severely limited by the diameter of the CD. They were not widely adopted. Sony, looking to re-establish itself as the ultimate purveyor of portable music, developed the Minidisc, a recordable format to replace the cassette. For a while in the mid nineties it looked as though this removable digital-storage unit would revive the personal-stereo industry. Especially if you watched the Sony adverts. But in fact it was the intangible and controversial MP3 format that was to give the long-awaited fillip to personal music. The secretive Apple caught Sony looking the other way and produced an MP3 player that could store your entire CD collection in a 'pod' the size of a packet of Nurofen.

Nostalgia is a wonderful thing. Today it is virtually impossible to achieve a high-quality tinnitus purely from the use of personal stereos. Manufacturers now limit the amount of decibels we can pump directly into our eardrums at short range, meaning that you will never more be able to turn your music up above the sound of Granny's Flymo. Talk about the Nanny State.

FAD RATING ✪✪✪✪ *'Tss Tss Tss Tss Tss Tss Tss Tss…'*

The Weeble

The Weebles wobbled, but they did not fall down. Sometimes, though, they came close. Those were giddy moments. But ultimately those Weebles did what it said on the tin. They wobbled. But they did not fall down. They could not, you see, for this family of Humpty lookalikes were eggs with weights in their undersides and a low centre of gravity. Good for target practice (*see* **The Airfix Kit**) and for wrapping carefully in a used Cadbury's Creme Egg foil and offering to a sibling.

 **RATING ✪✪✪** *'How do you eat yours?'*

The Whimsy

Range of collectible porcelain animal figurines in fixed positions and glazed attitudes. The Whimsy, so named for its whimsy, was best captured by Darth Vader (*see* **Star Wars**) and imprisoned in his **Lego** fortress of death where the author's sister would never find it.

 **FAD** **RATING** ✪✪ *'Ahhh, how whimsical.'*

Y2K

See The Millennium Bug.

Yoghurt

Yoghurt: the truth. In the beginning was **milk**. Then it all went sour. Here's how it could happen to you. If you are a Bulgar nomad wandering the plains of central Asia, you might put a bit of mare's milk in a goatskin bag for safekeeping. Natural bacteria inside the bag might then ferment the milk, turning its lactose sugar into tangy lactic acid. This acid might then cause the milk proteins to bulk up into a curd. If this happens to you, congratulations, for you have just invented yoghurt – although you will have to leave it to the Turks to give it a name.

Should you then find yourself developing a theory that the high proportion of 'friendly' lactobacillus bacteria in yoghurt contributed to the long lifespan of the Bulgars, and subsequently find yourself actively promoting its consumption across Europe, then you are probably Ilya Illyich Mechnikov, the Russian biologist. If you are definitely not him but find that you are opening a large plant for the commercial mass-production of yoghurt in Barcelona around 1919, then you are almost certainly Isaac Carasso, the Spanish founder of Danone ('Mm, Danone').

And that's yoghurt history.

Then the British invented the strawberry yoghurt, which was a user-friendly, entry-level variety. A brief plateau period followed, during which the range was tentatively expanded to include Fruits of the Forest, Peach Melba and Ski Black Cherry. They were austere but happy times. When Margaret Thatcher came to power in 1979, yoghurt was one of the first state-owned institutions to be deregulated and privatized. This caused a veritable explosion of taste sensations, as rival yoghurt manufacturers competed for a slice of the multimillion-pound yoghurt market.

Oh, the eighties was a wild old rollercoaster. Spurred on by the hedonistic demands of Britain's new über-consumers, or **Yuppies**, yoghurt-makers dared to be different. Before long, it was impossible to buy a plain, single-flavour yoghurt. Pioneering taste-combinations included Melon & Leather, Zinc & Banana, Pistachio & Eggs Benedict and the ever popular Game-Pie & Aspirin. The decade that gave us Nik Kershaw also gave birth to a rich and diverse range of fermented-milk product as supermarkets began proudly to display 'French Set' yoghurt (don't forget to pour off the liquid), wholegrain yoghurt with added fibre (do not use for sex fun) and 'live' yoghurt drinks such as Yakult.

The Fruit Corner, devised by Müller, took us back to a simpler era, allowing us to mix the flavouring to the natural yoghurt as our taste required. Now we can't get our yoghurt natural enough and the French Set has all but disappeared from British supermarkets. Why are we so keen on this fermented milk? Is it because it is healthy? Is it because it is a way for lactose-intolerant people to enjoy the natural goodness of dairy produce? Is it because it won't make you fat? The author is not entirely sure why the yoghurt is so particularly prone to craze activity, but of one thing he is sure: what a wild, zany and unpredictable dish it is.

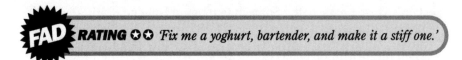

FAD **RATING ✪✪** *Fix me a yoghurt, bartender, and make it a stiff one.'*

The Yo-Yo

Pedro Flores never wanted to be a millionaire. He just wanted to work for himself. 'I have been working for other people for practically all my life and I don't like it,' he once told reporters. A college drop-out, he was working as a hotel bell-boy when he launched the company that made his product a household name. The joke was, of course, that it already existed.

Flores was born in Vintarilocos Norte, Philippines. There, as in almost any country you care to name, people had long played with a kind of spinning top on a string. The circular top had two rounded halves connected with a short, narrow spindle with a string attached. You coiled the string around the spindle, launched the top downwards and, hey presto, it came back up again. The toy, at least 2,500 years old, existed in Ancient Greece, where it was made from fired earth, but little more is known of its early life. Around the beginning of the nineteenth century the gadget began to appear in western Europe. The French called it *l'emigrette*, the English called it 'the bandalore'. In Philippines, where Pedro Flores lived, they apparently called it 'the yo-yo'. The name meant 'come back'. And it was indeed to stage an almighty comeback.

Flores moved to America in 1915 and studied law in California. But any dreams of making a fortune as a lawyer soon faded. He never finished his degree and instead worked for years at a series of odd jobs. One day he read a newspaper story about an entrepreneur who had made a million dollars from a ball attached to an elastic band. Flores remembered the yo-yo of his childhood and thought he could do better than a rubber band. In 1928, determined to lift himself off the breadline, he launched the Yo-Yo Manufacturing Company in Santa Barbara. Initial attempts to secure finance were unsuccessful, so he began making yo-yos by hand. His first run was for twelve, which he sold locally. It was not until he had flogged 2,000 of the homemade toys that he managed to woo backers. With money and machines, the team was able to increase production until, only one year later, they were making 300,000 yo-yos a day from three factories.

Flores, the first person ever to mass-produce the yo-yo, knew that markets did not create themselves. It was he who devised the yo-yo contest that kick-started the first craze, in 1929.

This brought the yo-yo spinning into the orbit of Donald Duncan. Duncan was a successful inventor and marketer, having already done well out of a hydraulic brake for cars. Duncan bought the rights and the factories from Flores – who made a canny move in selling out – and trademarked the name 'Yo-Yo'. Duncan made one addition to the design of the yo-yo that secured its future: the slip knot. Instead of simply attaching the string to the inner spindle, Duncan's Yo-Yo had a loop, which allowed the spinning Yo-Yo to 'sleep'. By skilful spinning, players could make the top hover until they brought it back up. Suddenly the Yo-Yo could 'walk the dog', among other tricks. Now the toy had the potential to become a sport. And so it came to pass.

Duncan was an arch-publicist, and his many deals with newspapers ensured mass coverage for his product. The ensuing demand was such that by 1931 Duncan's factory in Wisconsin was banging out 3,600 every hour. By 1932 Yo-Yo mania had hit Britain to such an extent that a *Times* 'correspondent' was moved to declare: 'Yo-Yo by-laws will have to come.' The journalist was upset that 'our public servants' were so busy playing Yo-Yo that they were not being properly subjugated. 'In another store I saw a fat and ugly woman unashamedly making her yo-yo climb the string like a squirrel,' he squawked. His feeling was that if Britain's 'bell-hops, newsboys, omnibus conductors and engine-stokers take violently to yo-yo we shall have to have some restrictions'. Well that seems fair.

Sadly for Duncan, the market for Yo-Yos went up and down like, er, well – but the cost of manufacture and promotion only went up. Even his top output of 45 million units in 1962 could not bring in enough to offset his overheads. The rights to the toy, along with the Duncan name, were rescued from the receivers by the Flambeau Plastic Company. Bankrupt, Duncan turned to making parking meters to try and turn an honest coin. Well, turn a coin anyway.

Meanwhile the Yo-Yo has gone from strength to strength. Much like the **Frisbee®** and the **Hacky Sack®**, the sport of Yo-Yo took on a life of its own. It is now possible to become a professional Yo-Yo 'player'. Something that might have pleased the work-weary Pedro Flores, who basically made his fortune selling something people already had. Like water and land, it's amazing what people will give you money for.

 FAD ⮚ *RATING* ✪✪✪✪ *'If it isn't a Duncan, it isn't a Yo-Yo top.'*

ELEVEN YO-YO TRICKS

1. **Split the Atom**
2. **Spank the Baby**
3. **Skin the Cat**
4. **Walk the Dog**
5. **Hop the Fence**
6. **Rock the Baby**
7. **Rock the Baby on the Eiffel Tower**
8. **In the Bucket**
9. **On the Trapeze**
10. **Man on Trapeze and His Brother Rocking in the Cradle**
11. **Buddha's Revenge**

The Yuppie

When the author took his first office job in London, a colleague told him: 'The pay here is good, but then it needs to be. My lifestyle demands it.' This was in 2000, and the ugly truth was that the Yuppie, bred in the eighties and unleashed, braying and spending, into our major cities, lived on. Did it stand for Young Urban Professional? They wished it did. Was it more a case of Youthful Unthinking Priggishness? For every action, we learn, there is an equal and opposite reaction (*see* **The Executive Toy**).

Where the hippies of the late sixties rejected the breadhead values of their square, besuited patriarchs, their Yuppie throwback children embraced them like a long-lost **Filofax**®. With the Conservative Prime Minister Margaret Thatcher goading them to earn, earn, earn and spend, spend, spend, with statements such as 'a man who, beyond the age of twenty-six, finds himself on a bus can count himself as a failure,' competitive acquisition became 'the new black'. A person's worth was measured by his or her performance, performance being measured by results, and results being rewarded with wealth. These were not life's failures, these were winners. Winners, you understand? Naturally, they 'worked hard and played hard'. Ostentatious consumption of expensive comestibles was a must, with champagne *de rigueur* at all times. Not that they could ever stop working. These were the first people to tote mobile phones, into which they said 'ya' and 'ciao' as loudly as possible, simply to draw attention to the fact that they

FAD Fact 'Children inundated with commerecialism... suffer not only from obesity but also from body-image and other emotional problems, eating disorders and tendencies towards violence.' (*The Lancet*)

were still winning. Even when relaxing, the Yuppie worked. Worked *out*.

Industries sprung up to service Yuppie needs. But what did they need? They needed lifestyles, and plenty of them. But Yuppies were busy people, 'time-poor' and 'cash-rich'. Happily, the sort of lifestyles they aspired to could be purchased swiftly, originally in Habitat, but that chain very soon became rather **Black Tower**. The true Yuppie bought 'bespoke' furniture and snorted the change up his nose. They frittered loose coins on **executive toys**.

Things! A person had to have *things*. Why buy orange juice when you can buy a juicer and compete over who has the most ridiculous juice-combination? Can't just drink juice, must win juice. Must win. The apogee of Yuppie professions was the merchant banker, whose job allowed him or her to both bray all day and close those deals. But there were deals to be closed all over the place. The author once worked for a Yuppie Prontaprint franchisee who would treat every miserable photocopy transaction as a deal to be won. 'How much for A4?' 'Thirty pee a click, mate.' 'That's a bit steep. [*Sotto voce*: shit, went in too high.] OK, let me put it another way, how much are you looking to spend today?'

Cars were important too, the redder the better. So was property. The ideal Yuppie accommodation would be a 'luxury', 'executive', 'converted' wharf. Yuppies would read the salmon-pink bits of newspapers to keep an eye on their stocks, but only in public places. Yuppies could work in the media too, ideally as a fashion- or lifestyle-editor on a glossy magazine. All Yuppies were absolutely fabulous at all times, especially when eating sushi.

Yuppies didn't sit in a quiet job for fourteen years and win promotion by default. Yuppies hacked, stabbed and damn well *won* their way up, up and ever upward. Yuppies didn't complete tasks, they hit targets; they didn't work well, they *performed*.

The fast-paced cut and thrust of corporate life can take its toll on the mind, body and spirit. That's where the health spa came in. The more expensive and luxurious, the better, 'because in business you need all the breaks you can get.'

The nineties brought some balance. For a start, more people were becoming affluent, so the boundary between Yuppie and lesser mortal was blurred. More winners were getting burned out, too, or having children. As the millennium drew to a close, people started to talk of 'downshifting'. The author prefers to call it 'working less', but you have to remember the Young Urban Professional is never idling in neutral. Always revving, ready to accelerate the moment the light changes, got to get ahead, can't be left behind. And so it goes on, rat racing rat.

The Yuppie craze embodied the materialistic values of the twenty-five to forty age-group in a decade driven by the embrace of capital gains and conservative taste. The old-school Yuppie still exists but is harder to spot: in an office where everyone can afford a Paul Smith suit, the aspiring Yuppie will be the one who left the labels on his cuffs so everyone can see he is a winner. But what has he won? Times change, people grow up, broaden their horizons, start to want less. God knows, we don't need any of it. A person could simply live in a shack by the sea and write books. On which note…

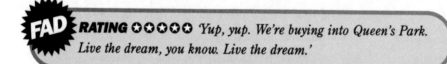

FAD RATING ✪✪✪✪✪ *'Yup, yup. We're buying into Queen's Park. Live the dream, you know. Live the dream.'*

Acknowledgements

I would like to give due credit, along with my sincere thanks, to Martin Toseland, who suggested a book along these lines to me, a long time ago it seems. Thank you Toby and Clara at Atlantic for your enthusiasm for the project from the outset. Thank you also Daniel, Angus, Karen, Clare, Louise, Bonnie and all at Atlantic who contributed their humour, memories and good fellowship. I would like to thank Susannah Godman, my agent at Lutyens Rubinstein and, on a personal note, my deepest gratitude goes to both Louis and Susannah, Andrew and Eliana and Jo and Val, for their generosity and friendship during this period and always. Booyakasha *adv. qv.*

Many people contributed to this book, in the form of personal memories. Still more helped me to compile my list. More still, it seems, kindly allowed me to quote from our conversations or from their message-board postings, or gave their consent for me to work from the information, figures or historical work they had published. Thank you to everyone who provided raw data and colour in this way. I enjoyed our correspondence immensely and appreciate the time you took. Thank you to the various company directors, marketing gurus, press officers and assistants who magicked information to me, often at very short notice. It is also much appreciated. I would like to give credit to the following written sources:

Adcuff, Dan S. *What Kids Buy and Why: The Psychology of Marketing to Kids*. New York, 1997.

Gilham, Roger. *Scalextric: The Definitive Guide*. London, 2004.

Green, Rod. *Scalextric: The Story of the World's Favourite Model Racing Cars*. London, 2001.

Harrison, Ian. *Action Man: The Official Dossier*. London, 2003.

King, Kevin. *Action Man: The Real Story 1966–*. Southwick, 2001.

Kline, Stephen. *Out of the Garden: Toys, TV, and Children's Culture in the Age of Marketing*. New York, 1993.

Lindstrom, Martin. *Brandchild*. London, 2003.

Opie, Iona & Peter. *Children's Games With Things*. Oxford & New York, 1997.

National Family and Parenting Institute. *Hard Sell, Soft Targets*. London, 2003.

Pine, Karen J. and Nash, Avril. *Dear Santa: The Effects of Television Advertising on Young Children*. Hatfield, 2001.

Pine, Karen J. and Nash, Avril. 'Barbie® or Bettie? Preschool Children's Preference for Branded Products and Evidence for Gender-Linked Differences' in *Developmental and Behavioural Pediatrics* Vol. 24, No. 4. August 2003.

Thimbleby, Witten and Inglis. *Displaying 3D Images: Alogorithms for Single Image Random Dot Stereograms*. Stirling & Hamilston, 1993.

Ward, Arthur. *Airfix: Celebrating 50 Years of the Greatest Modelling Kits in the World*. London, 2003.

Young, Nat. *History of Surfing*. London, 1994.

Dates for 'That was the year' lists were supplied by the British Toy Retailers Association.

Index